OBJECTIVE-C
PROGRAMMING
THE BIG NERD RANCH GUIDE

AARON HILLEGASS & MIKEY WARD

BiG
nerD
ranch

Objective-C Programming: The Big Nerd Ranch Guide

by Aaron Hillegass and Mikey Ward

Big Nerd Ranch, LLC.
1989 College Ave NE
Atlanta, GA 30317
(404) 478-9005
http://www.bignerdranch.com/
book-comments@bignerdranch.com

Exclusive worldwide distribution of the English edition of this book by

Pearson Technology Group
800 East 96th Street
Indianapolis, IN 46240 USA
http://www.informit.com

ISBN-10 032194206X
ISBN-13 978-0321942067

Second edition, November 2013

Acknowledgments

It is a great honor that we get to work with such amazing people. Several of them put a lot of time and energy into making this book great. We'd like to take this moment to thank them.

- The other instructors who teach our Objective-C class fed us with a never-ending stream of suggestions and corrections. They are Scott Ritchie, Bolot Kerimbaev, Christian Keur, Jay Campbell, Juan Pablo Claude, Owen Mathews, Step Christopher, TJ Usiyan, and Alex Silverman.

- Sarah Brown, Sowmya Hariharan, Nate Chandler, and James Majors kindly helped us find and fix flaws.

- Our brilliant editor, Susan Loper, took a stream-of-consciousness monologue that stumbled across everything a programmer needs to know and honed it into an approachable primer.

- Ellie Volckhausen designed the cover.

- Chris Loper at IntelligentEnglish.com designed and produced the print book and the EPUB and Kindle versions.

- The amazing team at Pearson Technology Group patiently guided us through the business end of book publishing.

Table of Contents

Part I
Getting Started

1
You and This Book

Let's talk about you for a minute. You want to write applications for iOS or OS X, but you have not done much (or any) programming in the past. Your friends have raved about other Big Nerd Ranch books (like *iOS Programming: The Big Nerd Ranch Guide* and *Cocoa Programming for Mac OS X*), but they are written for experienced programmers. What should you do?

Read this book.

There are similar books, but this one is the one you should read. Why? We have been teaching people how to write applications for iOS and the Mac for a long time now, and we have identified what you need to know at this point in your journey. We have worked hard to capture that knowledge and dispose of everything else. There is a lot of wisdom and very little fluff in this book.

Our approach is a little unusual. Instead of simply trying to get you to understand the syntax of Objective-C, we will show you how programming works and how experienced programmers think about it.

Because of this approach, we are going to cover some heavy ideas early in the book. You should not expect this to be an easy read. In addition, nearly every idea comes with a programming experiment. This combination of learning concepts and immediately putting them into action is the best way to learn programming.

C and Objective-C

When you run a program, a file is copied from the file system into memory (RAM), and the instructions in that file are executed by your computer. Those instructions are inscrutable to humans. So, humans write computer programs in a programming language. The very lowest-level programming language is called *assembly code*. In assembly code, you describe every step that the CPU (the computer's brain) must take. This code is then transformed into *machine code* (the computer's native tongue) by an *assembler*.

Assembly language is tediously long-winded and CPU-dependent (because the brain of your new iMac can be quite different from the brain of your well-loved, well-worn PowerBook). In other words, if you want to run the program on a different type of computer, you will need to rewrite the assembly code.

To make code that could be easily moved from one type of computer to another, we developed "high-level languages." With high-level languages, instead of having to think about a particular CPU, you can express the instructions in a general way, and a program (called a *compiler*) will transform that code into highly-optimized, CPU-specific machine code. One of these high-level languages is C. C programmers write code in the C language, and a C compiler converts the C code into machine code.

The C language was created in the early 1970s at AT&T. The Unix operating system, which is the basis for OS X and Linux, was written in C with a little bit of assembly code for very low-level operations. The Windows operating system is also mostly written in C.

The Objective-C programming language is based on C, but it adds support for object-oriented programming. Objective-C is the programming language that is used to write applications for Apple's iOS and OS X operating systems.

How this book works

In this book, you will learn enough of the C and Objective-C programming languages to learn to develop applications for the Mac or for iOS devices.

Why are we going to teach you C first? Every effective Objective-C programmer needs a pretty deep understanding of C. Also, many ideas that look complicated in Objective-C have very simple roots in C. We will often introduce an idea using C and then push you toward mastery of the same idea in Objective-C.

This book was designed to be read in front of a Mac. You will read explanations of ideas and carry out hands-on experiments that will illustrate those ideas. These experiments are not optional. You will not really understand the book unless you do them. The best way to learn programming is to type in code, make typos, fix your typos, and become physically familiar with the patterns of the language. Just reading code and understanding the ideas in theory will not do much for you and your skills.

For even more practice, there are exercises called *Challenges* at the end of each chapter. These exercises provide additional practice and will make you more confident with what you have just learned. We strongly suggest you do as many of the *Challenges* as you can.

You will also see sections called *For the More Curious* at the end of some chapters. These are more in-depth explanations of topics covered in the chapter. They are not absolutely essential to get you where you are going, but we hope you will find them interesting and useful.

Big Nerd Ranch hosts a forum where readers discuss this book and the exercises in it. You can find it at http://forums.bignerdranch.com/.

You will find this book and programming in general much more pleasant if you know how to touch-type. Touch-typing, besides being faster, enables you to look at your screen and book instead of at the keyboard. This makes it much easier to catch your errors as they happen. It is a skill that will serve you well for your entire career. There are numerous typing tutor programs available for the Mac.

How the life of a programmer works

By starting this book, you have decided to become a programmer. You should know what you have signed up for.

The life of a programmer is mostly a never-ending struggle. Solving problems in an always-changing technical landscape means that programmers are always learning new things. In this case, "learning new things" is a euphemism for "battling against our own ignorance." Even if a programmer is just fixing a bug in code that uses a familiar technology, sometimes the software we create is so complex that simply understanding what is going wrong can take an entire day.

If you write code, you will struggle. Most professional programmers learn to struggle hour after hour, day after day, without getting (too) frustrated. This is another skill that will serve you well. If you are curious about the life of programmers and modern software projects, we highly recommend the book *Dreaming in Code* by Scott Rosenberg.

Now it is time to jump in and write your first program.

2

Your First Program

Now that you know how this book is organized, it is time to see how programming for the Mac and for iOS devices works. To do that, you will:

- install Apple's Developer Tools

- create a simple project using those tools

- explore how these tools are used to make sure your project works

At the end of this chapter, you will have successfully written your first program for the Mac.

Installing Apple's developer tools

To write applications for OS X (the Mac) or iOS (the iPhone and friends), you will be using Apple's developer tools. The main application that you will need is called Xcode.

Xcode is only available on the Mac (not Windows or Linux), so you will need a Mac to work with this book. In addition, this book is based on Xcode 5, which is compatible with OS X 10.8 (Mountain Lion) and higher.

You can download the latest version of Xcode for free from the Mac App Store. You may want to drag the Xcode icon onto your Dock; you will be using it an awful lot.

Getting started with Xcode

Xcode is Apple's *Integrated Development Environment*. Everything you need to write, build, and run new applications is in Xcode.

A note on terminology: anything that is executable on a computer we call a *program*. Some programs have graphical user interfaces; we call these *applications*.

Some programs have no graphical user interface and run for days in the background; we call these *daemons*. Daemons sound scary, but they are not. You probably have about 60 daemons running on your Mac right now. They are waiting around, hoping to be useful. For example, one of the daemons running on your system is called pboard. When you do a copy and paste, the pboard daemon holds onto the data that you are copying.

Some programs have no graphical user interface and run for a short time in the terminal; we call these *command-line tools*. In this book, you will be writing mostly command-line tools to focus on programming essentials without the distraction of creating and managing a user interface.

Now you are going to create a simple command-line tool using Xcode so you can see how it all works.

When you write a program, you create and edit a set of files. Xcode keeps track of those files in a *project*. Launch Xcode. From the File menu, choose New and then Project....

To help you get started, Xcode suggests a number of project templates. You choose a template depending on what sort of program you want to write. In the lefthand column, select Application from the OS X section. Then choose Command Line Tool from the choices that appear to the right.

Figure 2.1 Choosing a template

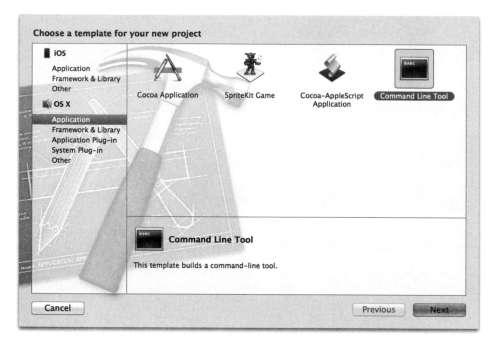

Click the Next button.

Name your new project AGoodStart. The organization name and company identifier will not matter for the exercises in this book, but they are required to continue. Use Big Nerd Ranch and com.bignerdranch. From the Type pop-up menu, select C.

Figure 2.2 Choosing project options

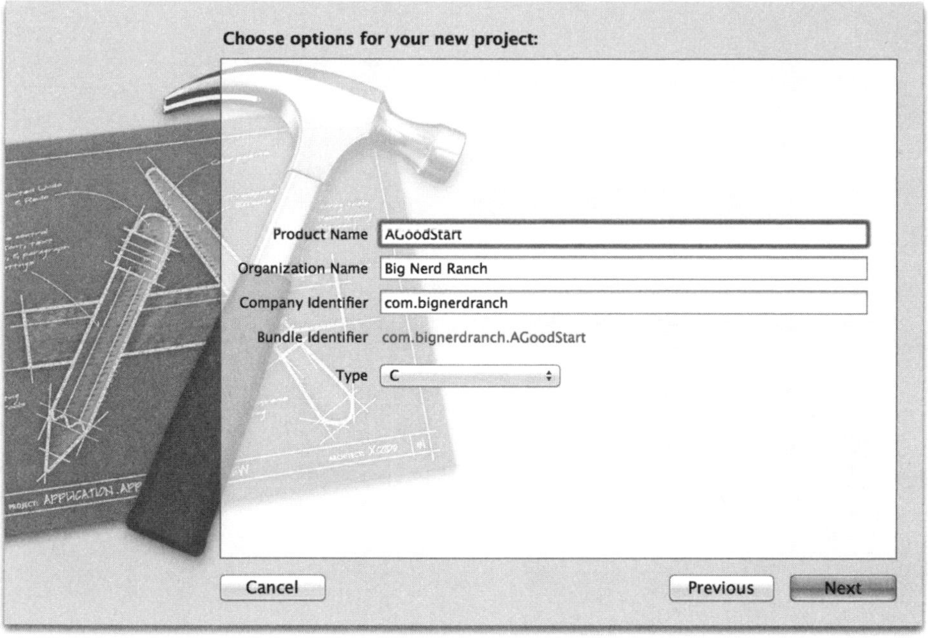

Click the Next button.

In the next window, choose the folder in which you want your project directory to be created. (If you are unsure, accept the default location that Xcode suggests.) You will not need a repository for version control, so uncheck the box labeled Create git repository. Finally, click the Create button.

You will be creating this same type of project for the next several chapters. In the future, we will just say, "Create a new C Command Line Tool named *program-name-here*" to get you to follow this same sequence.

Why are you creating C projects? Objective-C is built on top of the C programming language. You will need to have an understanding of parts of C before you can get to the particulars of Objective-C.

Where do I start writing code?

After creating your project, you will be greeted by a window displaying lots of information about AGoodStart.

Figure 2.3 First view of the AGoodStart project

This window is more detailed than you need, so let's make it a little simpler.

First, at the top right corner of the window, find three buttons that look like this: 🔲🔲🔲.

These buttons hide and show different areas of the window. You will not need the righthand area until later, so click the righthand button to hide it.

You now have two areas at your disposal: the *navigator area* on the left and the *editor area* on the right.

Figure 2.4 Navigator and editor areas in Xcode

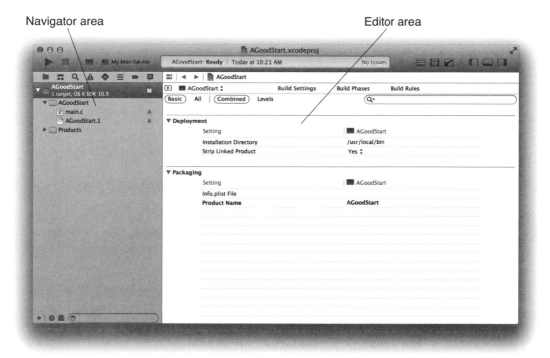

The navigator area displays the current navigator. There are several navigators, and each one provides a different way to examine the contents of your project. You are looking at the *project navigator*. This navigator lists the files that make up your project.

In the project navigator, find a file named main.c and click on it. (If you do not see main.c, click the triangle next to the folder labeled AGoodStart to reveal its contents.)

When you select main.c in the project navigator, the editor area changes to display the contents of this file (Figure 2.5).

Figure 2.5 Selecting main.c in the project navigator

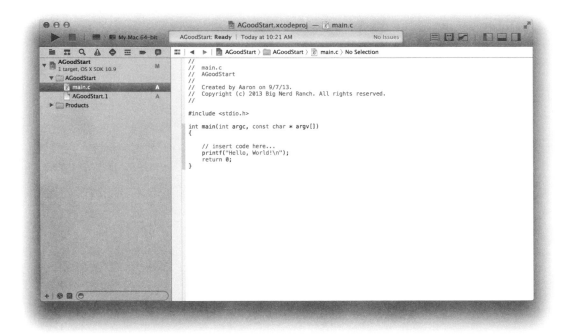

The main.c file contains a *function* named **main**. A function is a list of instructions for the computer to execute, and every function has a name. In a C or Objective-C program, **main** is the name of the function that is called when a program first starts.

```
#include <stdio.h>

int main(int argc, const char * argv[]) {

    // insert code here...
    printf("Hello, World!\n");
    return 0;
}
```

This function contains the two kinds of information that you write in a program: code and comments.

- Code is the set of instructions that tell the computer to do something.

- Comments are ignored by the computer, but we programmers use them to document code we have written. The more difficult the programming problem you are trying to solve, the more comments will help document how you solved the problem. The importance of this documentation becomes apparent when you return to your work months later, look at code you forgot to comment, and think, "I am sure this solution is brilliant, but I have absolutely no memory of how it works."

In C and Objective-C, there are two ways to distinguish comments from code:

- If you put // in a line of code, everything from those forward slashes to the end of that line is considered a comment. You can see this used in Apple's "insert code here..." comment.

- If you have more extensive remarks, you can use /* and */ to mark the beginning and end of comments that span more than one line.

These rules for marking comments are part of the *syntax* of C. Syntax is the set of rules that governs how code must be written in a given programming language. These rules are extremely specific, and if you fail to follow them, your program will not work.

While the syntax regarding comments is fairly simple, the syntax of code can vary widely depending on what the code does and how it does it. But there is one feature that remains consistent: every *statement* ends in a semicolon. (You will see examples of code statements in just a moment.) If you forget a semicolon, you will have made a syntax error, and your program will not work.

Fortunately, Xcode has ways to warn you of these kinds of errors. In fact, one of the first challenges you will face as a programmer is interpreting what Xcode tells you when something goes wrong and then fixing your errors. You will get to see some of Xcode's responses to common syntax errors as we go through the book.

Let's make some changes to main.c. First, you need to make some space. Find the curly braces ({ and }) that mark the beginning and end of the **main** function. Then delete everything between them.

Now replace the contents of the **main** function with what the contents shown below. You will add a comment, two code statements, and another comment. Do not worry if you do not understand what you are typing. The idea is to get started. You have an entire book ahead to learn what it all means.

```
#include <stdio.h>

int main (int argc, const char * argv[])
{
    // Print the beginning of the novel
    printf("It was the best of times.\n");
    printf("It was the worst of times.\n");
    /* Is that actually any good?
       Maybe it needs a rewrite. */

    return 0;
}
```

Notice that the new code that you need to type in is shown in a bold font. The code that is not bold is code that is already there and will show you where to add the new code. This is a convention that we will use for the rest of the book.

As you type, you may notice that Xcode tries to make helpful suggestions. This feature is called *code completion*, and it is very handy. You may want to ignore it right now and focus on typing things in yourself. But as you continue through the book, start playing with code completion and how it can help you write code more conveniently and more accurately.

(You can see and set the different options for code completion in Xcode's preferences. Select Xcode → Preferences and then open the Text Editing preferences.)

In addition, Xcode uses different font colors to make it easy to identify comments and different parts of your code. For example, comments are always green. After a while of working with Xcode, you will begin to instinctively notice when the colors do not look right. Often, this is a clue that you have made a syntax error. And the sooner you know that you have made an error, the easier it is to find and fix it.

How do I run my program?

It is time to run your program and see what it does. This is a two-step process. Xcode *builds* your program and then *runs* it. When building your program, Xcode prepares your code to run. This includes checking for syntax and other kinds of errors.

In the upper lefthand corner of the project window, find the button that looks suspiciously like the play button in iTunes or on a DVD player. If you leave your cursor over that button, you will see a tool tip that says Build and then run the current scheme. Click this button.

If all goes well, you will be rewarded with the following:

If not, you will get this:

What do you do then? Carefully compare your code with the code in the book. Look for typos and missing semicolons. Xcode will highlight the lines that it thinks are problematic. After you find and fix the problem, click the Run button again. Repeat until you have a successful build.

(Do not get disheartened when you have failed builds with this code or with any code that you write in the future. Making and fixing mistakes helps you understand what you are doing. In fact, it is actually better than lucking out and getting it right the first time.)

After your build has succeeded, a new area will appear at the bottom of the window (Figure 2.6). The right half of this area is the *console*. The console shows the output from your code being executed:

Figure 2.6 Output in console at bottom-right

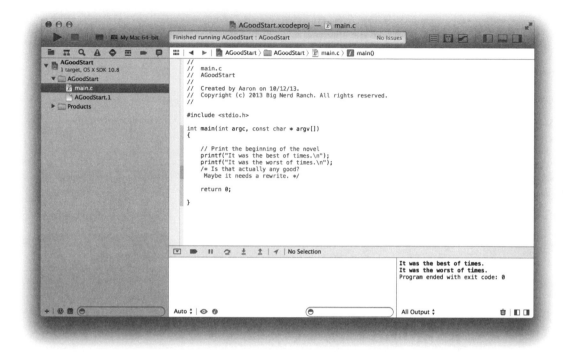

So, what is a program?

Now that you have built and run your first program, let's take a quick look inside to see how it works.

A program is a collection of functions. A function is a list of operations for the processor to execute. Every function has a name, and the function that you just wrote is named **main**.

When programmers talk about functions, we usually include a pair of empty parentheses. Thus, the **main** function is referred to as **main()**.

There was another function in your program – **printf()**. You did not write this function, but you did use it.

To a programmer, writing a function is a lot like writing a recipe card. Like a function, a recipe card has a name and a set of instructions. The difference is that you execute a recipe, and the computer executes a function.

Figure 2.7 A recipe card named Easy Broiled Chicken

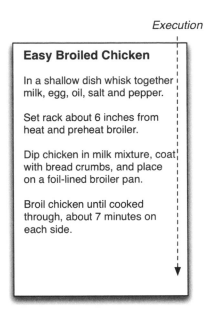

These cooking instructions are in English. In the first part of this book, your functions will be written in the C programming language. However, a computer processor expects its instructions in machine code. How do you get there?

When you write a program in C (which is relatively pleasant for you), the *compiler* converts your program's functions into machine code (which is pleasant and efficient for the processor). The compiler is itself a program that is run by Xcode when you press the Run button. Compiling a program is the same as building a program, and we will use these terms interchangeably.

When you run a program, the compiled functions are copied from the hard drive into memory, and the function named **main** is executed by the processor. The **main** function usually calls other functions. For example, your **main** function called the **printf** function. You will learn more about how functions work in Chapter 5.

Don't stop

At this point, you have probably dealt with several frustrations: installation problems, typos, and lots of new vocabulary. And maybe nothing you have done so far makes any sense. That is completely normal.

Aaron's son Otto is six. Otto is baffled several times a day. He is constantly trying to absorb knowledge that does not fit into his existing mental scaffolding. Bafflement happens so frequently that it does not really bother him. He never stops to wonder, "Why is this so confusing? Should I throw this book away?"

As we get older, we are baffled much less often – not because we know everything, but because we tend to steer away from things that leave us bewildered. For example, reading a book on history can be quite pleasant because we get nuggets of knowledge that we can hang from our existing mental scaffolding. This is easy learning.

Learning a new language is an example of difficult learning. You know that there are millions of people who speak that language effortlessly, but it seems incredibly strange and awkward in your mouth. And when people speak it to you, you are often flummoxed.

Learning to program a computer is also difficult learning. You will be baffled from time to time – especially here at the beginning. This is fine. In fact, it is kind of cool. It is a little like being six again.

Stick with this book; we promise that the bewilderment will cease before you get to the final page.

Part II
How Programming Works

In these next chapters, you will create many programs that demonstrate useful concepts. These command-line programs are nothing that you will show off to your friends, but there should be a small thrill of mastery when you run them. You are moving from computer user to computer programmer.

Your programs in these chapters will be written in C. Note that these chapters are not intended to cover the C language in detail. Quite the opposite: honed from years of teaching, this is the essential subset of information about programming and programming in C that new-to-programming people need to know before learning Objective-C programming.

3

Variables and Types

Continuing with the cooking metaphor from the last chapter, sometimes a chef will keep a small blackboard in the kitchen for storing data. For example, when unpacking a turkey, he notices a label that says "14.2 Pounds." Before he throws the wrapper away, he will scribble "weight = 14.2" on the blackboard. Then, just before he puts the turkey in the oven, he will calculate the cooking time (15 minutes + 15 minutes per pound) by referring to the weight on the blackboard.

Figure 3.1 Keeping track of data with a blackboard

During execution, a program often needs places to store data that will be used later. A place where one piece of data can go is known as a *variable*. Each variable has a name (like cookingTime) and a *type* (like a number). In addition, when the program executes, the variable will have a value (like 228.0).

Types

In a program, you create a new variable by *declaring* its type and name. Here is an example of a variable declaration:

```
float weight;
```

The type of this variable is float (which we will define in a moment), and its name is weight. At this point, the variable does not have a value.

In C, you must declare the type of each variable for two reasons:

- The type lets the compiler check your work for you and alert you to possible mistakes or problems. For instance, say you have a variable of a type that holds text. If you ask for its logarithm, the compiler will tell you something like "It does not make any sense to ask for this variable's logarithm."

- The type tells the compiler how much space in memory (how many bytes) to reserve for that variable.

Here is an overview of the commonly used types. We will return in to each type in more detail in later chapters.

short, int, long	These three types are whole numbers; they do not require a decimal point. A short usually has fewer bytes of storage than a long, and an int is in between. Thus, you can store a much larger number in a long than in a short.
float, double	A float is a floating point number – a number that can have a decimal point. In memory, a float is stored as a mantissa and an exponent. For example, 346.2 is represented as 3.462×10^2 A double is a double-precision number, which typically has more bits to hold a longer mantissa and larger exponents.
char	A char is a one-byte integer that is usually treated as a character, like the letter 'a'.
pointer	A pointer holds a memory address. It is declared using the asterisk character. For example, a variable declared as int * can hold a memory address where an int is stored. It does not hold the actual number's value, but if you know the address of the int, then you can get to its value. Pointers are very useful, and there will be more on pointers later. Much more.
struct	A struct (or *structure*) is a type made up of other types. You can also create new struct definitions. For example, imagine that you wanted a GeoLocation type that contains two float members: latitude and longitude. In this case, you would define a struct type.

These are the types that a C programmer uses every day. It is quite astonishing what complex ideas can be captured in these five simple ideas.

A program with variables

Back in Xcode, you are going to create another project. First, close the AGoodStart project so that you do not accidentally type new code into the old project.

Now create a new project (File → New → Project...). This project will be a C Command Line Tool named Turkey.

In the project navigator, find this project's main.c file and open it. Edit main.c so that it matches the following code.

```c
#include <stdio.h>

int main (int argc, const char * argv[])
{
    // Declare the variable called 'weight' of type float
    float weight;

    // Store a number in that variable
    weight = 14.2;

    // Log it to the user
    printf("The turkey weighs %f.\n", weight);

    // Declare another variable of type float
    float cookingTime;

    // Calculate the cooking time and store it in the variable
    // In this case, '*' means 'multiplied by'
    cookingTime = 15.0 + 15.0 * weight;

    // Log that to the user
    printf("Cook it for %f minutes.\n", cookingTime);

    // End this function and indicate success
    return 0;
}
```

(Wondering about the \n that keeps turning up in your code? You will learn what it does in Chapter 6.)

Build and run the program. You can either click the Run button at the top left of the Xcode window or use the keyboard shortcut Command-R. Your output in the console should look like this:

```
The turkey weighs 14.200000.
Cook it for 228.000000 minutes.
```

Back in your code, let's review what you have done. In the line of code that looks like this:

```c
float weight;
```

we say that you are "declaring the variable weight to be of type float."

In the next line, your variable gets a value:

```c
weight = 14.2;
```

You are copying data into that variable. We say that you are "assigning a value of 14.2 to that variable."

In modern C, you can declare a variable and assign it an initial value in one line, like this:

```c
float weight = 14.2;
```

Here is another assignment:

```c
cookingTime = 15.0 + 15.0 * weight;
```

The stuff on the righthand side of the = is an *expression*. An expression is something that gets evaluated and results in some value. Actually, every assignment has an expression on the righthand side of the =.

For example, in this line:

```
weight = 14.2;
```

the expression is just 14.2.

An expression can have multiple steps. For example, when evaluating the expression 15.0 + 15.0 * weight, the computer first multiplies weight by 15.0 and then adds that result to 15.0. Why does the multiplication come first? We say that multiplication has *precedence* over addition.

To change the order in which operations are normally executed, you use parentheses:

```
cookingTime = (15.0 + 15.0) * weight;
```

Now the expression in the parentheses is evaluated first, so the computer first does the addition and then multiplies weight by 30.0.

Challenge

Welcome to your first challenge!

Most chapters in this book will finish with a challenge exercise to do on your own. Some challenges (like the one you are about to do) are easy and provide practice doing the same thing you did in the chapter. Other challenges are harder and require more problem-solving. Doing these exercises cements what you have learned and builds confidence in your skills. We cannot encourage you enough to take them on.

(If you get stuck while working on a challenge, take a break and come back and try again fresh. If that does not work, visit the forum for this book at forums.bignerdranch.com for help.)

Create a new C Command Line Tool named TwoFloats. In its **main()** function, declare two variables of type float and assign each of them a number with a decimal point, like 3.14 or 42.0. Declare another variable of type double and assign it the sum of the two floats. Print the result using **printf()**. Refer to the code in this chapter if you need to check your syntax.

4
if/else

An important idea in programming is taking different actions depending on circumstances:

- Have all the billing fields in the order form been filled out? If so, enable the Submit button.

- Does the player have any lives left? If so, resume the game. If not, show the picture of the grave and play the sad music.

This sort of behavior is implemented using if and else, the syntax of which is:

```
if (conditional) {
   // Execute this code if the conditional evaluates to true
} else {
   // Execute this code if the conditional evaluates to false
}
```

You will not create a project in this chapter. Instead, consider the code examples carefully based on what you have learned in the last two chapters.

Here is an example of code using if and else:

```
float truckWeight = 34563.8;

// Is it under the limit?
if (truckWeight < 40000.0) {
    printf("It is a light truck\n");
} else {
    printf("It is a heavy truck\n");
}
```

If you do not have an else clause, you can just leave that part out:

```
float truckWeight = 34563.8;

// Is it under the limit?
if (truckWeight < 40000.0) {
    printf("It is a light truck\n");
}
```

The conditional expression is always either true or false. In C, it was decided that 0 would represent false, and anything that is not zero would be considered true.

In the conditional in the example above, the < operator takes a number on each side. If the number on the left is less than the number on the right, the expression evaluates to 1 (a very common way of expressing trueness), If the number on the left is greater than or equal to the number on the right, the expression evaluates to 0 (the only way to express falseness).

Operators often appear in conditional expressions. Table 4.1 shows the common operators used when comparing numbers (and other types that the computer evaluates as numbers):

Table 4.1 Comparison operators

<	Is the number on the left less than the number on the right?
>	Is the number on the left greater than the number on the right?
<=	Is the number on the left less than or equal to the number on the right?
>=	Is the number on the left greater than or equal to the number on the right?
==	Are they equal?
!=	Are they *not* equal?

The == operator deserves an additional note: In programming, the == operator is what is used to *check for* equality. We use the single = to *assign* a value. Many, many bugs have come from programmers using = when they meant to use ==. So stop thinking of = as "the equals sign." From now on, it is "the assignment operator."

Some conditional expressions require logical operators. What if you want to know if a number is in a certain range, like greater than zero and less than 40,000? To specify a range, you can use the logical AND operator (&&):

```
if ((truckWeight > 0.0) && (truckWeight < 40000.0)) {
    printf("Truck weight is within legal range.\n");
}
```

Table 4.2 shows the three logical operators:

Table 4.2 Logical operators

&&	Logical AND -- true if and only if both are true
||	Logical OR -- false if and only if both are false
!	Logical NOT -- true becomes false, false becomes true

(If you are coming from another language, note that there is no logical exclusive OR in Objective-C, so we will not discuss it here.)

The logical NOT operator (!) negates the expression to its right.

```
// Is it lighter than air?
if (!(truckWeight > 0.0)) {
    printf("The truck has zero or negative weight. Hauling helium?\n");
}
```

Boolean variables

As you can see, expressions can become quite long and complex. Sometimes it is useful to put the value of the expression into a handy, well-named variable.

```
BOOL isNotLegal = !((truckWeight > 0.0) && (truckWeight <  40000.0));
if (isNotLegal) {
    printf("Truck weight is not within legal range.\n");
}
```

A variable that can be true or false is a *boolean* variable. Historically, C programmers have always used an int to hold a boolean value. Objective-C programmers typically use the type BOOL for boolean variables, so that is what we use here. (BOOL is an alias for an integer type.) To use BOOL in a C function, like **main()**, you would need to include in your program the file where this type is defined:

```
#include <objc/objc.h>
```

You will learn more about including files in the next chapter.

When curly braces are optional

A syntax note: if the code that follows the conditional expression consists of only one statement, then the curly braces are optional. So the following code is equivalent to the previous example.

```
BOOL isNotLegal = !((truckWeight > 0.0) && (truckWeight <  40000.0));
if (isNotLegal)
    printf("Truck weight is not within legal range.\n");
```

However, the curly braces are necessary if the code consists of more than one statement.

```
BOOL isNotLegal = !((truckWeight > 0.0) && (truckWeight <  40000.0));
if (isNotLegal) {
    printf("Truck weight is not within legal range.\n");
    printf("Impound truck.\n");
}
```

Why? Imagine if you removed the curly braces.

```
BOOL isNotLegal = !((truckWeight > 0.0) && (truckWeight <  40000.0));
if (isNotLegal)
    printf("Truck weight is not within legal range.\n");
    printf("Impound truck.\n");
```

This code would make you very unpopular with truck drivers. In this case, every truck gets impounded regardless of weight. When the compiler does not find a curly brace after the conditional, only the next statement is considered part of the if construct. Thus, the second statement is always executed. (What about the indention of the second statement? While indention is very helpful for human readers of code, it means nothing to the compiler.)

In this book, we will always include the curly braces.

else if

What if you have more than two possibilities? You can test for them one by one using else if. For example, suppose a truck belongs to one of three weight categories: floating, light, and heavy.

```
if (truckWeight <= 0) {
    printf("A floating truck\n");
} else if (truckWeight < 40000.0) {
    printf("A light truck\n");
} else {
    printf("A heavy truck\n");
}
```

You can have as many else if clauses as you wish. They will each be tested in the order in which they appear until one evaluates as true. The "in the order in which they appear" part is important. Be sure to order your conditions so that you do not get a false positive. For instance, if you swapped the first two tests in the above example, you would never find a floating truck because floating trucks are also light trucks. The final else clause is optional, but it is useful when you want to catch everything that did not meet the earlier conditions.

For the more curious: conditional operators

It is not uncommon to use if and else to set the value of an instance variable. For example, you might have the following code:

```
int minutesPerPound;
if (isBoneless) {
    minutesPerPound = 15;
} else {
    minutesPerPound = 20;
}
```

Whenever you have a scenario where a value is assigned to a variable based on a conditional, you have a candidate for the *conditional operator*, which is ?. (You will sometimes see it called the *ternary operator* because it takes three operands).

```
int minutesPerPound = isBoneless ? 15 : 20;
```

This one line is equivalent to the previous example. Instead of writing if and else, you write an assignment. The part before the ? is the conditional. The values after the ? are the alternatives for whether the conditional is found to be true or false.

Challenge

Consider the following code snippet:

```
int i = 20;
int j = 25;
int k = ( i > j ) ? 10 : 5;

if ( 5 < j - k ) { // First expression
    printf("The first expression is true.");
} else if ( j > i ) { // Second expression
    printf("The second expression is true.");
} else {
    printf("Neither expression is true.");
}
```

What will be printed to the console?

5

Functions

In Chapter 3, you learned that a variable is a name associated with a chunk of data. A function is a name associated with a chunk of code. You can pass information to a function. You can make the function execute code. You can make a function return information to you.

Functions are fundamental to programming, so there is a lot in this chapter – three new projects, a new tool, and many new ideas. Let's get started with an exercise that will demonstrate what functions are good for.

When should I use a function?

Suppose you are writing a program to congratulate students for completing a Big Nerd Ranch course. Before worrying about retrieving the student list from a database or about printing certificates on spiffy Big Nerd Ranch paper, you want to experiment with the message that will be printed on the certificates.

Create a new C Command Line Tool named ClassCertificates. (Select File → New → Project... or use the keyboard shortcut Command-Shift-N to get started.)

Your first thought in writing this program might be:

```
int main (int argc, const char * argv[])
{
    printf("Kate has done as much Cocoa Programming as I could fit into 5 days.\n");
    printf("Bo has done as much Objective-C Programming as I could fit into 2 days.\n");
    printf("Mike has done as much Python Programming as I could fit into 5 days.\n");
    printf("Liz has done as much iOS Programming as I could fit into 5 days.\n");

    return 0;
}
```

Does the thought of typing all this in bother you? Does it seem annoyingly repetitive? If so, you have the makings of an excellent programmer. When you find yourself repeating work that is very similar in nature (in this case, the words in the **printf()** statement), you want to start thinking about a function as a better way of accomplishing the same task.

How do I write and use a function?

Now that you have realized that you need a function, you need to write one. Open main.c in your ClassCertificates project and write a new function named **congratulateStudent**. This function should go just before **main()** in the file.

```
#include <stdio.h>

void congratulateStudent(char *student, char *course, int numDays)
[
    printf("%s has done as much %s Programming as I could fit into %d days.\n",
        student, course, numDays);
}

int main(int argc, const char * argv[])
{
    ...
```

(Wondering what the %s and %d mean? Puzzled by the type char *? Hold on for now; we will get there.)

Now edit **main()** to use your new function:

```
int main (int argc, const char * argv[])
{
    congratulateStudent("Kate", "Cocoa", 5);
    congratulateStudent("Bo", "Objective-C", 2);
    congratulateStudent("Mike", "Python", 5);
    congratulateStudent("Liz", "iOS", 5);

    return 0;
}
```

Build and run the program. Find your output in the console. You may need to resize the bottom area. You can do this by clicking on the area's grey header and then dragging to adjust its size. (You can resize any of the areas in Xcode the same way.)

The output should be identical to what you would have seen if you had typed in everything yourself.

```
Kate has done as much Cocoa Programming as I could fit into 5 days.
Bo has done as much Objective-C Programming as I could fit into 2 days.
Mike has done as much Python Programming as I could fit into 5 days.
Liz has done as much iOS Programming as I could fit into 5 days.
```

Think about what you have done here. You noticed a repetitive pattern. You took all the shared characteristics of the problem (the repetitive text) and moved them into a separate function. That left the differences (student name, course name, number of days). You handled those differences by adding three *parameters* to the function. Let's look again at the line where you name the function.

```
void congratulateStudent(char *student, char *course, int numDays)
```

Each parameter has two parts: the type of data the argument represents and the name of the parameter. Parameters are separated by commas and placed in parentheses to the right of the name of the function.

What about the void to the left of your function name? That is the type of information returned from the function. When you do not have any information to return, you use the keyword void. We will talk more about *returning* later in this chapter.

You also used, or *called*, your new function in **main()**. When you called **congratulateStudent()**, you passed it values. Values passed to a function are known as *arguments*. The argument's value is then assigned to the corresponding parameter name. That parameter name can be used inside the function as a variable that contains the passed-in value.

In your first call to **congratulateStudent()**, you passed three arguments: "Kate", "Cocoa", 5.

```
congratulateStudent("Kate", "Cocoa", 5);
```

For now, focus on the third argument. When 5 is passed to **congratulateStudent()**, it is assigned to the third parameter, numDays. Arguments and parameters are matched up in the order in which they appear. They must also be the same (or very close to the same) type. Here, 5 is an integer value, and the type of numDays is int.

Now, when **congratulateStudent()** uses the numDays variable within the function, its value will be 5. Finally, you can prove that all of this worked by looking at the first line of the output, which correctly displays the number of days.

Look back to the first proposed version of ClassCertificates with all the repetitive typing. What is the point of using a function instead? To save on the typing? Well, yes, but that is definitely not all. Partitioning your code into functions makes it easier to make changes and to find and fix bugs. You can make a change or fix a typo in one place, and it will have the effects you want everywhere you call that function.

Another benefit to writing functions is reusability. Now that you have written this handy function, you could use it in another program.

How functions work together

A program is a collection of functions. When you run a program, those functions are copied from the hard drive into memory, and the processor finds the function called "main" and executes it.

Remember that a function is like a recipe card. If you began to execute the "Easy Broiled Chicken" card, you would discover that the third instruction says "Execute the Seasoned Bread Crumbs recipe," which is explained on another card. A programmer would say, "The Easy Broiled Chicken function *calls* the Seasoned Bread Crumbs function."

Figure 5.1 Recipe cards

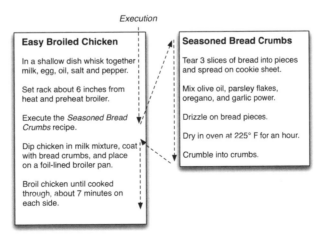

Similarly, **main()** can call other functions. For example, **main()** in ClassCertificates called the **congratulateStudent()**, which in turn called **printf()**.

While you are preparing the bread crumbs, you stop executing the steps on the "Easy Broiled Chicken" card. When the bread crumbs are ready, you resume working through the "Easy Broiled Chicken" card.

Similarly, the main function stops executing and "blocks" until the function it called is done executing. To see this happen, you are going to call a **sleep** function that does nothing but wait a number of seconds. This function is declared in the file unistd.h. At the top of main.c, include this file:

```
#include <stdio.h>
#include <unistd.h>

void congratulateStudent(char *student, char *course, int numDays)
{
...
```

In your **main** function, call the **sleep** function after the calls to **congratulateStudent()**.

```
int main (int argc, const char * argv[])
{
    congratulateStudent("Kate", "Cocoa", 5);
    sleep(2);
    congratulateStudent("Bo", "Objective-C", 2);
    sleep(2);
    congratulateStudent("Mike", "Python", 5);
    sleep(2);
    congratulateStudent("Liz", "iOS", 5);

    return 0;
}
```

Build and run the program. You should see a two-second pause between each message of congratulations. That is because the **main** function stops running until the **sleep** function is done sleeping.

Standard libraries

Your computer came with many functions built-in. Actually, that is a little misleading – here is the truth: Before OS X was installed on your computer, it was nothing but an expensive space heater. Among the things that were installed as part of OS X were files containing a collection of precompiled functions. These collections are called the *standard libraries*.

Two of the files that make up the standard libraries are stdio.h and unistd.h. When you include these files in your program, you can then use the functions that they contain. **printf()** is in stdio.h; **sleep()** is in unistd.h.

The standard libraries have two purposes:

- They represent big chunks of code that you do not need to write and maintain. Thus, they empower you to build much bigger, better programs than you would be able to do otherwise.

- They ensure that most programs look and feel similar.

Programmers spend a lot of time studying the standard libraries for the operating systems that they work on. Every company that creates an operating system also has documentation for the standard libraries that come with it. You will learn how to browse the documentation for iOS and OS X in Chapter 16.

Local variables, frames, and the stack

Every function can have *local variables*. Local variables are variables declared inside a function. They exist only during the execution of that function and can only be accessed from within that function. For example, consider a function that computed how long to cook a turkey. It might look like this:

```
void showCookTimeForTurkey(int pounds)
{
    int necessaryMinutes = 15 + 15 * pounds;
    printf("Cook for %d minutes.\n", necessaryMinutes);
}
```

necessaryMinutes is a local variable. It will come into existence when **showCookTimeForTurkey()** starts to execute and will cease to exist once that function completes execution. The parameter of the function, pounds, is also a local variable. A parameter is a local variable that gets initialized to the value of the corresponding argument.

A function can have many local variables, and all of them are stored in the *frame* for that function. Think of the frame as a blackboard that you can scribble on while the function is running. When the function is done executing, the blackboard is discarded.

Imagine for a moment that you are working on the Easy Broiled Chicken recipe. In your kitchen, each recipe that is in progress gets its own blackboard, so you have a blackboard for the Easy Broiled Chicken recipe ready. Now, when you call the Seasoned Bread Crumbs recipe, you need a new blackboard. Where are you going to put it? Right on top of the blackboard for Easy Broiled Chicken. After all, you have suspended execution of Easy Broiled Chicken to make Seasoned Bread Crumbs. You will not need the Easy Broiled Chicken frame until the Seasoned Bread Crumbs recipe is complete and its frame is discarded. What you have now is a stack of frames.

Figure 5.2 Two blackboards in a stack

Programmers use the word *stack* to describe where the frames are stored in memory. When a function is called, its frame is pushed onto the top of the stack. When a function finishes executing, we say that it *returns*. That is, it pops its frame off the stack and lets the function that called it resume execution.

Let's look more closely at how the stack works by putting **showCookTimeForTurkey()** into a program. Create a new C Command Line Tool named TurkeyTimer. Edit main.c to look like this:

```
#include <stdio.h>

void showCookTimeForTurkey(int pounds)
{
    int necessaryMinutes = 15 + 15 * pounds;
    printf("Cook for %d minutes.\n", necessaryMinutes);
}

int main(int argc, const char * argv[])
{
    int totalWeight = 10;
    int gibletsWeight = 1;
    int turkeyWeight = totalWeight - gibletsWeight;
    showCookTimeForTurkey(turkeyWeight);
    return 0;
}
```

Build and run the program. You should see the following output:

```
Cook for 150 minutes.
```

Recall that `main()` is always executed first. `main()` calls `showCookTimeForTurkey()`, which begins executing. What, then, does this program's stack look like just after `necessaryMinutes` is computed?

Figure 5.3 Two frames on the stack

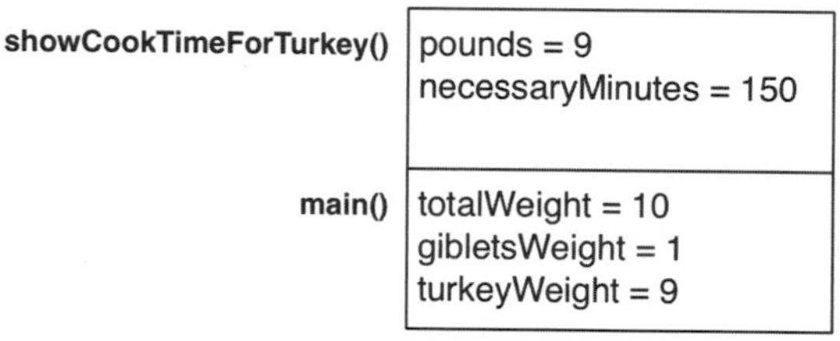

showCookTimeForTurkey()	pounds = 9 necessaryMinutes = 150
main()	totalWeight = 10 gibletsWeight = 1 turkeyWeight = 9

The stack is last-in, first-out. That is, `showCookTimeForTurkey()`'s frame is popped off the stack before `main()`'s frame is popped off the stack.

Notice that pounds, the single parameter of `showCookTimeForTurkey()`, is part of the frame. Recall that a parameter is a local variable that has been assigned the value of the corresponding argument. For this example, the variable turkeyWeight with a value of 9 is passed as an argument to `showCookTimeForTurkey()`. Then that value is assigned to the parameter pounds, that is, it is copied into the function's frame.

Scope

In a function definition, any pair of curly braces { ... }) define the *scope* of the code that is in between them. A variable cannot be accessed outside of the scope that it is declared in. In fact, it does not exist outside of the scope that it is declared in.

Any pair of braces, whether they are a part of a function definition, an `if` statement, or a loop, defines its own scope that restricts the availability of any variables declared within them.

Add the following code to your **showCookTimeForTurkey** function:

```
void showCookTimeForTurkey(int pounds)
{
    int necessaryMinutes = 15 + 15 * pounds;
    printf("Cook for %d minutes.\n", necessaryMinutes);
    if (necessaryMinutes > 120) {
        int halfway = necessaryMinutes / 2;
        printf("Rotate after %d of the %d minutes.\n", halfway, necessaryMinutes);
    }
}
```

Build and run the program.

The **printf** statement in this example can access variables that are in the scope defined by the curly braces of the if statement, like halfway. It can also access variables in the outer scope defined by the **showCookTimeForTurkey** function itself, like necessaryMinutes.

Now move the **printf** call outside of the if statement's scope:

```
void showCookTimeForTurkey(int pounds)
{
    int necessaryMinutes = 15 + 15 * pounds;
    printf("Cook for %d minutes.\n", necessaryMinutes);
    if (necessaryMinutes > 120) {
        int halfway = necessaryMinutes / 2;
        printf("Rotate after %d of the %d minutes.\n", halfway, necessaryMinutes);
    }
    printf("Rotate after %d of the %d minutes.\n", halfway, necessaryMinutes);
}
```

Build and run the program again. The program will not run, and you will get a build error: Use of undeclared identifier 'halfway'. Outside of the if statement's scope, the halfway variable does not exist. Stylish programmers would say that, "When the **printf()** call is made, the halfway variable has fallen out of scope."

Recursion

Can a function call itself? You bet! We call that *recursion*. There is a notoriously dull song called "99 Bottles of Beer." Create a new C Command Line Tool named BeerSong. Open main.c and add a function to write out the words to this song and then kick it off in **main()**:

```
#include <stdio.h>

void singSongFor(int numberOfBottles)
{
    if (numberOfBottles == 0) {
        printf("There are simply no more bottles of beer on the wall.\n\n");
    } else {
        printf("%d bottles of beer on the wall. %d bottles of beer.\n",
                numberOfBottles, numberOfBottles);
        int oneFewer = numberOfBottles - 1;
        printf("Take one down, pass it around, %d bottles of beer on the wall.\n\n",
                oneFewer);
        singSongFor(oneFewer); // This function calls itself!

        // Print a message just before the function ends
        printf("Put a bottle in the recycling, %d empty bottles in the bin.\n",
                numberOfBottles);
    }
}


int main(int argc, const char * argv[])
{

    // We could sing 99 verses, but 4 is easier to think about
    singSongFor(4);
    return 0;
}
```

Build and run the program. The output looks like this:

```
4 bottles of beer on the wall. 4 bottles of beer.
Take one down, pass it around, 3 bottles of beer on the wall.

3 bottles of beer on the wall. 3 bottles of beer.
Take one down, pass it around, 2 bottles of beer on the wall.

2 bottles of beer on the wall. 2 bottles of beer.
Take one down, pass it around, 1 bottles of beer on the wall.

1 bottles of beer on the wall. 1 bottles of beer.
Take one down, pass it around, 0 bottles of beer on the wall.

There are simply no more bottles of beer on the wall.

Put a bottle in the recycling, 1 empty bottles in the bin.
Put a bottle in the recycling, 2 empty bottles in the bin.
Put a bottle in the recycling, 3 empty bottles in the bin.
Put a bottle in the recycling, 4 empty bottles in the bin.
```

What does the stack look like when the last bottle is taken off the wall, but none have been put in the recycling bin?

Figure 5.4 Frames on the stack for a recursive function

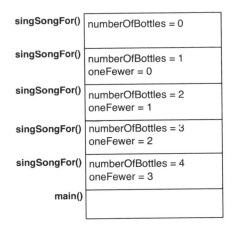

Confused? Here is what happened:

- **main()** called **singSongFor(4)**.

- **singSongFor(4)** printed a verse and called **singSongFor(3)**.

- **singSongFor(3)** printed a verse and called **singSongFor(2)**.

- **singSongFor(2)** printed a verse and called **singSongFor(1)**.

- **singSongFor(1)** printed a verse and called **singSongFor(0)**.

- **singSongFor(0)** printed "There are simply no more bottles of beer on the wall." And returned.

- **singSongFor(1)** resumed execution, printed the recycling message, and returned.

- **singSongFor(2)** resumed execution, printed the recycling message, and returned.

- **singSongFor(3)** resumed execution, printed the recycling message, and returned.

- **singSongFor(4)** resumed execution, printed the recycling message, and returned.

- **main()** resumed, returned, and the program ended.

Discussing frames and the stack is usually not covered in a beginning programming course, but we have found the ideas to be exceedingly useful to new programmers. First, these concepts give you a more concrete understanding of the answers to questions like "What happens to my local variables when the function finishes executing?" Second, they help you understand the *debugger*. The debugger is a program that helps you understand what your program is actually doing, which, in turn, helps you find and fix "bugs" (problems in your code). When you build and run a program in Xcode, the debugger is *attached* to the program so that you can use it.

Looking at frames in the debugger

You can use the debugger to browse the frames on the stack. To do this, however, you have to stop your program in mid-execution. Otherwise, **main()** will finish executing, and there will not be any frames left to look at. To see as many frames as possible in your BeerSong program, you want to halt execution on the line that prints "There are simply no more bottles of beer on the wall."

How do you do this? In main.c, find the line

```
printf("There are simply no more bottles of beer on the wall.\n");
```

There are two gray columns to the left of your code. Click the wider, lighter-gray column next to this line of code to set a *breakpoint*.

Figure 5.5 Setting a breakpoint

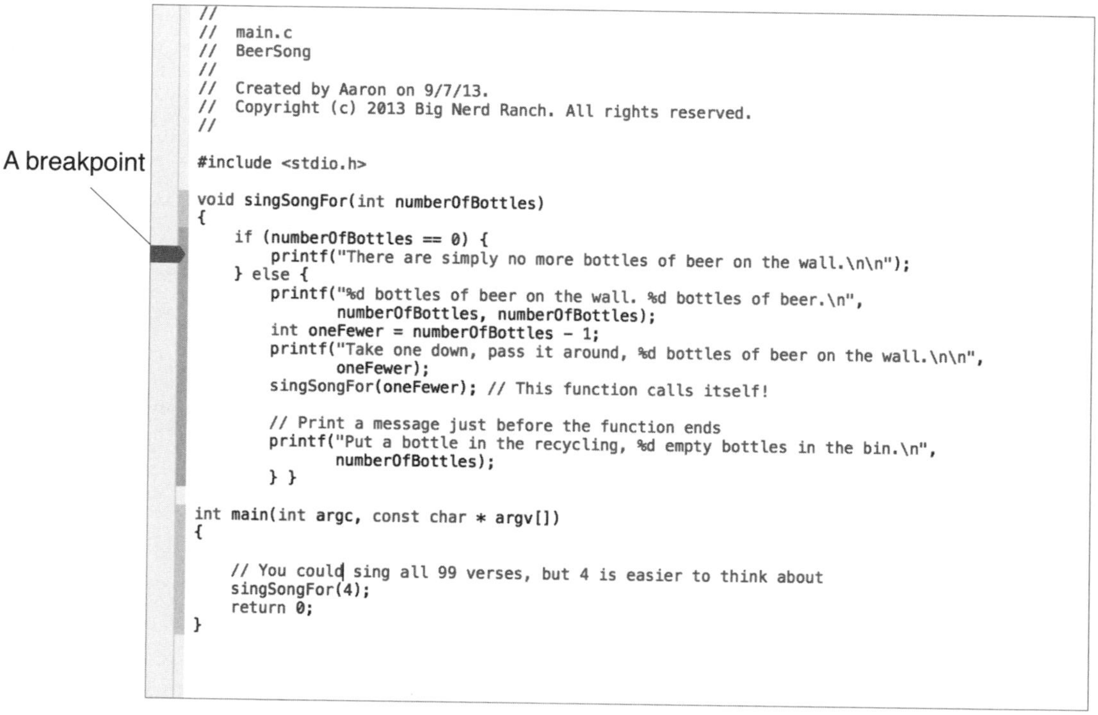

A breakpoint is a location in code where you want the debugger to pause the execution of your program. Run the program again. You can see from the output in the console that your program stopped (or "broke") right before executing the line on which you set the breakpoint.

The program is temporarily frozen, and you can examine it more closely. The navigator area has switched to displaying the *debug navigator*, which shows all the frames currently on the stack, also called a *stack trace*.

In the stack trace, frames are identified by the name of their function. Since your program consists almost entirely of a recursive function, these frames have the same name and you must distinguish them by the value of oneFewer that gets passed to them. At the bottom of the stack is the frame for **main()**.

You can select a frame from the stack to see the variables in that frame and the source code for the line of code that is currently being executed. Select the frame for the first time **singSongFor()** is called.

Figure 5.6 Selecting frame for singSongFor(4)

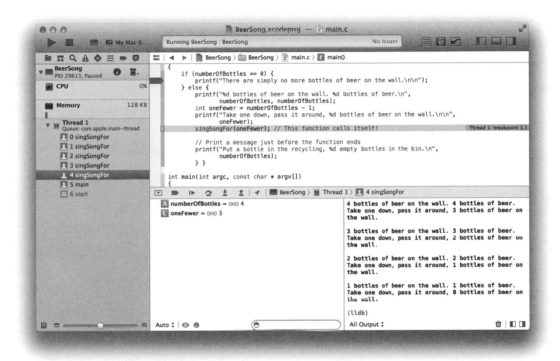

You can see this frame's variables and their values in the bottom area to the left of the console. This area is called the *variables view*.

Now you need to remove the breakpoint so that the program will run normally. Right-click the blue indicator and select Delete Breakpoint.

To resume execution of your program, click the ▮► button on the grey bar above the variables view.

Figure 5.7 Resuming BeerSong

Continue program execution

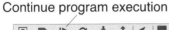

We just took a quick look at the debugger here to demonstrate how frames work. However, using the debugger to set breakpoints and browse the frames in a program's stack will be helpful when your program is not doing what you expect and you need to look at what is really happening.

return

Many functions return a value when they complete execution. You know what type of data a function will return by the type that precedes the function name. (If a function does not return anything, its return type is void.)

Create a new C Command Line Tool named Degrees. In main.c, add a function before **main()** that converts a temperature from Celsius to Fahrenheit. Then update **main()** to call the new function.

```
#include <stdio.h>

float fahrenheitFromCelsius(float cel)
{
    float fahr = cel * 1.8 + 32.0;
    printf("%f Celsius is %f Fahrenheit\n", cel, fahr);
    return fahr;
}

int main(int argc, const char * argv[])
{
    float freezeInC = 0;
    float freezeInF = fahrenheitFromCelsius(freezeInC);
    printf("Water freezes at %f degrees Fahrenheit.\n", freezeInF);
    return 0;
}
```

See how you take the return value of **fahrenheitFromCelsius()** and assign it to the freezeInF variable of type float? Build and run the program.

The execution of a function stops when it returns. For example, take a look at this function:

```
float average(float a, float b)
{
    return (a + b)/2.0;
    printf("The mean justifies the end.\n");
}
```

If you called this function, the **printf()** call would never get executed.

A natural question, then, is "Why do we always return 0 from **main()**?" When you return 0 to the system, you are saying "Everything went OK." If you are terminating the program because something has gone wrong, you return 1.

This may seem contradictory to how 0 and 1 work in if statements; because 1 is true and 0 is false, it is natural to think of 1 as success and 0 as failure. So think of **main()** as returning an error report. In that case, 0 is good news! Success is a lack of errors.

To make this clearer, some programmers use the constants EXIT_SUCCESS and EXIT_FAILURE, which are just aliases for 0 and 1, respectively. These constants are defined in the header file stdlib.h:

```
#include <stdio.h>
#include <stdlib.h>

float fahrenheitFromCelsius(float cel)
{
    float fahr = cel * 1.8 + 32.0;
    printf("%f Celsius is %f Fahrenheit.\n", cel, fahr);
    return fahr;
}

int main(int argc, const char * argv[])
{
    float freezeInC = 0;
    float freezeInF = fahrenheitFromCelsius(freezeInC);
    printf("Water freezes at %f degrees Fahrenheit.\n", freezeInF);
    return EXIT_SUCCESS;
}
```

In this book, we will generally use 0 instead of EXIT_SUCCESS.

Global and static variables

In this chapter, we talked about local variables that only exist while a function is running. There are also variables that can be accessed from any function at any time. We call these *global variables*. To make a variable global, you declare it outside of a particular function. For example, you could add a lastTemperature variable that holds the temperature that was converted from Celsius. Add a global variable to Degrees:

```
#include <stdio.h>
#include <stdlib.h>

// Declare a global variable
float lastTemperature;

float fahrenheitFromCelsius(float cel)
{
    lastTemperature = cel;
    float fahr = cel * 1.8 + 32.0;
    printf("%f Celsius is %f Fahrenheit.\n", cel, fahr);
    return fahr;
}
int main(int argc, const char * argv[])
{
    float freezeInC = 0;
    float freezeInF = fahrenheitFromCelsius(freezeInC);
    printf("Water freezes at %f degrees Fahrenheit.\n", freezeInF);
    printf("The last temperature converted was %f.\n", lastTemperature);
    return EXIT_SUCCESS;
}
```

Any complex program will involve dozens of files containing different functions. Global variables are available to the code in every one of those files. Sometimes sharing a variable between different files is what you want. But, as you can imagine, having a variable that can be accessed by multiple functions can also lead to great confusion. To deal with this, we have *static variables*. A static variable is like a global variable in that it is declared outside of any function. However, a static variable is only accessible from the code in the file where it was declared. So you get the non-local, "exists outside of any function" benefit while avoiding the "you touched my variable!" issue.

You can change your global variable to a static variable, but because you have only one file, main.c, it will have no effect whatsoever.

```
// Declare a static variable
static float lastTemperature;
```

Both static and global variables can be given an initial value when they are created:

```
// Initialize lastTemperature to 50 degrees
static float lastTemperature = 50.0;
```

If you do not give them an initial value, they are automatically initialized to zero.

In this chapter, you have learned about functions. When you get to Objective-C in Part III, you will hear the word *method* – a method is very, very similar to a function.

Challenge

The interior angles of a triangle must add up to 180 degrees. Create a new C Command Line Tool named Triangle. In main.c, write a function that takes the first two angles and returns the third. Here is what it will look like when you call it:

```
#include <stdio.h>

// Add your new function here

int main(int argc, const char * argv[])
{
    float angleA = 30.0;
    float angleB = 60.0;
    float angleC = remainingAngle(angleA, angleB);
    printf("The third angle is %.2f\n", angleC);
    return 0;
}
```

The output should be:

```
The third angle is 90.00
```

6
Format Strings

Now that you know how functions work, let's take a closer look at the **printf** function that you have been using to write to the log.

The **printf** function accepts a *string* as an argument and prints it to the log. A string is a "string" of characters strung together like beads on a necklace. Typically, a string is text.

A *literal string* is text surrounded by double quotes. In the AGoodStart project from Chapter 2, you called **printf()** with literal string arguments:

```
// Print the beginning of the novel
printf("It was the best of times.\n");
printf("It was the worst of times.\n");
```

Your output looked like this:

```
It was the best of times.
It was the worst of times.
```

You can store a literal string in a variable of type char *:

```
char *myString = "Here is a string";
```

This is a *C string*. You could have created C strings in AGoodStart and passed them to **printf()**:

```
// Write the beginning of the novel
char *firstLine = "It was the best of times.\n";
char *secondLine = "It was the worst of times.\n";

// Print the beginning of the novel
printf(firstLine);
printf(secondLine);
```

Your output would have looked exactly the same.

Using tokens

The **printf** function can do more than just print literal strings. You can also use **printf()** to create custom strings at runtime using tokens and variables.

Reopen your ClassCertificates project. In main.c, find **congratulateStudent()**. Within this function, you call **printf()** and pass it a string with three tokens and three variables as arguments.

```
void congratulateStudent(char *student, char *course, int numDays)
{
    printf("%s has done as much %s Programming as I could fit into %d days.\n",
        student, course, numDays);
}
```

When you pass a string containing one or more tokens to **printf()**, the string that you pass is called the *format string*. In this example, the format string includes three tokens: %s, %s, and %d.

When the program is run, the tokens are replaced with the values of the corresponding variable arguments. In this case, those variables are student, course, and numDays. Your output looked something like this:

```
Liz has done as much iOS Programming as I could fit into 5 days.
```

Tokens are replaced in order in the output: the first variable replaces the first token, and so on. Thus, if you swapped student and course in the list of variables, you would see

```
iOS has done as much Liz Programming as I could fit into 5 days.
```

On the other hand, not all tokens and variables are interchangeable. The token you choose tells **printf()** how the variable's value should be formatted. The %s token tells **printf()** to format the value as a string. The %d tells **printf()** to format the value an integer. (The d stands for "decimal.")

If you use the wrong token, such as using %d when the substitution is the string "Ted", **printf()** will try to represent "Ted" with an integer value, which will give you strange results.

There are other tokens for other types. You will learn and use several more as you continue working through this book.

Escape sequences

The \n that you put at the end of your strings is an *escape sequence*. An escape sequence begins with \, which is the *escape character*. This character tells the compiler that the character that comes immediately after does not have its usual meaning.

The \n represents the new-line character. In **printf()** statements, you include a new-line character when you want output to continue on a new line. Try removing one of these new-lines and see what happens to your output.

Another escape sequence is \". You use it when you need to include quotation marks within a literal string. The escape character tells the compiler to treat the " as part of the literal string and not as an instruction to end the string. Here is an example:

```
printf("\"It doesn't happen all at once,\" said the Skin Horse.\n");
```

And here is the output:

```
"It doesn't happen all at once," said the Skin Horse.
```

Challenge

Create a new project (C Command Line Tool) named Squarer. Write a program that computes and displays the square of integer. Put the numbers in quotation marks. Your output should look something like this:

```
"5" squared is "25".
```

7

Numbers

You have used numbers to measure and display temperature, weight, and how long to cook a turkey. Now let's take a closer look at how numbers work in C programming. On a computer, numbers come in two flavors: integers and floating-point numbers. You have already used both.

Integers

An integer is a number without a decimal point – a whole number. Integers are good for tasks like counting. Some tasks, like counting every person on the planet, require really large numbers. Other tasks, like counting the number of children in a classroom, require numbers that are not as large.

To address these different tasks, integer variables come in different sizes. An integer variable has a certain number of bits in which it can encode a number, and the more bits the variable has, the larger the number it can hold. Typical sizes are 8-bit, 16-bit, 32-bit, and 64-bit.

Similarly, some tasks require negative numbers, while others do not. So integer types come in signed and unsigned varieties.

An unsigned 8-bit number can hold any integer from 0 to 255. Why? $2^8 = 256$ possible numbers. And we choose to start at 0.

A signed 64-bit number can hold any integer from -9,223,372,036,854,775,808 to 9,223,372,036,854,775,807. One bit for the sign leaves $2^{63} = 9,223,372,036,854,775,808$. There is only one zero.

When you declare an integer, you can be very specific:

```
UInt32 x; // An unsigned 32-bit integer
SInt16 y; // A signed 16-bit integer
```

However, it is more common for programmers just to use the descriptive types that you learned in Chapter 3.

```
char a;      // 8 bits
short b;     // Usually 16 bits (depending on the platform)
int c;       // Usually 32 bits (depending on the platform)
long d;      // 32 or 64 bits  (depending on the platform)
long long e; // 64 bits
```

Why is char an 8-bit integer? When C was designed, nearly everyone used ASCII to represent characters. ASCII gave each commonly used character a number. For example, 'B' was represented by the number 66. The numbers went up to 127, so we could easily fit any ASCII character into 8 bits. To deal with other character systems (like Cyrillic or Kanji), we needed a lot more than 8 bits. For now, live with ASCII characters, and we will talk about dealing with other encodings (like Unicode) in Chapter 26.

What about sign? char, short, int, long, and long long are signed by default, but you can prefix them with unsigned to create the unsigned equivalent.

Also, the sizes of integers depend on the platform. (A *platform* is a combination of an operating system and a particular computer or mobile device.) Some platforms are 32-bit and others are 64-bit. The difference is in the size of the memory address, and we will talk more about that in Chapter 9.

Tokens for displaying integers

Create a new project: a C Command Line Tool called Numbers. In main.c, create an integer and print it out in base-10 (i.e., as a decimal number) using **printf()**:

```
#include <stdio.h>

int main (int argc, const char * argv[])
{
    int x = 255;
    printf("x is %d.\n", x);
    return 0;
}
```

You should see something like

```
x is 255.
```

As you have seen, %d prints an integer as a decimal number. What other tokens work? You can print the integer in base-8 (octal) or base-16 (hexadecimal). Add a couple of lines to the program:

```
#include <stdio.h>

int main (int argc, const char * argv[])
{
    int x = 255;
    printf("x is %d.\n", x);
    printf("In octal, x is %o.\n", x);
    printf("In hexadecimal, x is %x.\n", x);

    return 0;
}
```

When you run it, you should see something like:

```
x is 255.
In octal, x is 377.
In hexadecimal, x is ff.
```

(We will return to hexadecimal numbers in Chapter 38.)

What if the integer has lots of bits? You slip an l (for long) or an ll (for long long) between the % and the format character. Change your program to use a long instead of an int:

```c
#include <stdio.h>

int main (int argc, const char * argv[])
{
    long x = 255;
    printf("x is %ld.\n", x);
    printf("In octal, x is %lo.\n", x);
    printf("In hexadecimal, x is %lx.\n", x);

    return 0;
}
```

If you are printing an unsigned decimal number, you should use %u:

```c
#include <stdio.h>

int main (int argc, const char * argv[])
{
    unsigned long x = 255;
    printf("x is %lu.\n", x);

    // Octal and hex already assume the number was unsigned
    printf("In octal, x is %lo.\n", x);
    printf("In hexadecimal, x is %lx.\n", x);

    return 0;
]
```

Integer operations

The arithmetic operators +, -, and * work as you would expect. They also have the precedence rules that you would expect: * is evaluated before + or -. In main.c, replace the previous code with a calculation:

```c
#include <stdio.h>

int main (int argc, const char * argv[])
{

    printf("3 * 3 + 5 * 2 = %d\n", 3 * 3 + 5 * 2);

    return 0;
}
```

You should see

```
3 * 3 + 5 * 2 = 19
```

Integer division

Most beginning C programmers are surprised by how integer division works. Try it:

```
#include <stdio.h>

int main (int argc, const char * argv[])
{
    printf("3 * 3 + 5 * 2 = %d\n", 3 * 3 + 5 * 2);
    printf("11 / 3 = %d\n", 11 / 3);

    return 0;
}
```

You will get 11 / 3 = 3.666667, right? Nope. You get 11 / 3 = 3. When you divide one integer by another, you always get a third integer. The system rounds off toward zero. (So, -11 / 3 is -3.)

This actually makes sense if you think "11 divided by 3 is 3 with a remainder of 2." And it turns out that the remainder is often quite valuable. The modulus operator (%) is like /, but it returns the remainder instead of the quotient. Add the modulus operator to get a statement that includes the remainder:

```
#include <stdio.h>

int main (int argc, const char * argv[])
{
    printf("3 * 3 + 5 * 2 = %d\n", 3 * 3 + 5 * 2);
    printf("11 / 3 = %d remainder of %d \n", 11 / 3, 11 % 3);

    return 0;
}
```

What if you *want* to get 3.666667? You convert the int to a float using the *cast operator*. The cast operator is the type that you want placed in parentheses to the left of the variable you want converted. Cast your denominator as a float before you do the division:

```
int main (int argc, const char * argv[])
{
    printf("3 * 3 + 5 * 2 = %d\n", 3 * 3 + 5 * 2);
    printf("11 / 3 = %d remainder of %d \n", 11 / 3, 11 % 3);
    printf("11 / 3.0 = %f\n", 11 / (float)3);

    return 0;
}
```

Now, floating point division will be done instead of integer division, and you will get 3.666667. Here is the rule for integer vs. floating-point division: / is integer division only if both the numerator and denominator are integer types. If either is a floating-point number, floating-point division is done instead.

NSInteger and NSUInteger

At this moment, Xcode supports the development of both 32-bit and 64-bit applications. In an effort to make it easy for you to write code that will work elegantly on either system, Apple introduced NSInteger and NSUInteger. These are 32-bit integers on 32-bit systems; They are 64-bit integers on 64-bit systems. NSInteger is signed. NSUInteger is unsigned.

`NSInteger` and `NSUInteger` are used extensively in Apple's libraries, so when you start working in Objective-C, you will use them a lot.

The recommended way of outputting them with **`printf()`** is a little surprising. Because Apple does not want you to make too many assumptions about what is really behind them, it is recommended that you cast them to the appropriate `long` before trying to display them:

```
NSInteger x = -5;
NSUInteger y = 6;
printf("Here they are: %ld, %lu", (long)x, (unsigned long)y);
```

Operator shorthand

All the operators that you have seen so far yield a new result. So, for example, to increase x by 1, you would use the + operator and then assign the result back into x:

```
int x = 5;
x = x + 1; // x is now 6
```

C programmers do these sorts of operations so often that operators were created that change the value of the variable without an assignment. For example, you can increase the value held in x by 1 with the *increment operator* (++):

```
int x = 5;
x++; // x is now 6
```

There is also a *decrement operator* (--) that decreases the value by 1:

```
int x = 5;
x--; // x is now 4
```

What if you want to increase x by 5 instead of just 1? You could use addition and assignment:

```
int x = 5;
x = x + 5; // x is 10
```

But there is a shorthand for this, too:

```
int x = 5;
x += 5; // x is 10
```

You can think of the second line as "assign x the value of x + 5." In addition to +=, there are also -=, *=, /=, and %=.

To get the absolute value of an `int`, you use a function instead of an operator. The function is **`abs()`**. If you want the absolute value of a `long`, use **`labs()`**. Both functions are declared in `stdlib.h`:

```
#include <stdio.h>
#include <stdlib.h>

int main (int argc, const char * argv[])
{
    printf("3 * 3 + 5 * 2 = %d\n", 3 * 3 + 5 * 2);
    printf("11 / 3 = %d remainder of %d \n", 11 / 3, 11 % 3);
    printf("11 / 3.0 = %f\n", 11 / (float)3);
    printf("The absolute value of -5 is %d\n", abs(-5));

    return 0;
}
```

Floating-point numbers

If you need a number with a decimal point, like 3.2, you use a floating-point number. Most programmers think of a floating-point number as a mantissa multiplied by 10 to an integer exponent. For example, 345.32 is thought of as 3.4532×10^2. And this is essentially how they are stored: a 32-bit floating number has 8 bits dedicated to holding the exponent (a signed integer) and 23 bits dedicated to holding the mantissa, with the remaining 1 bit used to hold the sign.

Like integers, floating-point numbers come in several sizes. Unlike integers, floating-point numbers are *always* signed:

```
float g;        // 32 bits
double h;       // 64 bits
long double i;  // 128 bits
```

Tokens for displaying floating-point numbers

`printf()` can also display floating point numbers, most commonly using the tokens %f and %e. In main.c, replace the integer-related code:

```
int main (int argc, const char * argv[])
{
    double y = 12345.6789;
    printf("y is %f\n", y);
    printf("y is %e\n", y);

    return 0;
}
```

When you build and run it, you should see:

```
y is 12345.678900
y is 1.234568e+04
```

So %f uses normal decimal notation, and %e uses scientific notation.

Notice that %f is currently showing 6 digits after the decimal point. This is often a bit much. Limit it to two digits by modifying the token:

```
int main (int argc, const char * argv[])
{
    double y = 12345.6789;
    printf("y is %.2f\n", y);
    printf("y is %.2e\n", y);
    return 0;
}
```

When you run it, you should see:

```
y is 12345.68
y is 1.23e+04
```

The math library

If you will be doing a lot of math, you will need the math library. To see what is in the math library, open the Terminal application on your Mac and type man math. You will get a great summary of everything in the math library: trigonometry, rounding, exponentiation, square and cube root, etc.

If you use any of these math functions in your code, be sure to include the math library header at the top that file:

```
#include <math.h>
```

One warning: all of the trig-related functions are done in radians, not degrees!

Challenge

Use the math library! Add code to `main.c` that displays the sine of 1 radian. Show the number rounded to three decimal points. It should be `0.841`. The sine function is declared like this:

```
double sin(double x);
```

A note about comments

As you type in exercises, do not be shy about adding comments of your own to help you remember what code is doing. Get in the habit of commenting code. Write useful and specific comments that could be understood by someone else reading your code or by you in the future coming back to review the code.

Comments can be helpful when you tackle challenges. For example, say you get a challenge working but are not sure it is solved in an elegant way. Leave yourself a note about what bugged you. When you are further along in the book, review old challenges and see if you can improve your solutions. This will also test your ability to write useful comments. Something like

```
// Not sure if this is right
...
```

will be useless to your future self.

8
Loops

In Xcode, create yet another new project: a C Command Line Tool named Coolness.

The first program I ever wrote printed the words, "Aaron is Cool". (I was 10 at the time.) Write a program to do that now:

```
#include <stdio.h>

int main(int argc, const char * argv[])
{
    printf("Aaron is Cool\n");
    return 0;
}
```

Build and run the program.

Let's suppose for a moment that you could make my 10-year-old self feel more confident if the program printed the affirmation a dozen times. How would you do that?

Here is the dumb way:

```
#include <stdio.h>

int main(int argc, const char * argv[])
{
    printf("Aaron is Cool\n");
    printf("Aaron is Cool\n");
    printf("Aaron is Cool\n");
    printf("Aaron is Cool\n");
    printf("Aaron is Cool\n");
    printf("Aaron is Cool\n");
    printf("Aaron is Cool\n");
    printf("Aaron is Cool\n");
    printf("Aaron is Cool\n");
    printf("Aaron is Cool\n");
    printf("Aaron is Cool\n");
    printf("Aaron is Cool\n");

    return 0;
}
```

The smart way is to create a loop.

The while loop

The first loop you will use is a while loop. The while construct works something like the it construct discussed in Chapter 4. You give it an expression and a block of code contained by curly braces. In the if construct, if the expression is true, the block of code is run once. In the while construct, the block is run again and again until the expression becomes false.

Rewrite the **main()** function to look like this:

```
#include <stdio.h>

int main(int argc, const char * argv[])
{
    int i = 0;
    while (i < 12) {
        printf("%d. Aaron is Cool\n", i);
        i++;
    }
    return 0;
}
```

Build and run the program.

The conditional (i < 12) is being checked before each execution of the block. The first time it evaluates to false, execution leaps to the code after the block.

Notice that the second line of the block increments i. This is important. If i was not incremented, then this loop, as written, would continue forever because the expression would always be true.

Here is a flow-chart of this while loop:

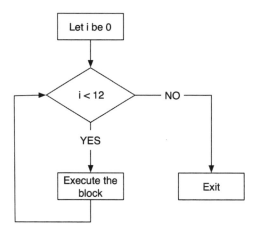

The for loop

The `while` loop is a general looping structure, but C programmers use the same basic pattern a lot:

```
some initialization
while (some check) {
    some code
    some last step
}
```

So, the C language has a shortcut: the `for` loop. In the `for` loop, the pattern shown above becomes:

```
for (some initialization; some check; some last step) {
    some code;
}
```

Change the program to use a `for` loop:

```
#include <stdio.h>

int main(int argc, const char * argv[])
{
    for (int i = 0; i < 12; i++) {
        printf("%d. Aaron is Cool\n", i);
    }
    return 0;
}
```

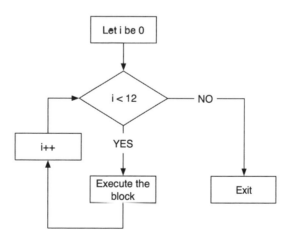

Note that in this simple loop example, you used the loop to dictate the number of times something happens. More commonly, however, loops are used to *iterate* through a collection of items, such as a list of names. For instance, you could modify this program to use a loop in conjunction with a list of friends' names. Each time through the loop, a different friend would get to be cool. You will learn more about collections and loops starting in Chapter 17.

break

Sometimes it is necessary to stop the loop's execution from inside the loop. For example, let's say you want to step through the positive integers looking for the number x, where $x + 90 = x^2$. Your plan is to step through the integers 0 through 11 and pop out of the loop when you find the solution. Change the code:

```c
#include <stdio.h>

int main(int argc, const char * argv[])
{
    int i;
    for (i = 0; i < 12; i++) {
        printf("Checking i = %d\n", i);
        if (i + 90 == i * i) {
            break;
        }
    }
    printf("The answer is %d.\n", i);
    return 0;
}
```

Build and run the program. You should see

```
Checking i = 0
Checking i = 1
Checking i = 2
Checking i = 3
Checking i = 4
Checking i = 5
Checking i = 6
Checking i = 7
Checking i = 8
Checking i = 9
Checking i = 10
The answer is 10.
```

Notice that when break is called, execution skips directly to the end of the code block.

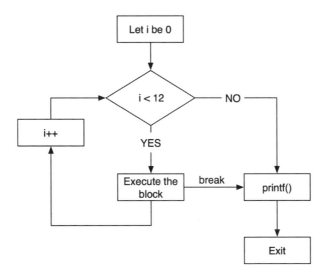

continue

Sometimes you find yourself in the middle of the code block and you need to say, "Forget the rest of this run through the code block and start the next run through the code block." This is done with the `continue` command. For example, what if you were pretty sure that no multiples of 3 satisfied the equation? How would you avoid wasting precious time checking those?

```
#include <stdio.h>

int main(int argc, const char * argv[])
{
    int i;
    for (i = 0; i < 12; i++) {
        if (i % 3 == 0) {
            continue;
        }
        printf("Checking i = %d\n", i);
        if (i + 90 == i * i) {
            break;
        }
    }
    printf("The answer is %d.\n", i);
    return 0;
}
```

Build and run it:

```
Checking i = 1
Checking i = 2
Checking i = 4
Checking i = 5
Checking i = 7
Checking i = 8
Checking i = 10
The answer is 10.
```

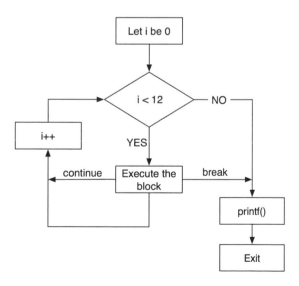

The do-while loop

The cool kids seldom use the do-while loop, but for completeness, here it is. The do-while loop does not check the expression until it has executed the block. Thus, it ensures that the block is always executed at least once. If you rewrote the original exercise to use a do-while loop, it would look like this:

```
int main(int argc, const char * argv[])
{
    int i = 0;
    do {
        printf("%d. Aaron is Cool\n", i);
        i++;
    } while (i < 12);
    return 0;
}
```

Notice the trailing semicolon. That is because unlike the other loops, a do-while loop is actually one long statement:

do { something } while (something else stays true);

Here is a flow-chart of this do-while loop:

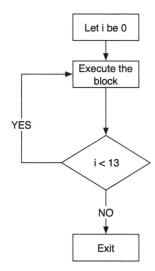

Challenge: counting down

Create a new project (C Command Line Tool) named CountDown and write a program that counts backward from 99 through 0 by 3, printing each number.

If the number is divisible by 5, it should also print the words "Found one!". Thus, the output should look something like this:

```
99
96
93
90
Found one!
87
...
0
Found one!
```

Challenge: user input

So far, the programs you have written do some work and then output text to the console. In this challenge, you will modify your CountDown solution to ask for input from the user. In particular, you will ask the user what number the countdown should start from.

To make this happen, you need to know about two new functions: **readline()** and **atoi()** (pronounced "A to I").

The **readline** function is the opposite of **printf()**. Rather than printing text to the screen, it gets text that user has entered.

Before you can use **readline()**, you must first add the library that contains it to your program.

In the project navigator, click the top-level Coolness item. In the editor area, click Build Phases and then the disclosure triangle next to the line that says Link Binary With Libraries.

Figure 8.1 Link binary with libraries

Click the + button. A sheet will a appear with a list of available code libraries. Use the search box to search for libreadline. When it appears in the list, select it and click Add.

Figure 8.2 Libraries

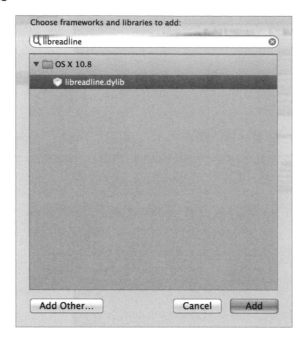

Select main.c in the project navigator to get back to your code.

What were these steps for? Sometimes, you want to use a function that is not already provided for you. So you need to tell Xcode which *code library* contains the function you want to use.

Let's look at an example that uses the **readline()** function. You started this chapter with code that printed Aaron is Cool. What if the user could enter the name of the person that is cool? Here is what the program would look like when run. (The user input is shown in bold)

```
Who is cool? Mikey
Mikey is cool!
```

The code would look like this:

```
#import <stdio.h>
int main(int argc, const char * argv[])
{
    printf("Who is cool? ");
    const char *name = readline(NULL);
    printf("%s is cool!\n\n",name);
    return 0;
}
```

(Type this code into your Coolness project and run it, if you would like to see it in action.)

The first line of this **main** function is a variable declaration:

```
const char *name;
```

Remember that char * is a type you can use for strings.

In the third line, you call the **readline** function, and pass NULL as its argument. This line gets what the user typed in and stores it in the name variable.

Now let's turn to the **atoi** function. This function takes a string and converts it into an integer. (The 'i' stands for integer, and the 'a' stands for ASCII.)

What good is **atoi()**? The following example code would cause an error because it attempts to store a string in a variable of type int.

```
int num = "23";
```

You can use **atoi()** to convert that string into an integer with a value of 23, which you can happily store in a variable of type int:

```
int num = atoi("23");
```

(If the string passed into **atoi()** cannot be converted into an integer, then **atoi()** returns 0.)

With these two functions in mind, modify your code to prompt the user for input and then kick off the countdown from the desired spot. Your output should look something like this:

```
Where should I start counting? 42
42
39
36
33
30
Found one!
27
...
```

Note that Xcodo has an interesting behavior when using the **readline** function. It will duplicate text input as output:

Figure 8.3 **readline()** output

This is expected behavior in Xcode.

9

Addresses and Pointers

Your computer is, at its core, a processor (the Central Processing Unit or CPU) and a vast meadow of switches (the Random-Access Memory or RAM) that can be turned on or off by the processor. We say that a switch holds one *bit* of information. You will often see 1 used to represent "on" and 0 used to represent "off."

Eight of these switches make a *byte* of information. The processor can fetch the state of these switches, do operations on the bits, and store the result in another set of switches. For example, the processor might fetch a byte from here and another byte from there, add them together, and store the result in a byte someplace else.

Figure 9.1 Memory and the CPU

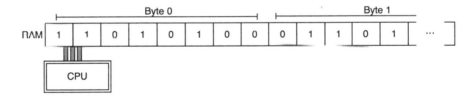

The memory is numbered, and we typically talk about the *address* of a particular byte of data. When people talk about a 32-bit CPU or a 64-bit CPU, they are usually talking about how big the address is. A 64-bit CPU can deal with much, much more memory than a 32-bit CPU.

Getting addresses

In Xcode, create a new project: a C Command Line Tool named Addresses.

The address of a variable is the location in memory where the value for that variable is stored. To get the variable's address, you use the & operator:

```
#include <stdio.h>

int main(int argc, const char * argv[])
{
    int i = 17;
    printf("i stores its value at %p\n", &i);
    return 0;
}
```

Notice the %p token. This is the token that you can replace with a memory address. Build and run the program.

Your output will look something like:

```
i stores its value at 0xbffff738
```

although your computer may put i at a different address. Memory addresses are nearly always printed in hexadecimal format.

In a computer, everything is stored in memory, and thus everything has an address. For example, a function starts at some particular address. To get that address, you just use the function's name:

```
int main(int argc, const char * argv[])
{
    int i = 17;
    printf("i stores its value at %p\n", &i);
    printf("this function starts at %p\n", main);
    return 0;
}
```

Build and run the program.

Storing addresses in pointers

What if you wanted to store an address in a variable? You could stuff it into an unsigned integer that was the right size, but the compiler will help you catch your mistakes if you are more specific when you give that variable its type. For example, if you wanted a variable named ptr that holds the address where a float can be found, you would declare it like this:

```
float *ptr;
```

We say that ptr is a variable that is a *pointer* to a float. It does not store the value of a float; it can hold an address where a float may be stored.

Declare a new variable named addressOfI that is a pointer to an int. Assign it the address of i.

```
int main(int argc, const char * argv[])
{
    int i = 17;
    int *addressOfI = &i;
    printf("i stores its value at %p\n", addressOfI);
    printf("this function starts at %p\n", main);
    return 0;
}
```

Build and run the program. You should see no change in its behavior.

You are using integers right now for simplicity. But if you are wondering what the point of pointers is, we hear you. It would be just as easy to pass the integer value assigned to this variable as it is to pass its address. Soon, however, your data will be much larger and much more complex than single integers. That is why we pass addresses. It is not always possible to pass a copy of data you want to work with, but you can always pass the *address* of where that data begins. And it is easy to access data once you have its address.

Getting the data at an address

If you have an address, you can get the data stored there using the * operator. Have the log display the value of the integer stored at addressofI.

```
int main(int argc, const char * argv[])
{
    int i = 17;
    int *addressOfI = &i;
    printf("i stores its value at %p\n", addressOfI);
    printf("this function starts at %p\n", main);
    printf("the int stored at addressOfI is %d\n", *addressOfI);
    return 0;
}
```

Notice that the asterisk is used two different ways in this example:

- When you declared addressOfI to be an int *. That is, you told the compiler "It will hold an address where an int can be stored."

- When you read the int value that is stored at the address stored in addressOfI. (Pointers are also called references. Thus, using the pointer to read data at the address is sometimes called *dereferencing* the pointer.)

You can also use the * operator on the left-hand side of an assignment to store data at a particular address:

```
int main(int argc, const char * argv[])
{
    int i = 17;
    int *addressOfI = &i;
    printf("i stores its value at %p\n", addressOfI);
    *addressOfI = 89;
    printf("Now i is %d\n", i);
    return 0;
}
```

Build and run your program.

Do not worry if you do not have pointers squared away in your mind just yet. You will spend a lot of time working with pointers as you go through this book, so you will get plenty of practice.

How many bytes?

Given that everything lives in memory and that you now know how to find the address where data starts, the next question is "How many bytes does this data type consume?"

Using **sizeof()** you can find the size of a data type. For example,

```
int main(int argc, const char * argv[])
{
    int i = 17;
    int *addressOfI = &i;
    printf("i stores its value at %p\n", addressOfI);
    *addressOfI = 89;
    printf("Now i is %d\n", i);
    printf("An int is %zu bytes\n", sizeof(int));
    printf("A pointer is %zu bytes\n", sizeof(int *));
    return 0;
}
```

Here there is yet another new token in the calls to **printf()**: %zu. The **sizeof()** function returns a value of type size_t, for which %zu is the correct placeholder token.

Build and run the program. If your pointer is 4 bytes long, your program is running in 32-bit mode. If your pointer is 8 bytes long, your program is running in 64-bit mode.

sizeof() will also take a variable as an argument, so you could have written the previous program like this:

```
int main(int argc, const char * argv[])
{
    int i = 17;
    int *addressOfI = &i;
    printf("i stores its value at %p\n", addressOfI);
    *addressOfI = 89;
    printf("Now i is %d\n", i);
    printf("An int is %zu bytes\n", sizeof(i));
    printf("A pointer is %zu bytes\n", sizeof(addressOfI));
    return 0;
}
```

NULL

Sometimes you need a pointer to nothing. That is, you have a variable that can hold an address, and you want to store something in it that makes it explicit that the variable is not set to anything. We use NULL for this:

```
float *myPointer;
// Set myPointer to NULL for now, I'll store an address there
// later in the program
myPointer = NULL;
```

What is NULL? Remember that an address is just a number. NULL is zero. This is very handy in if statements:

```
float *myPointer;
...
// Has myPointer been set?
if (myPointer) {
    // myPointer is not NULL
    ...do something with the data at myPointer...
} else {
    // myPointer is NULL
}
```

Sometimes NULL indicates that there is no value, so you might see something like this:

```
float *measuredGravityPtr = NULL;

// Some code that might set measuredGravityPtr to be non-NULL
...

float actualGravity;

// Did we measure the gravity?
if (measuredGravityPtr) {
    actualGravity = *measuredGravityPtr;
} else {
    actualGravity = estimatedGravity(planetRadius);
}
```

Or, you can use the ternary operator to do the same thing more tersely:

```
// If measuredGravityPtr is NULL, estimate the gravity
float actualGravity =
        measuredGravityPtr ? *measuredGravityPtr : estimatedGravity(planetRadius);
```

Later, when you are learning about pointers to objects, you will use nil instead of NULL. They are equivalent, but Objective-C programmers use nil to mean the address where no object lives.

Stylish pointer declarations

When you declare a pointer to float, it looks like this:

```
float *powerPtr;
```

Because the type is a pointer to a float, you may be tempted to write it like this:

```
float* powerPtr;
```

This is fine, and the compiler will let you do it. However, stylish programmers do not.

Why? You can declare multiple variables in a single line. For example, if you wanted to declare variables x, y, and z, you could do it like this:

```
float x, y, z;
```

Each one is a float.

What do you think these are?

```
float* b, c;
```

Surprise! b is a pointer to a float, but c is just a float. If you want them both to be pointers, you must put a * in front of each one:

```
float *b, *c;
```

Putting the * directly next to the variable name makes this clearer.

A final note: Pointers can be difficult to get your head around at first. Do not worry if you have not mastered these ideas yet. You will be working with them for the rest of the book, and they will make more sense each time you do.

Challenge: how much memory?

Write a program that shows you how much memory a float consumes.

Challenge: how much range?

On a Mac, a short is a 2-byte integer, and one bit is used to hold the sign (positive or negative). What is the smallest number that a short can store? What is the largest?

An unsigned short only holds non-negative numbers. What is the largest number that an unsigned short can store?

10
Pass-By-Reference

There is a standard C function called **modf()**. You give **modf()** a double, and it calculates the integer part and the fraction part of the number. For example, if you give it 3.14, 3 is the integer part and 0.14 is the fractional part.

You, as the caller of **modf()**, want both parts. However, a C function can only return one value. How can **modf()** give you both pieces of information?

When you call **modf()**, you will supply an address where it can stash one of the numbers. In particular, it will return the fractional part and copy the integer part to the address you supply. Create a new project: a C Command Line Tool named PBR.

Edit main.c:

```
#include <stdio.h>
#include <math.h>

int main(int argc, const char * argv[])
{
    double pi = 3.14;
    double integerPart;
    double fractionPart;

    // Pass the address of integerPart as an argument
    fractionPart = modf(pi, &integerPart);

    // Find the value stored in integerPart
    printf("integerPart = %.0f, fractionPart = %.2f\n", integerPart, fractionPart);

    return 0;
}
```

This is known as *pass-by-reference*. That is, you supply an address (also known as "a reference"), and the function puts the data there.

Figure 10.1 The stack as **modf()** returns

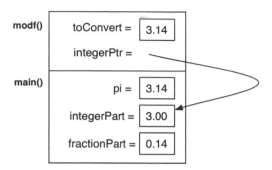

Here is another way to think about pass-by-reference. Imagine that you give out assignments to spies. You might tell one, "I need photos of the finance minister with his girlfriend. I've left a short length of steel pipe at the foot of the angel statue in the park. When you get the photos, roll them up and leave them in the pipe. I'll pick them up Tuesday after lunch." In the spy biz, this is known as a "dead drop."

modf() works just like a dead drop. You are asking it to execute and telling it a location where the result can be placed so you can find it later. The only difference is that instead of a steel pipe, you are giving it a location in memory where the result can be placed.

Writing pass-by-reference functions

The world is just awesome. The variety of cultures and peoples around the world inspires a great deal of excellent output from the arts and sciences.

One complication of this diversity is that different people use different units for measuring the world around them. The scientific and engineering communities tend to have a preference for metric units (such as meters) over imperial units (such as feet and inches), due to their ease of use in mathematical calculation.

If you were to write an application for consumption by users in certain parts of the world, however, you might want to be able to print the results of your meter-based calculations using feet and inches.

How would you write a function that converts a distance in meters to the equivalent distance in feet and inches? It would need to read a floating-point number and return two others. The declaration of such a function would look like this:

```
void metersToFeetAndInches(double meters, unsigned int *ftPtr, double *inPtr);
```

When the function is called, it will be passed a value for meters. It will also be supplied with locations where the values for feet and inches can be stored.

Now write the function near the top of your main.c file and call it from **main()**:

```c
#include <stdio.h>
#include <math.h>

void metersToFeetAndInches(double meters, unsigned int *ftPtr, double *inPtr)
{
    // This function assumes meters is non-negative.

    // Convert the number of meters into a floating-point number of feet
    double rawFeet = meters * 3.281; // e.g. 2.4536

    // How many complete feet as an unsigned int?
    unsigned int feet = (unsigned int)floor(rawFeet);

    // Store the number of feet at the supplied address
    printf("Storing %u to the address %p\n", feet, ftPtr);
    *ftPtr = feet;

    // Calculate inches
    double fractionalFoot = rawFeet - feet;
    double inches = fractionalFoot * 12.0;

    // Store the number of inches at the supplied address
    printf("Storing %.2f to the address %p\n", inches, inPtr);
    *inPtr = inches;
}


int main(int argc, const char * argv[])
{
    double meters = 3.0;
    unsigned int feet;
    double inches;

    metersToFeetAndInches(meters, &feet, &inches);
    printf("%.1f meters is equal to %d feet and %.1f inches.", meters, feet, inches);

    return 0;
}
```

Build and run the program.

Figure 10.2 The stack as **metersToFeetAndInches()** returns

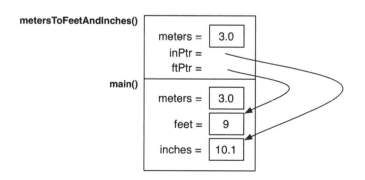

Avoid dereferencing NULL

Sometimes a function can supply many values by reference, but you may only care about some of them. How do you avoid declaring these variables and passing their addresses when you are not going to use them anyway? Typically, you pass NULL as an address to tell the function "I do not need this particular value."

This means that you should always check to make sure the pointers are non-NULL before you dereference them. Add these checks in **metersToFeetAndInches()**:

```
void metersToFeetAndInches(double meters, unsigned int *ftPtr, double *inPtr)
{
    double rawFeet = meters * 3.281;
    unsigned int feet = (unsigned int)floor(rawFeet);

    // Store the number of feet at the supplied address
    if (ftPtr) {
        printf("Storing %u to the address %p\n", feet, ftPtr);
        *ftPtr = feet;
    }

    double fractionalFoot = rawFeet - feet;
    double inches = fractionalFoot * 12.0;

    if (inPtr) {
        printf("Storing %.2f to the address %p\n", inches, inPtr);
        *inPtr = inches;
    }
}
```

Challenge

In **metersToFeedAndInches()**, you used **floor()** and subtraction to break rawFeet into its integer and fractional parts. Change **metersToFeedAndInches()** to use **modf()** instead.

11
Structs

Sometimes you need a variable to hold several related chunks of data. In C, you can do this with a *structure*, commonly called a *struct*. Each chunk of data is known as a *member* of the struct.

For example, consider a program that computes a person's Body Mass Index, or BMI. BMI is a person's weight in kilograms divided by the square of the person's height in meters. (BMI is a very imprecise tool for measuring a person's fitness, but it makes a fine programming example.)

Create a new project: a C Command Line Tool named BMICalc. Edit main.c to declare a struct named Person that has two members: a float named heightInMeters and an int named weightInKilos. Then create two Person structs:

```
#include <stdio.h>

// Here is the declaration of the struct
struct Person {
    float heightInMeters;
    int weightInKilos;
};

int main(int argc, const char * argv[])
{
    struct Person mikey;
    mikey.heightInMeters = 1.7;
    mikey.weightInKilos = 96;

    struct Person aaron;
    aaron.heightInMeters = 1.97;
    aaron.weightInKilos = 84;

    printf("mikey is %.2f meters tall\n", mikey.heightInMeters);
    printf("mikey weighs %d kilograms\n", mikey.weightInKilos);
    printf("aaron is %.2f meters tall\n", aaron.heightInMeters);
    printf("aaron weighs %d kilograms\n", aaron.weightInKilos);
    return 0;
}
```

Notice that you access the members of a struct using a period (stylish programmers like to say "dot"). Build and run the program and confirm the output.

Here is the frame for **main()** after the struct's members have been assigned values.

Figure 11.1 Frame after member assignments

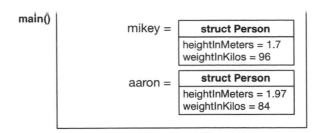

Most of the time, you use a struct declaration over and over again. So it is common to create a typedef for the struct type. A typedef defines an alias for a type declaration and allows you to use it more like the usual data types. Change main.c to create and use a typedef for struct Person. Notice that the code to replace is shown struck-through.

```
#include <stdio.h>
// Here is the declaration of the struct
struct Person {
    float heightInMeters;
    int weightInKilos;
};

// Here is the declaration of the type Person
typedef struct {
    float heightInMeters;
    int weightInKilos;
} Person;

int main(int argc, const char * argv[])
{
    struct Person mikey;
    Person mikey;
    mikey.heightInMeters = 1.7;
    mikey.weightInKilos = 96;

    struct Person aaron;
    Person aaron;
    aaron.heightInMeters = 1.97;
    aaron.weightInKilos = 84;

    printf("mikey is %.2f meters tall\n", mikey.heightInMeters);
    printf("mikey weighs %d kilograms\n", mikey.weightInKilos);
    printf("aaron is %.2f meters tall\n", aaron.heightInMeters);
    printf("aaron weighs %d kilograms\n", aaron.weightInKilos);
    return 0;
}
```

You can pass a Person to another function. Add a function named **bodyMassIndex()** that accepts a Person as a parameter and calculates BMI. Then update **main()** to call this function:

```
#include <stdio.h>


// Here is the declaration of the type Person
typedef struct {
    float heightInMeters;
    int weightInKilos;
} Person;

float bodyMassIndex(Person p)
{
  return p.weightInKilos / (p.heightInMeters * p.heightInMeters);
}

int main(int argc, const char * argv[])
{
    Person mikey;
    mikey.heightInMeters = 1.7;
    mikey.weightInKilos = 96;

    Person aaron;
    aaron.heightInMeters = 1.97;
    aaron.weightInKilos = 84;

    printf("mikey is %.2f meters tall\n", mikey.heightInMeters);
    printf("mikey weighs %d kilograms\n", mikey.weightInKilos);
    printf("aaron is %.2f meters tall\n", aaron.heightInMeters);
    printf("aaron weighs %d kilograms\n", aaron.weightInKilos);

    float bmi;
    bmi = bodyMassIndex(mikey);
    printf("mikey has a BMI of %.2f\n", bmi);

    bmi = bodyMassIndex(aaron);
    printf("aaron has a BMI of %.2f\n", bmi);

    return 0;
}
```

Here you create a local variable bmi to hold the return value of **bodyMassIndex()**. You retrieve and print out the Mikey's BMI. Then you reuse the variable to retrieve and print out Aaron's BMI.

Challenge

The first struct I had to deal with as a programmer was struct tm, which the standard C library uses to hold time broken down into its components. The struct is defined:

```
struct tm {
    int     tm_sec;      /* seconds after the minute [0-60] */
    int     tm_min;      /* minutes after the hour [0 59] */
    int     tm_hour;     /* hours since midnight [0-23] */
    int     tm_mday;     /* day of the month [1-31] */
    int     tm_mon;      /* months since January [0-11] */
    int     tm_year;     /* years since 1900 */
    int     tm_wday;     /* days since Sunday [0-6] */
    int     tm_yday;     /* days since January 1 [0-365] */
    int     tm_isdst;    /* Daylight Savings Time flag */
    long    tm_gmtoff;   /* offset from CUT in seconds */
    char    *tm_zone;    /* timezone abbreviation */
};
```

The function **time()** returns the number of seconds since the first moment of 1970 in Greenwich, England. **localtime_r()** can read that duration and pack a struct tm with the appropriate values. (It actually takes the *address* of the number of seconds since 1970 and the *address* of an struct tm.) Thus, getting the current time as a struct tm looks like this:

```
long secondsSince1970 = time(NULL);
printf("It has been %ld seconds since 1970\n", secondsSince1970);

struct tm now;
localtime_r(&secondsSince1970, &now);
printf("The time is %d:%d:%d\n", now.tm_hour, now.tm_min, now.tm_sec);
```

Your challenge is to write a program that will tell you what the date (4-30-2015 format is fine) will be in 4 million seconds.

(One hint: tm_mon = 0 means January, so be sure to add 1. Also, include the <time.h> header at the start of your program.)

12
The Heap

So far, your programs have used one kind of memory – frames on the stack. Recall that every function has a frame where its local variables are stored. This memory is automatically allocated when a function starts and automatically deallocated when the function ends. In fact, local variables are sometimes called *automatic variables* because of this convenient behavior.

Sometimes, however, you need to claim a contiguous chunk of memory yourself – a *buffer*. Programmers often use the word buffer to mean a long line of bytes of memory. The buffer comes from a region of memory known as the *heap*, which is separate from the stack.

On the heap, the buffer is independent of any function's frame. Thus, it can be used across many functions. For example, you could claim a buffer of memory intended to hold some text. You could then call a function that would read a text file into the buffer, call a second function that would count all the vowels in the text, and call a third function to spellcheck it. When you were finished using the text, you would return the memory that was in the buffer to the heap.

You request a buffer of memory using the function **malloc()**. When you are done using the buffer, you call the function **free()** to release your claim on that memory and return it to the heap.

Let's say, for example, you needed a chunk of memory big enough to hold 1,000 floats. Note the crucial use of **sizeof()** to get the right number of bytes for your buffer.

```c
#include <stdio.h>
#include <stdlib.h> // malloc() and free() are in stdlib.h

int main(int argc, const char * argv[])
{
    // Declare a pointer
    float *startOfBuffer;

    // Ask to use some bytes from the heap
    startOfBuffer = malloc(1000 * sizeof(float));

    // ...use the buffer here...

    // Relinquish your claim on the memory so it can be reused
    free(startOfBuffer);

    // Forget where that memory is
    startOfBuffer = NULL;

    return 0;
}
```

startOfBuffer is a pointer to the address of the first floating point number in the buffer.

Figure 12.1 A pointer on the stack to a buffer on the heap

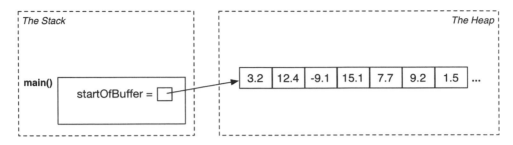

At this point, most C books would spend a lot of time talking about how to use startOfBuffer to read and write data in different locations in the buffer of floating pointer numbers. This book, however, is trying to get you to objects as quickly as possible. So, we will put off these concepts until later.

In Chapter 11, you created a struct as a local variable in **main()**'s frame on the stack. You can also allocate a buffer on the heap for a struct. To create a Person struct on the heap, you could write a program like this:

```c
#include <stdio.h>
#include <stdlib.h>

typedef struct {
    float heightInMeters;
    int weightInKilos;
} Person;

float bodyMassIndex(Person *p)
{
   return p->weightInKilos / (p->heightInMeters * p->heightInMeters);
}

int main(int argc, const char * argv[])
{
    // Allocate memory for one Person struct
    Person *mikey = (Person *)malloc(sizeof(Person));

    // Fill in two members of the struct
    mikey->weightInKilos = 96;
    mikey->heightInMeters = 1.7;

    // Print out the BMI of the original Person
    float mikeyBMI = bodyMassIndex(mikey);
    printf("mikey has a BMI of %f\n", mikeyBMI);

    // Let the memory be recycled
    free(mikey);

    // Forget where it was
    mikey = NULL;

    return 0;
}
```

Notice the operator ->. The code p->weightInKilos says, "Dereference the pointer p to the struct and get me the member called weightInKilos."

Figure 12.2 A pointer on the stack to a struct on the heap

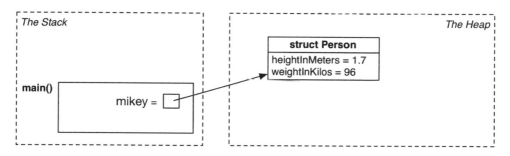

This idea of structs on the heap is a very powerful one. It forms the basis for Objective-C objects, which we turn to next.

Part III
Objective-C and Foundation

Now that you have an understanding of the basics of programs, functions, variables, and data types, you are ready to learn Objective-C. We will stick with command-line programs for now to keep the focus on programming essentials.

All Objective-C programming is done with the Foundation framework. A *framework* is library of classes that you use to write programs. What is a class? That is what we will talk about first…

13
Objects

In this chapter, you will write your first Objective-C program. This program will be a command-line tool like the ones you have written so far, but it will be written in Objective-C.

In the early 1980's, Brad Cox and Tom Love created the Objective-C language. For objects, they built upon the idea of structs allocated on the heap and added a message-sending syntax.

As you move from C programming to Objective-C programming, you are entering the world of objects and object-oriented programming. Be prepared to encounter new concepts and to be patient. You will be using these patterns again and again, and they will become clear with time and practice.

Objects

An *object* is similar to a struct (such as the `struct Person` you created in Chapter 11). Like a struct, an object can contain several pieces of related data. In a struct, we called them *members*. In an object, we call them *instance variables* (or you might hear "ivars").

An object differs from a struct in that an object can also have its own functions that act on the data it contains. These functions are called *methods*.

Classes

A *class* describes a certain type of object by listing the instance variables and methods that object will have. A class can describe an object that represents

- a concept, like a date, a string, or a set

- something in the real world, like a person, a location, or a checking account

A class defines a kind of object. It also produces objects of that kind. You can think of a class as both blueprint and factory.

In Chapter 18, you will rewrite the BMI-calculating program using objects instead of structs. You are going to create a class named **Person**. The objects that it produces will be *instances* of the **Person** class. These instances will have instance variables for height and weight and a method for calculating the BMI.

Figure 13.1 A **Person** class and two **Person** instances

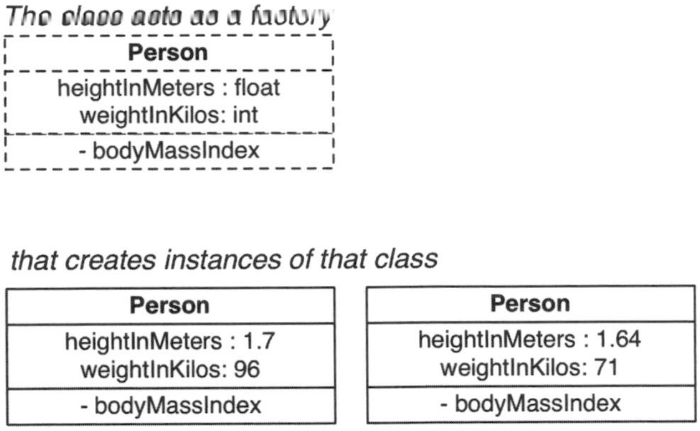

The class acts as a factory

Person
heightInMeters : float weightInKilos: int
- bodyMassIndex

that creates instances of that class

Person		Person
heightInMeters : 1.7 weightInKilos: 96		heightInMeters : 1.64 weightInKilos: 71
- bodyMassIndex		- bodyMassIndex

A note about our object diagrams: Classes, like the **Person** class, are diagrammed with a dashed border. Instances are drawn with solid borders. This is a common diagramming convention for distinguishing between classes and instances of a class.

At this point in this chapter, we are going to switch from theory to practice. Do not worry if objects, classes, instances, and methods do not make perfect sense yet. Practice will help.

Instead of starting off by writing a new custom class, you are going to create instances of a class that Apple has provided. This class is named **NSDate**. An instance of **NSDate** represents a point in time. You can think of it as a timestamp. You will also be using methods from the **NSDate** class.

Creating your first object

Create a new Command Line Tool project named TimeAfterTime. Make its type Foundation – not C like with your past projects (Figure 13.2).

Figure 13.2 Creating a Foundation command-line tool

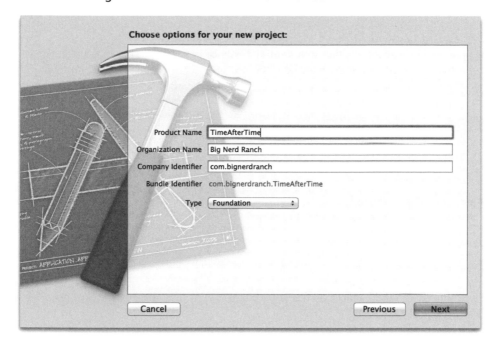

Files containing Objective-C code are given the suffix .m. Find and open main.m.

At the top of this file, find the line that reads

```
#import <Foundation/Foundation.h>
```

When Xcode created your project, it imported the Foundation framework for you. A *framework* is a set of related classes, functions, constants, and types. The Foundation framework contains fundamental classes that are used in all iOS apps and OS X applications. The **NSDate** class is in the Foundation framework.

What is the difference between #import and #include? #import is faster and more efficient. When the compiler sees the #include directive, it makes a dumb copy-and-paste of the contents of the file to include. When the compiler sees the #import directive, it first checks to see if another file may have already imported or included the file.

In main.m, add the following line of code:

```
#import <Foundation/Foundation.h>

int main (int argc, const char * argv[])
{
    @autoreleasepool {

        NSDate *now = [NSDate date];

    }
    return 0;
}
```

On the left side of the assignment operator (=), you have a variable named now. You can tell from the *
that this variable is a pointer. This pointer holds the address in memory where the instance of **NSDate**
lives.

The code on the right side returns the address of an instance of **NSDate**. This code is known as a
message send, and you will learn about messages in the next section. First, add the following line that
writes the address of the **NSDate** instance using the function **NSLog()**.

```
#import <Foundation/Foundation.h>

int main (int argc, const char * argv[])
{
    @autoreleasepool {

        NSDate *now = [NSDate date];
        NSLog(@"This NSDate object lives at %p", now);
    }
    return 0;
}
```

NSLog() is a function in the Foundation framework that is a lot like **printf()**. It accepts a format string
and can have replaceable tokens.

Build and run the program. You should see something like:

```
2013-08-05 11:53:54.366 TimeAfterTime[4862:707] This NSDate object lives at 0x100116240
```

Unlike **printf()**, **NSLog()** prefaces its output with the date, time, program name, and process ID.
From now on, when we show output from **NSLog()**, we will skip this data – the page is just too narrow.

```
This NSDate object lives at 0x100116240
```

You have created an instance of **NSDate**, and it lives at the address stored in now. To understand how
this happened, you need to know about methods and messages.

Methods and messages

Methods are like functions. They contain code to be executed on command. In Objective-C, to execute
the code in a method, you send a *message* to the object or class that has that method.

The **NSDate** class has a **date** method. In the code you just wrote, you sent the **date** message to the
NSDate class to execute the **date** method.

```
NSDate *now = [NSDate date];
```

This was your first message send.

Message sends

A message send is surrounded by square brackets and has two parts: the receiver and the selector.

Figure 13.3 A message send

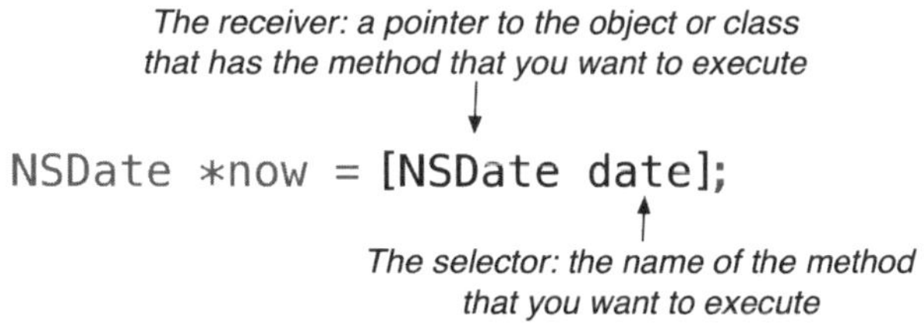

The receiver: a pointer to the object or class that has the method that you want to execute

NSDate ∗now = [NSDate date];

The selector: the name of the method that you want to execute

What does sending the **date** message do? When the **date** method is executed, the **NSDate** class claims some memory on the heap for an instance of **NSDate**, initializes the instance to the current date/time, and returns the address of the new object.

Add another **NSLog()** call to your program.

```
#import <Foundation/Foundation.h>

int main (int argc, const char * argv[])
{
    @autoreleasepool {

        NSDate *now = [NSDate date];
        NSLog(@"This NSDate object lives at %p", now);
        NSLog(@"The date is %@", now);

    }
    return 0;
}
```

Here you use a new token, %@. This Objective-C token asks the object for a description of itself. (You will learn more about %@ in Chapter 20.)

Build and run the program. You should see something like this:

```
This NSDate object lives at 0x100116240
The date is 2013-08-05 16:09:14 +0000
```

Another message

Now that you have an instance of **NSDate**, you can send messages to this new object. You are going to send it the message **timeIntervalSince1970**.

When you send this message to an instance of **NSDate**, you get back the difference in seconds between the date/time that the **NSDate** instance represents and 12:00AM on Jan 1, 1970 in Greenwich, England. (Why 1970? OS X and iOS are based on Unix, and 1970 is the start of the "Unix epoch.")

Send the **timeIntervalSince1970** message to the **NSDate** instance pointed to by now. The **timeIntervalSince1970** method returns a double. (Recall that a double is a floating-point number that has more precision than a float.) Put the result in a variable named seconds.

```
#import <Foundation/Foundation.h>

int main (int argc, const char * argv[])
{
    @autoreleasepool {

        NSDate *now = [NSDate date];
        NSLog(@"This NSDate object lives at %p", now);
        NSLog(@"The date is %@", now);

        double seconds = [now timeIntervalSince1970];
        NSLog(@"It has been %f seconds since the start of 1970.", seconds);

    }
    return 0;
}
```

Build and run the program to see the results.

Class methods vs. instance methods

Consider two messages that you have sent:

Figure 13.4 Two message sends

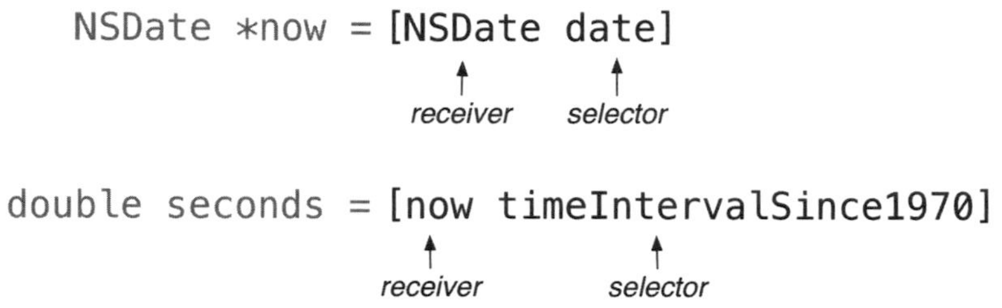

$$NSDate\ *now = [NSDate\ date]$$

$$\underset{receiver}{\uparrow} \qquad \underset{selector}{\uparrow}$$

$$double\ seconds = [now\ timeIntervalSince1970]$$

$$\underset{receiver}{\uparrow} \qquad \underset{selector}{\uparrow}$$

You sent the **date** message to the **NSDate** class. **date** is a *class method*. Typically, class methods create an instance of the class and initialize its instance variables.

In the second message send, you sent the **timeIntervalSince1970** message to the **NSDate** instance pointed to by now. **timeIntervalSince1970** is an *instance method*. Typically, instance methods give you information about or perform an operation on an instance's instance variables.

Instance methods tend to be more common in Objective-C programs. You send a message to a class to create an instance. This message causes a class method to be executed. But once you have that instance, the instance will likely receive many messages over the run of the program. These messages will cause instance methods to be executed.

Sending bad messages

What would happen if you sent the **date** class method to an **NSDate** instance or the **timeIntervalSince1970** instance method to the **NSDate** class? Try it:

```
#import <Foundation/Foundation.h>

int main (int argc, const char * argv[])
{
    @autoreleasepool {

        NSDate *now = [NSDate date];
        NSLog(@"This NSDate object lives at %p", now);
        NSLog(@"The date is %@", now);

        double seconds = [now timeIntervalSince1970];
        NSLog(@"It has been %f seconds since the start of 1970.", seconds);

        // Sending bogus messages to see errors...
        double testSeconds = [NSDate timeIntervalSince1970];
        NSDate *testNow = [now date];

    }
    return 0;
}
```

Build your program (Command-B), and Xcode will report build errors. On the first new line, find an error that reads No known class method for selector 'timeIntervalSince1970'.

(There is another error on this line about initializing a double. Ignore that one for now.)

The error is clear: The receiver in this message send is the **NSDate** class, so the selector should be the name of an **NSDate** class method. This selector is not.

On your next faulty message send, find an error that reads No visible @interface for 'NSDate' declares the selector 'date'.

This error is less clear: It is telling you that **NSDate** has no instance method whose name matches the **date** selector.

These errors are important for beginners to recognize. They appear when you mistype a message name. Try it:

```
#import <Foundation/Foundation.h>

int main (int argc, const char * argv[])
[
    @autoreleasepool {

        NSDate *now = [NSDate date];
        NSLog(@"This NSDate object lives at %p", now);
        NSLog(@"The date is %@", now);

        double seconds = [now timeIntervalSince1970];
        NSLog(@"It has been %f seconds since the start of 1970.", seconds);

        // Sending bogus messages to see errors...
         double testSeconds = [NSDate timeIntervalSince1970];
         NSDate *testNow = [now date];

        // Mistyped selector name
        testSeconds = [now fooIntervalSince1970];

    }
    return 0;
}
```

Build your program and you will be told that **NSDate** does not have an instance method named **fooIntervalSince1970**.

Capitalization counts!

Objective-C code is case-sensitive. Thus, **timeIntervalSince1970** and **timeintervalsince1970** are two distinct messages. Only one of these messages matches the name of an **NSDate** method. Try it:

```
#import <Foundation/Foundation.h>

int main (int argc, const char * argv[])
{
    @autoreleasepool {

        NSDate *now = [NSDate date];
        NSLog(@"This NSDate object lives at %p", now);
        NSLog(@"The date is %@", now);

        double seconds = [now timeIntervalSince1970];
        NSLog(@"It has been %f seconds since the start of 1970.", seconds);

        // Sending bogus messages to see errors...
        NSDate *testNow = [now date];
        double testSeconds = [NSDate timeIntervalSince1970];

        // Mistyped selector name
        testSeconds = [now fooIntervalSince1970];

        // Typo! Lowercase 'i' and 's'
        testSeconds = [now timeintervalsince1970];

    }
    return 0;
}
```

Keep the case-sensitivity of method names in mind. This is the source of many beginner errors. Remove your bogus message sends before continuing:

```
#import <Foundation/Foundation.h>

int main (int argc, const char * argv[])
{
    @autoreleasepool {

        NSDate *now = [NSDate date];
        NSLog(@"This NSDate object lives at %p", now);
        NSLog(@"The date is %@", now);

        double seconds = [now timeIntervalSince1970];
        NSLog(@"It has been %f seconds since the start of 1970.", seconds);

        // Sending bogus messages to see errors...
        NSDate *testNow = [now date];
        double testSeconds = [NSDate timeIntervalSince1970];

        // Mistyped selector name
        testSeconds = [now fooIntervalSince1970];

        // Typo! Lowercase 'i' and 's'
        testSeconds = [now timeintervalsince1970];
    }
    return 0;
}
```

Objective-C naming conventions

- Variable names that point to instances use "camel case." They begin with lowercase letters and the first letter of each subsequent word is capitalized: now, weightLifter, myCurrentLocation

- Method names also use camel case: **date**, **bodyMassIndex**, **timeIntervalSince1970**

- Class names are capitalized, that is, they begin with capital letters but after that use camel case: **NSDate**, **Person**, **CLLocation**, **NSMutableArray**

  Typically, class names begin with prefixes to avoid confusion between similarly named classes. Prefixes can also tell you what framework something belongs to. The **NS** prefix is used for the Foundation framework: **NSDate**, **NSLog()**. **NS** is short for NeXTSTEP, the platform for which Foundation was originally conceived.

- Many Apple-created types and constants are also capitalized. For example, NSInteger is not a class, it is just a type of integer. NSOKButton is a constant that is equal to 1.

A note on terminology

When talking about code, typically, developers say "an **NSDate**" to refer to an instance of **NSDate**. It is also common to refer to an instance by what it represents. You might refer to an instance of **NSDate** as "a date object" or even just "a date."

To refer to a class, developers typically use just the class name. For example, "**NSDate** was included in OS X 10.0."

The ideas of classes, objects, messages, and methods can be difficult to get your head around at the beginning. Do not worry if you still feel uncertain about objects. This is just the beginning. You will be using these concepts over and over again, and they will make more sense each time you do.

Challenge

In this challenge, you will write a Foundation Command Line Tool that prints out the name of your computer. This program will use two classes from the Foundation framework: **NSHost** and **NSString**.

First, you will get an instance of **NSHost** that has your computer's information. Then you will ask the **NSHost** object for your computer's name. Finally, you will use **NSLog()** to print out this name.

Here are more details that you will need:

- To get an instance of **NSHost**, send the **currentHost** message to the **NSHost** class.

- Once you have an instance of **NSHost**, send it the **localizedName** message. The **localizedName** method returns a pointer to an instance of **NSString**. Thus, you can store the result of sending this message in a variable of type NSString *.

- Use **NSLog()** and the %@ token to print out your computer's name.

This challenge is very much like what you did in this chapter: getting a new object, sending it a message, and storing the result of that message in a variable. Do not let the new classes and methods throw you. Also, this program can take a surprisingly long time to run.

14

More Messages

Objects are very chatty by nature. They send and receive lots of messages about the work they are doing. In this chapter, you will learn about messages with arguments, nested message sends, and more.

A message with an argument

The TimeAfterTime program has an **NSDate** initialized to the date and time at which it is created. What if you want to represent a date in the future – say, 100,000 seconds from the first date? You can create such a date by sending the **dateByAddingTimeInterval:** message to the original instance of **NSDate**.

Notice the colon at the end of the **dateByAddingTimeInterval:** method's name. This tells you that **dateByAddingTimeInterval:** accepts an argument. Methods, like functions, can have zero, one, or more arguments.

Figure 14.1 A message send with an argument

The **dateByAddingTimeInterval:** method accepts the number of seconds by which the new **NSDate** should differ from the original one. (A negative number would give you an **NSDate** in the past.)

In TimeAfterTime, use **dateByAddingTimeInterval:** to create a second date that is 100,000 seconds (a bit over a day) later than the date pointed to by now:

```
#import <Foundation/Foundation.h>

int main (int argc, const char * argv[])
{
    @autoreleasepool {

        NSDate *now = [NSDate date];
        NSLog(@"This NSDate object lives at %p", now);
        NSLog(@"The date is %@", now);

        double seconds = [now timeIntervalSince1970];
        NSLog(@"It has been %f seconds since the start of 1970.", seconds);

        NSDate *later = [now dateByAddingTimeInterval:100000];
        NSLog(@"In 100,000 seconds it will be %@", later);

    }
    return 0;
}
```

When a method has an argument, the colon is an essential part of the method's name. There is no method named **dateByAddingTimeInterval**. There is only **dateByAddingTimeInterval:**.

Multiple arguments

What if you want to know the day of the month (e.g., June 1st) for an **NSDate** object? An **NSDate** does not know this information. Instead, you must ask an instance of **NSCalendar**.

NSCalendar is another Foundation class. You can create an instance of **NSCalendar** by sending the **NSCalendar** class the **currentCalendar** message.

The class method **currentCalendar** will return the address of an **NSCalendar** instance that matches the user's settings. (In most western countries, the Gregorian calendar is the default, but there are several other calendars, like the Hebrew calendar and the Islamic calendar.) Ask the **NSCalendar** class for an instance of **NSCalendar**.

```
#import <Foundation/Foundation.h>

int main (int argc, const char * argv[])
{
    @autoreleasepool {

        NSDate *now = [NSDate date];
        NSLog(@"This NSDate object lives at %p", now);
        NSLog(@"The date is %@", now);

        double seconds = [now timeIntervalSince1970];
        NSLog(@"It has been %f seconds since the start of 1970.", seconds);

        NSDate *later = [now dateByAddingTimeInterval:100000];
        NSLog(@"In 100,000 seconds it will be %@", later);

        NSCalendar *cal = [NSCalendar currentCalendar];
        NSLog(@"My calendar is %@", [cal calendarIdentifier]);
    }
    return 0;
}
```

NSCalendar has a method **ordinalityOfUnit:inUnit:forDate:** that can tell you more information about an **NSDate**. This method takes three arguments. You can tell by the number of colons in the method name.

Let's start with the third argument. It is the **NSDate** object that you want more information about. The first and second arguments are constants from the **NSCalendar** class that describe the type of information you want. To get the day of the month, you pass NSDayCalendarUnit for the first argument and NSMonthCalendarUnit for the second argument.

Figure 14.2 A message send with three arguments

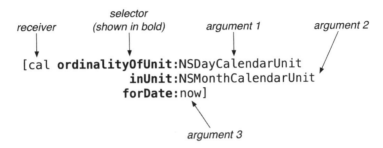

This method takes three arguments, so its name has three parts, but this is *one* message send and it triggers *one* method.

There are **NSCalendar** constants you can use to find information on hours, days, weeks, months, quarters, etc. For instance, to find out what week of the month an **NSDate** falls in, you would send the same message and pass NSWeekCalendarUnit and NSMonthCalendarUnit as the first and second arguments.

In TimeAfterTime, ask the instance of **NSCalendar** to find the day of the month for the **NSDate** pointed to by now.

```
#import <Foundation/Foundation.h>

int main (int argc, const char * argv[])
{
    @autoreleasepool {

        NSDate *now = [NSDate date];
        NSLog(@"This NSDate object lives at %p", now);
        NSLog(@"The date is %@", now);

        double seconds = [now timeIntervalSince1970];
        NSLog(@"It has been %f seconds since the start of 1970.", seconds);

        NSDate *later = [now dateByAddingTimeInterval:100000];
        NSLog(@"In 100,000 seconds it will be %@", later);

        NSCalendar *cal = [NSCalendar currentCalendar];
        NSLog(@"My calendar is %@", [cal calendarIdentifier]);
        unsigned long day = [cal ordinalityOfUnit:NSDayCalendarUnit
                                           inUnit:NSMonthCalendarUnit
                                          forDate:now];
        NSLog(@"This is day %lu of the month", day);

    }
    return 0;
}
```

Notice that you split the **ordinalityOfUnit:inUnit:forDate:** message send into three lines. Objective-C programmers often line up the colons so that it is easy to tell the parts of the method name from the arguments. (Xcode should do this for you: every time you start a new line, the previous line should indent properly. If that is not happening, check your Xcode preferences for indention.)

Nesting message sends

Message sends can be *nested*. For instance, to find out the number of seconds since the start of 1970, you could write your code this way:

```
NSDate *now = [NSDate date];
double seconds = [now timeIntervalSince1970];
NSLog(@"It has been %f seconds since the start of 1970", seconds);
```

Or you could nest the two message sends like this:

```
double seconds = [[NSDate date] timeIntervalSince1970];
NSLog(@"It has been %f seconds since the start of 1970", seconds);
```

When message sends are nested, the system will handle the message send on the inside first and then the message that contains it. So **date** is sent to the **NSDate** class, and the result of that (a pointer to the newly-created instance) is sent **timeIntervalSince1970**.

You will often see nested message sends in code, and you need to know how to read them. However, when writing your own code, you may find that nesting messages is counterproductive. It makes your code harder to read and harder to debug because more than one thing is happening on one line.

alloc and init

There is one case where it is always right and proper to nest two message sends. You always nest the messages **alloc** and **init**.

The **alloc** method is a class method that every class has. It returns a pointer to a new instance that needs to be initialized. An uninitialized instance may exist in memory, but it is not ready to receive messages. The **init** method is an instance method that every class has. It *initializes* an instance so that it is ready to work.

Practice using nested messages in your program. Create an **NSDate** object by sending **alloc** and **init** messages instead of the **date** message.

```
#import <Foundation/Foundation.h>

int main (int argc, const char * argv[])
{
    @autoreleasepool {
        NSDate *now = [NSDate date];
        NSDate *now = [[NSDate alloc] init];
        NSLog(@"This NSDate object lives at %p", now);
        NSLog(@"The date is %@", now);

        double seconds = [now timeIntervalSince1970];
        NSLog(@"It has been %f seconds since the start of 1970.", seconds);

        NSDate *later = [now dateByAddingTimeInterval:100000];
        NSLog(@"In 100,000 seconds it will be %@", later);

        NSCalendar *cal = [NSCalendar currentCalendar];
        NSLog(@"My calendar is %@", [cal calendarIdentifier]);

        unsigned long day = [cal ordinalityOfUnit:NSDayCalendarUnit
                                           inUnit:NSMonthCalendarUnit
                                          forDate:now];
        NSLog(@"This is day %lu of the month", day);

    }
    return 0;
}
```

There is no difference in the two ways of creating an instance of **NSDate**. The **init** method of **NSDate** initializes the **NSDate** object to the current date and time – just like the **date** method does. The **date** method is a convenient way to get an **NSDate** instance with minimal code. In fact, we call this sort of method a *convenience method*.

Sending messages to nil

Nearly all object-oriented languages have the idea of nil, the pointer to no object. In Objective-C, we use nil instead of NULL, which was discussed in Chapter 9. They really are the same thing: the zero pointer. By convention, though, we use nil when referring to the value of an empty pointer declared as pointing to an Objective-C object type, and NULL when referring to any other pointer, such as to a struct.

In most object-oriented languages, sending a message to nil is not allowed. As a result, you have to check for non-nil-ness before accessing an object. So you see this sort of thing a lot:

```
if (fido != nil) {
    [fido goGetTheNewspaper];
}
```

When Objective-C was designed, it was decided that sending a message to nil would be OK; it would simply do nothing. Thus, this code is completely legal:

```
Dog *fido = nil;
[fido goGetTheNewspaper];
```

Important thing #1: If you are sending messages and nothing is happening, make sure you are not sending messages to a pointer that has been set to nil.

Important thing #2: If you send a message to nil, the return value is meaningless and should be disregarded.

```
Dog *fido = nil;
Newspaper *daily = [fido goGetTheNewspaper];
```

In this case, daily will be zero. (In general, if you expect a number or a pointer as a result, sending a message to nil will return zero. However, for other types like structs, you will get strange and unexpected return values.)

id

When declaring a pointer to hold the address of an object, most of the time you specify the class of the object that the pointer will refer to:

```
NSDate *expiration;
```

However, often you need a way to create a pointer without knowing exactly what kind of object the pointer will refer to. For this case, you use the type id to mean "a pointer to some kind of Objective-C object" Here is what it looks like when you use it:

```
id delegate;
```

Notice that there is no asterisk in this declaration. id implies the asterisk.

Challenge

Use two instances of **NSDate** to figure out how many seconds you have been alive.

First, **NSDate** has an instance method **timeIntervalSinceDate:**. This method takes one argument – another instance of **NSDate**. It returns the number of seconds between the **NSDate** that received the message and the **NSDate** that was passed in as the argument.

It looks something like this:

```
double secondsSinceEarlierDate = [laterDate timeIntervalSinceDate:earlierDate];
```

Second, you will need to create a new date object that is set to a given year, month, etc. You will do this with the help of an **NSDateComponents** object and an **NSCalendar** object. Here is an example:

```
NSDateComponents *comps = [[NSDateComponents alloc] init];
[comps setYear:1969];
[comps setMonth:4];
[comps setDay:30];
[comps setHour:13];
[comps setMinute:10];
[comps setSecond:0];

NSCalendar *g = [[NSCalendar alloc] initWithCalendarIdentifier:NSGregorianCalendar];
NSDate *dateOfBirth = [g dateFromComponents:comps];
```

Good luck!

15

Objects and Memory

In this chapter, you will learn about the life of objects on the heap and how heap memory is managed.

On pointers and their values

Objects can only be accessed via a pointer, and it is practical, if inaccurate, to refer to an object by its pointer, as in "now is an **NSDate**." However, is important to remember that the pointer and the object that it points at are not the same thing. Here is a more accurate statement: "now is a pointer that can hold an address of a location in memory where an instance of **NSDate** lives."

Create a new Command-line Tool named TimesTwo. Make its type Foundation. In main.m, declare a variable that points to an instance of **NSDate**.

```
#import <Foundation/Foundation.h>

int main (int argc, const char * argv[])
{
    @autoreleasepool {
        NSDate *currentTime = nil;
        NSLog(@"currentTime's value is %p", currentTime);
    }
    return 0;
}
```

Here you have initialized the pointer variable to nil. Run the program, and you will find that currentTime points at 0x0 which is the value of nil.

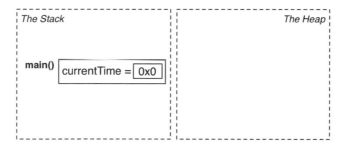

This diagram shows the currentTime local variable that is part of the frame for **main()**. Its current value is nil, and there are no objects yet created on the heap.

Next, create an **NSDate** for currentTime to point at instead of pointing at nil.

```
...
    @autoreleasepool {
        NSDate *currentTime = [NSDate date];
        NSLog(@"currentTime's value is %p", currentTime);
    }
    return 0;
}
```

Build and run the program. The output will report the address of the object pointed to by currentTime. An **NSDate** object now exists on the heap.

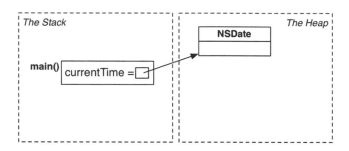

currentTime is a variable, so you can change it to point at a different **NSDate**. Make the program sleep for two seconds after the first log statement and then point currentTime at a second instance of **NSDate**.

```
    @autoreleasepool {
        NSDate *currentTime = [NSDate date];
        NSLog(@"currentTime's value is %p", currentTime);

        sleep(2);

        currentTime = [NSDate date];
        NSLog(@"currentTime's value is now %p", currentTime);
    }
    return 0;
}
```

Build and run the program. Two seconds after the first line of output, you will see a second line reporting a different address for currentTime. currentTime now points at a different **NSDate**:

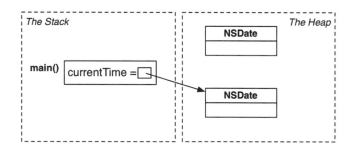

What about the original date object? From your code's perspective, this object and the information it contained are lost. If you lose your only pointer to an object, then you can no longer access it – even if it continues to exist on the heap.

If you wanted to change currentTime's value and still be able to access the original date, you could declare another pointer to store the address of the original date.

```
@autoreleasepool {
    NSDate *currentTime = [NSDate date];
    NSLog(@"currentTime's value is %p", currentTime);

    NSDate *startTime = currentTime;

    sleep(2);

    currentTime = [NSDate date];
    NSLog(@"currentTime's value is now %p", currentTime);
    NSLog(@"The address of the original object is %p", startTime);
}
    return 0;
}
```

Build and run the program.

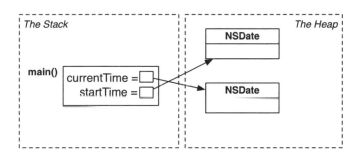

Now let's look at this code progression from the perspective of memory management.

Memory management

When we talk about memory management, we are talking about managing heap memory. Consider the difference between the stack and the heap. Recall from Chapter 5 that the stack is an orderly stack of frames. Each frame is automatically deallocated when the function using it ends. The heap, on the other hand, is a heaping pile of memory, and that is where your objects live.

Managing the heap is important because objects can be large and because your program only gets so much heap memory for its own use. Each object that is created takes up some of that memory.

Running low on memory is a problem. It will cause a Mac app to perform badly and will cause an iOS app to crash. Thus, it is essential that any objects that are no longer necessary are destroyed so that their memory can be reclaimed and reused.

Take another look again at the program when you first change currentTime to a new value and before you have startTime.

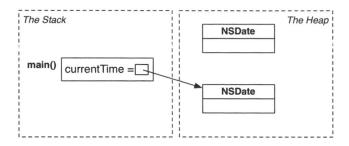

Nothing points to the original date object. From a memory management perspective, this object is useless and is taking up valuable heap memory. It needs to be destroyed.

ARC

The setting that instructs the compiler to ensure the destruction of unreferenced objects is called ARC. ARC is short for Automatic Reference Counting. If you recall that "reference" is another word for pointer, then it is easy to understand what ARC is for: Each object keeps a count of how many references to itself there are. When this reference count reaches zero, the object knows it is no longer needed and will self-destruct. When your project has ARC enabled, the compiler adds code to your project to tell each object when it gains or loses a reference. Once upon a time, developers were required to write code to keep an object's reference count up to date – hence the "Automatic" in Automatic Reference Counting.

When you change currentTime to point at a new object, the original object loses a reference, and ARC decrements its reference count. The new date object's reference count is incremented.

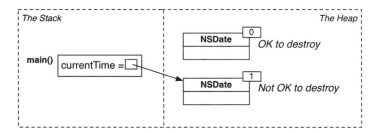

Given that currentTime was the only reference to the original **NSDate**, the object will be destroyed so that its memory can be used for something else.

When you create the startTime pointer and give it the same value as currentTime, the date object gains another reference.

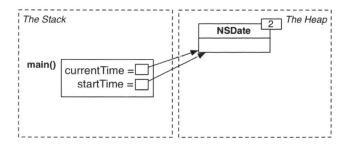

When you change `currentTime` to point to a new date, the new date gains a reference and the original date loses a reference.

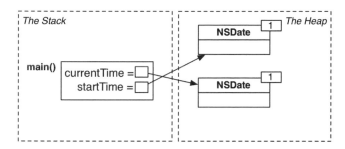

This time, however, the original date still has another reference. So you still have access to this object, and the object still exists.

Thus, as long as you have a pointer to an object, you can be sure that it will continue to exist. You will never explicitly destroy an object, as you would a buffer with **free()** (as you learned in Chapter 12). You can only add or remove a reference to the object. The object will destroy itself when its reference count reaches zero.

What if you are done with an object? You set the pointer to `nil`, or let the pointer be destroyed when it falls out of scope. To illustrate what happens, go ahead and manually nullify `currentTime` in your program:

```
@autoreleasepool {
    NSDate *currentTime = [NSDate date];
    NSLog(@"currentTime's value is %p", currentTime);
    NSDate *startTime = currentTime;

    sleep(2);

    currentTime = [NSDate date];
    NSLog(@"currentTime's value is now %p", currentTime);
    NSLog(@"The original object lives at %p", startTime);

    currentTime = nil;
    NSLog(@"currentTime's value is %p", currentTime);
}
    return 0;
}
```

Build and run the program. At the end of the output, you will see that `currentTime`'s value is back to `0x0`.

Setting `currentTime` to `nil` causes the **NSDate** object to lose a reference, and in this case, it will be destroyed.

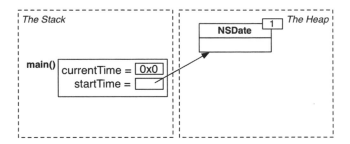

An object also loses a reference when the pointer variable itself is destroyed. Things get a little more complicated when you have objects with instance variables pointing to other objects. You will learn how to handle those cases starting in Chapter 21.

16

NSString

NSString is another class like **NSDate**. Instances of **NSString** hold character strings. Objective-C developers use **NSString** instances to hold and manipulate text in their programs.

Creating instances of NSString

In code, you can create an instance of **NSString** like this:

```
NSString *lament = @"Why me!?";
```

Notice that there is no explicit message sent to the **NSString** class to create the instance. The @"..." is Objective-C shorthand for creating an **NSString** object with the given character string. This shorthand is known as literal syntax. When you use it, we say that you are creating a *literal* instance of **NSString**, or more commonly, an **NSString** literal.

Instances of **NSString** can contain any Unicode character. To insert non-ASCII characters, use \u followed by the Unicode number for that character in hexadecimal. For example, the symbol for the white heart suit in cards is 0x2661:

```
NSString *slogan = @"I \u2661 New York!";
```

Because **NSString** objects can hold Unicode characters, they make it easy to create applications that can deal with strings from many languages.

Frequently, you will need to create strings *dynamically*. That is, you will need to create a string whose contents will not be known until the program is running. To create an instance of **NSString** dynamically, you can use the **stringWithFormat:** class method:

```
NSString *dateString = [NSString stringWithFormat:@"The date is %@", now];
```

In the **stringWithFormat:** message, you send as an argument a format string with one or more tokens and the variable(s) whose values will be used in place of the token(s). It works the same as the format string that you have been passing to the **NSLog** function.

NSString methods

NSString is a class that developers use a lot. Like all Objective-C classes, it comes with useful methods. If you want to do something with a string, there is likely an **NSString** method that can help.

Below are a few examples of **NSString** methods. To introduce these methods, we are showing you the declaration of the method and then an example of it being used. The declaration tells you what you need to know about a method: whether it is an instance or a class method, what it returns, its name, and the types of its arguments, if any.

To get the number of characters in a string, you use the **length** method:

```
- (NSUInteger)length;
```

This method is an instance method. You can tell by the '-' at the start of the declaration. (A class method would have a '+' instead.) This method returns an NSUInteger and does not have any arguments. NSUInteger is a type in the Foundation framework. It is equivalent to the unsigned long type that you learned about in Chapter 7.

```
    NSUInteger charCount = [dateString length];
```

To see if one string is equal to another, you can use the **isEqualToString:** method:

```
- (BOOL)isEqualToString:(NSString *)other;
```

This instance method will go through the two strings comparing them character by character to see if they are the same. Its one argument is the string that you want to compare with the string that will receive the **isEqualToString:** message. The method returns a BOOL that reports whether the two strings are, in fact, equal.

```
    if ([slogan isEqualToString:lament]) {
        NSLog(@"%@ and %@ are equal", slogan, lament);
    }
```

To get an uppercase version of a string, you use the **uppercaseString** method.

```
- (NSString *)uppercaseString;
```

This instance method returns an instance of **NSString** that is equivalent to the receiver except all uppercase:

```
    NSString *angryText = @"That makes me so mad!";
    NSString *reallyAngryText = [angryText uppercaseString];
```

Class references

So where do you find methods that you need? Apple maintains a *class reference* for each class in its APIs. The class reference lists all of the methods of a class and basic information on how to use them.

In Xcode, select Help → Documentation and API Reference. This will open Xcode's documentation browser.

In the search field at the top of the window, enter **NSString**.

Figure 16.1 **NSString** class reference

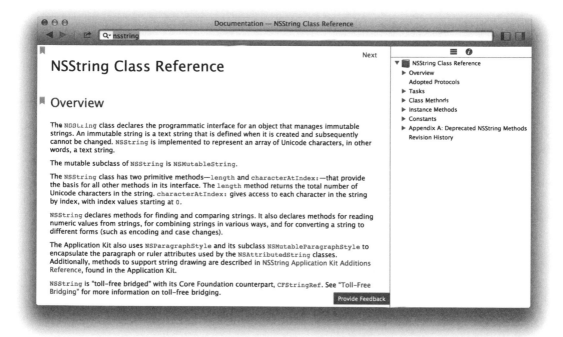

(You can also access the documentation via Apple's developer website. To get to the **NSString** class reference, simply search for "NSString class reference." The first result returned is usually the **NSString** reference page at developer.apple.com.)

In the righthand pane is the table of contents for the **NSString** class reference. The Overview describes the **NSString** class in general. There are also headings that list the class methods and instance methods. If you know the name of the method you are looking for, then you can find it by name under one of these headings and read all about its details.

Reveal the contents of the Class Methods category. Find and select **stringWithFormat:** from the list to see useful information about this method, like descriptions of its parameters and return value.

Figure 16.2 Documentation for **stringWithFormat:**

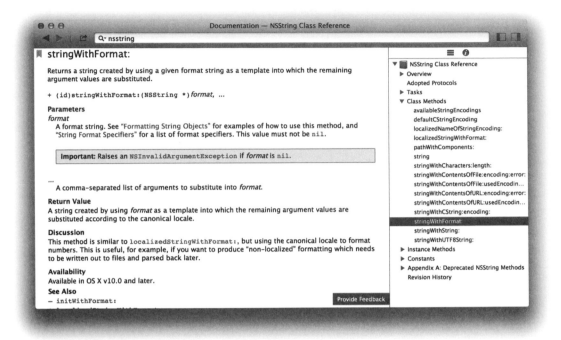

If you need to do something with an object but do not know of a specific method, then the best place to start is the Tasks heading. One task that developers often need to accomplish with **NSString** is searching one string to see if it contains a certain *substring*. A substring is a string that may make up part or all of another string.

For instance, say you read in a comma-delimited list of names as an **NSString** object. Now you need to check if a particular name is in the list. That single name would be a substring of the larger string.

Reveal the contents under the Tasks heading. Find and select Finding Characters and Substrings. This will reveal several potentially useful methods.

Figure 16.3 Methods for finding characters and substrings

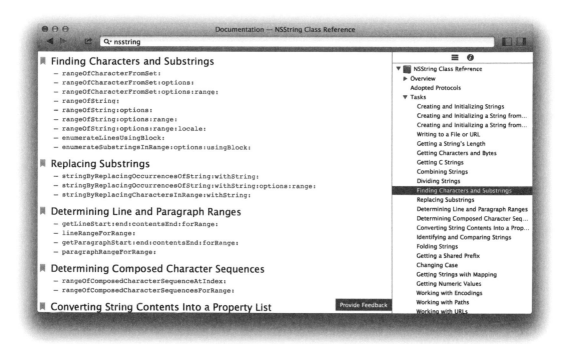

In the real world, you would browse through the details of candidate methods until you found one that would work. For this example, we will give you a head start: click **rangeOfString:** in the list of methods to see its details (Figure 16.4).

Figure 16.4 Documentation for **rangeOfString:**

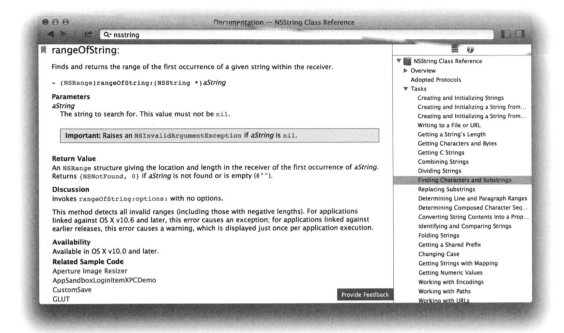

You can see that **rangeOfString:** has one parameter that is an instance of **NSString**. This is the "substring" for which you want to search – the single name to find in the list of names.

You can also see that this method returns an NSRange. What is an NSRange? Click NSRange to view its definition (Figure 16.5).

Figure 16.5 Documentation for NSRange

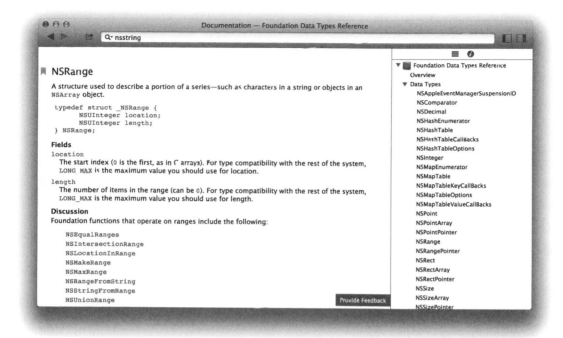

NSRange is a `typedef` for a `struct`, like you used in Chapter 11. It has two members, `location` and `length`, that you can use to pinpoint a substring within a string.

However, in the current problem, you only want to see if the name occurs in the list or not. To figure out how to do this, press the back button at the top lefthand corner of the documentation browser to return to the previous page. Then find the Return Value section in the **rangeOfString:** documentation. This section states that when the passed-in substring does not occur, **rangeOfString:** returns an NSRange whose `location` is the constant NSNotFound.

Thus, to determine whether the name is in the list of names, you can simply check the return value's `location` member. The code would look something like this:

```
NSString listOfNames = @"..."; // a long list of names
NSString name = @"Ward";
NSRange match = [listOfNames rangeOfString:name];
if (match.location == NSNotFound) {
    NSLog(@"No match found!");
    // Other actions to be taken
} else {
    NSLog(@"Match found!");
    // Other actions to be taken
}
```

Other parts of the documentation

Before you close the documentation, let's look at few more items that can be especially helpful for new Objective-C developers. Return to the top of the righthand pane and click the ❶ button to reveal some basic details about the **NSString** class.

Figure 16.6 Details for **NSString**

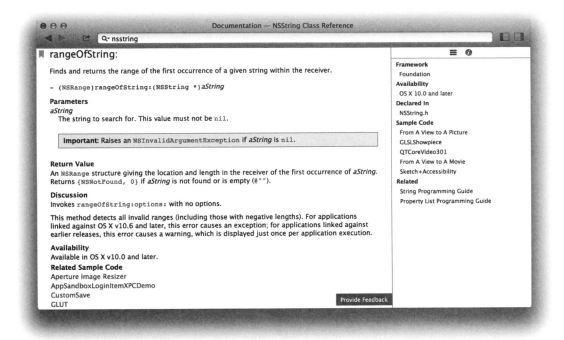

Below these details are links to other parts of Apple's documentation related to **NSString**.

Under the **Sample Code** heading are small, complete projects that demonstrate how Apple expects the class in question to be used. Many classes (especially commonly-used ones, like **NSString**) have sample code links on their reference pages.

Under the **Related** heading are two of Apple's *developer guides*. These guides are organized by topic rather than by class or method, so they are excellent for learning about specific topics in Objective-C, iOS development, and OS X development.

You can browse all of the developer guides at https://developer.apple.com/library. Select iOS or OS X to get to the developer library for that platform. The two platforms share the Foundation framework, so anything you are learning now will be in either library.

Select **Guides** from the contents on the left to see a list of guides with a handy search field at the top. Or you can select **Getting Started** to see a smaller group of beginning tutorial guides.

It would be difficult to overstate how important Apple's documentation will be to you and how important it is for programmers of all levels. As you go through this book, take a moment to look up new classes and methods as you encounter them and see what else they can do. Also read through developer guides and download sample code projects that peak your interest. The more comfortable you get using the documentation, the faster your development will go.

Challenge: finding more NSString methods

The **rangeOfString:** method is case-sensitive. Return to the **NSString** class reference and find the method that you would use if you needed to do a case-insensitive search.

Then find the **NSString** method that will return the actual portion of the string that was found.

Challenge: using readline()

The return value of the **readline** function from Chapter 8 is of type `const char *`, or a C string. It is possible to get an **NSString** instance with the same characters as any given C string by sending the **stringWithUTF8String:** class message to the **NSString** class and passing in the C string as its argument.

Re-write the **readline()** challenge from Chapter 8 to use an **NSString** and **NSLog()** rather than a C string and **printf()**. You will want to create a new Foundation Command Line Tool.

17
NSArray

NSArray is another commonly used Objective-C class. An instance of **NSArray** holds a list of pointers to other objects.

Create a new project: a Foundation Command Line Tool called DateList. This program will create an array that holds a list of pointers to **NSDate** objects.

Creating arrays

Open main.m and change **main()**:

```
#import <Foundation/Foundation.h>

int main(int argc, const char * argv[])
{
    @autoreleasepool {

        // Create three NSDate objects
        NSDate *now = [NSDate date];
        NSDate *tomorrow = [now dateByAddingTimeInterval:24.0 * 60.0 * 60.0];
        NSDate *yesterday = [now dateByAddingTimeInterval:-24.0 * 60.0 * 60.0];

        // Create an array containing all three
        NSArray *dateList = @[now, tomorrow, yesterday];

    }
    return 0;
}
```

Like **NSString**, **NSArray** has a literal syntax for creating instances. The array's contents are in a comma-delimited list, surrounded by square brackets, and preceded with @. No explicit message send is necessary.

Figure 17.1 is an object diagram of your program. Notice that the instance of **NSArray** has pointers to the **NSDate** objects.

Figure 17.1 Object diagram for DateList

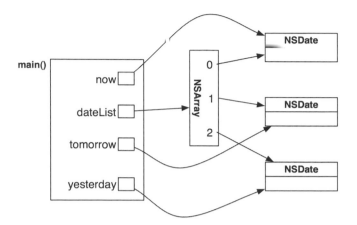

An instance of **NSArray** is *immutable*. Once an **NSArray** has been created, you can never add or remove a pointer from that array. Nor can you change the order of the pointers in that array.

Accessing arrays

Arrays are ordered lists, and you access an item in an array by its *index*. Arrays are zero-based: the first item is stored at index 0, the second item is stored at index 1, and so on.

You can access an individual item in the array using the name of the array followed by the index of the item in square brackets. Add the following code to your program to access and print two items in the array:

```
#import <Foundation/Foundation.h>

int main(int argc, const char * argv[])
{
    @autoreleasepool {

        // Create three NSDate objects
        NSDate *now = [NSDate date];
        NSDate *tomorrow = [now dateByAddingTimeInterval:24.0 * 60.0 * 60.0];
        NSDate *yesterday = [now dateByAddingTimeInterval:-24.0 * 60.0 * 60.0];

        // Create an array containing all three
        NSArray *dateList = @[now, tomorrow, yesterday];

        // Print a couple of dates
        NSLog(@"The first date is %@", dateList[0]);
        NSLog(@"The third date is %@", dateList[2]);

        // How many dates are in the array?
        NSLog(@"There are %lu dates", [dateList count]);

    }
    return 0;
}
```

Build and run the program and check your output.

You sent dateList the message **count**. To find out what the **count** method does, you could go to **NSDate**'s class reference page. But there is a way to get a quick, on-the-spot summary right in Xcode.

Hold down the Option key and click on **count**. The Quick Help window will appear with information about that method:

Figure 17.2 Quick Help pop-up window

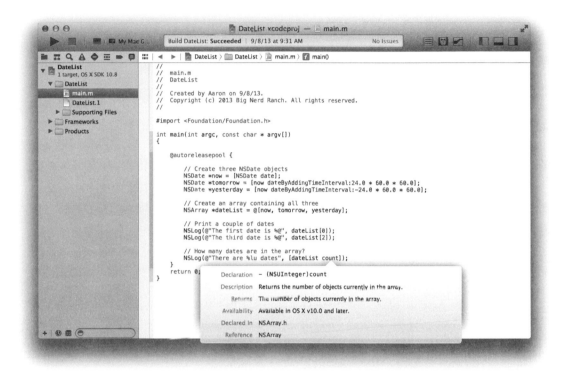

Notice that there are links in the Quick Help window. If you click a link, it will open the appropriate documentation in the Xcode's documentation browser.

You can also open Quick Help in the utilities area in Xcode to see its information all the time.

In the upper righthand corner of the Xcode window, click the rightmost button of this group: ▣▣▣.

This will reveal the utilities area. At the top of the utilities area, click the ▤ button to reveal Quick Help.

Back in your code, click **NSArray** to see its documentation:

Figure 17.3 Quick Help in utilities area

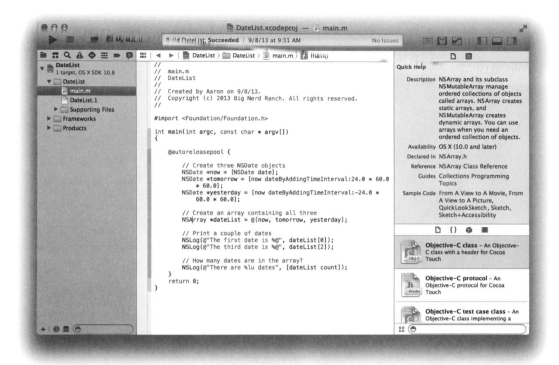

When you move the cursor somewhere else, Quick Help immediately updates if there is documentation available.

Let's get back to the purpose of the **count** method. You saw that this method returns the number of items in the array. Knowing an array's item count is more important than you might think. If the **count** method reports that there are 100 items in the array, then you can ask for items at indices 0 to 99. If you ask for an item with an index beyond 99, then you will get an *out-of-range error* that will crash your program.

To see an example of an out-of-range error, add the following deadly line of code:

```
#import <Foundation/Foundation.h>

int main(int argc, const char * argv[])
{
    @autoreleasepool {

        ...

        // How many dates are in the array?
        NSLog(@"There are %lu dates", [dateList count]);

        NSLog(@"The fourth date is %@", dateList[3]);  // Crash!

    }
    return 0;
}
```

You are requesting the object at index 3 (the fourth object) in dateList when dateList only has three objects. Build and run your program. When it crashes on this line, first stop the program using the stop button in Xcode's top left corner. Then delete the problematic line.

```
#import <Foundation/Foundation.h>

int main(int argc, const char * argv[])
{
    @autoreleasepool {

        ...

        // How many dates are in the array?
        NSLog(@"There are %lu dates", [dateList count]);

        NSLog(@"The fourth date is %@", dateList[3]);   // Crash!

    }
    return 0;
}
```

Build and run again to confirm that the problem is fixed. Out-of-range errors are common with beginning programmers. Use the **count** method as a check and remember that arrays are always zero-based.

Iterating over arrays

Programmers often need to loop and perform operations on each item in an array (or "iterate over an array"). You can do this with a for-loop. Edit main.m:

```
#import <Foundation/Foundation.h>

int main(int argc, const char * argv[])
[
    @autoreleasepool [

        // Create three NSDate objects
        NSDate *now = [NSDate date];
        NSDate *tomorrow = [now dateByAddingTimeInterval:24.0 * 60.0 * 60.0];
        NSDate *yesterday = [now dateByAddingTimeInterval:-24.0 * 60.0 * 60.0];

        // Create an array containing all three
        NSArray *dateList = @[now, tomorrow, yesterday];

        // Print a couple of dates
        NSLog(@"The first date is %@", dateList[0]);
        NSLog(@"The third date is %@", dateList[2]);

        // How many dates are in the array?
        NSLog(@"There are %lu dates", [dateList count]);

        // Iterate over the array
        NSUInteger dateCount = [dateList count];
        for (int i = 0; i < dateCount; i++) {
            NSDate *d = dateList[i];
            NSLog(@"Here is a date: %@", d);
        }

    }
    return 0;
}
```

In the for-loop, notice that you use the array's item count to limit the number of times the loop will run to prevent an out-of-range error.

Programmers iterate over arrays so often that they made a special addition to the for-loop called *fast enumeration*. This type of loop is an extremely efficient way to walk through the items in an array. When you use fast enumeration, checking the array's item count is handled for you. Edit your code to use fast enumeration:

```
#import <Foundation/Foundation.h>

int main(int argc, const char * argv[])
{
    @autoreleasepool {

        // Create three NSDate objects
        NSDate *now = [NSDate date];
        NSDate *tomorrow = [now dateByAddingTimeInterval:24.0 * 60.0 * 60.0];
        NSDate *yesterday = [now dateByAddingTimeInterval:-24.0 * 60.0 * 60.0];

        // Create an array containing all three
        NSArray *dateList = @[now, tomorrow, yesterday];

        // Iterate over the array
        NSUInteger dateCount = [dateList count];
        for (int i = 0; i < dateCount; i++) {
            NSDate *d = dateList[i];
        for (NSDate *d in dateList) {
            NSLog(@"Here is a date: %@", d);
        }

    }
    return 0;
}
```

Build and run your program. The output will be the same as before, but your code is simpler and more efficient.

NSMutableArray

An instance of **NSMutableArray** is similar to an instance of **NSArray**, but you can add, remove, and reorder pointers. (**NSMutableArray** is a *subclass* of **NSArray**. You will learn about subclasses in Chapter 20.)

Change your program to use an **NSMutableArray** and methods from the **NSMutableArray** class:

```
#import <Foundation/Foundation.h>

int main(int argc, const char * argv[])
{
    @autoreleasepool {

        // Create three NSDate objects
        NSDate *now = [NSDate date];
        NSDate *tomorrow = [now dateByAddingTimeInterval:24.0 * 60.0 * 60.0];
        NSDate *yesterday = [now dateByAddingTimeInterval:-24.0 * 60.0 * 60.0];

        // Create an array containing all three
        NSArray *dateList = @[now, tomorrow, yesterday];

        // Create an empty mutable array
        NSMutableArray *dateList = [NSMutableArray array];

        // Add two dates to the array
        [dateList addObject:now];
        [dateList addObject:tomorrow];

        // Add yesterday at the beginning of the list
        [dateList insertObject:yesterday atIndex:0];

        // Iterate over the array
        for (NSDate *d in dateList) {
            NSLog(@"Here is a date: %@", d);
        }

        // Remove yesterday
        [dateList removeObjectAtIndex:0];
        NSLog(@"Now the first date is %@", dateList[0]);

    }
    return 0;
}
```

You used the class method **array** to create the **NSMutableArray**. This method returns an empty array, to which you can then add objects. You can also use **alloc** and **init** to get the same result:

```
NSMutableArray *dateList = [[NSMutableArray alloc] init];
```

You used the **addObject:** method to populate the **NSMutableArray**. This method adds the object to the end of the list. To add an object at a specific index, you can use **insertObject:atIndex:**. As objects are added, an array will grow as big as necessary to hold them.

You removed an object from the array using **removeObject:atIndex:**. An array's item count will change as objects are removed. For example, if you were to ask for the object at index 2 in dateList after removing the yesterday pointer, then the program would crash.

For future reference, when using fast enumeration with an **NSMutableArray**, you are not allowed to add or remove items while iterating over the array. If you need to add or remove items while iterating, you must use a standard for-loop.

Old-style array methods

Before a literal syntax was introduced for creating instances of **NSArray**, developers used the class method **arrayWithObjects:**.

```
// Create an array containing three pointers (nil terminates the list)
NSArray *dateList = [NSArray arrayWithObjects:now, tomorrow, yesterday, nil];
```

The nil at the end tells the method to stop. Thus, this date array has three objects. (If you forget the nil, it will probably crash your program, but you will at least get a compiler warning.)

The syntax that you used to access items in the dateList array is known as *subscripting*. Before subscripting was introduced, developers used the **objectAtIndex:** method to access an item in an array:

```
// Print a couple of dates
NSLog(@"The first date is %@", [dateList objectAtIndex:0]);
NSLog(@"The third date is %@", [dateList objectAtIndex:2]);
```

The **arrayWithObjects:** and **objectAtIndex:** methods still exist and are not deprecated. Feel free to use the literal syntax and subscripting or the old-style methods when working with arrays.

One problem that can occur with literal syntax and subscripting is that the different uses for square brackets can make your code difficult to read. Consider that you now have three distinct uses for square brackets:

1. sending messages	`NSUInteger dateCount = [dateList count];`
2. creating an **NSArray**	`NSArray *dateList = @[now, tomorrow, yesterday];`
3. asking for the item at a particular index of an array	`NSDate *firstDate = dateList[0];`

At times in your code, these different uses will be mixed in together. When this happens, reverting to the old-style array methods can make your code easier to read. For example, this might be confusing:

```
id selectedDog = dogs[[tableView selectedRow]];
```

In such situations, you might consider using the old style array access. Here is the same line of code rewritten:

```
id selectedDog = [dogs objectAtIndex:[tableView selectedRow]];
```

Challenge: a grocery list

Create a new Foundation Command Line Tool named Groceries. Start by creating an empty **NSMutableArray** object. Then add several grocery-like strings to the array. (You will have to create those, too.) Finally, use fast enumeration to print out your grocery list.

```
My grocery list is:
Loaf of bread
Container of milk
Stick of butter
```

Challenge: interesting names

This challenge is more challenging. Read through the following program, which finds common proper names that contain two adjacent A's.

```
#import <Foundation/Foundation.h>

int main (int argc, const char * argv[])
[
    @autoreleasepool [

        // Read in a file as a huge string (ignoring the possibility of an error)
        NSString *nameString =
                   [NSString stringWithContentsOfFile:@"/usr/share/dict/propernames"
                                          encoding:NSUTF8StringEncoding
                                             error:NULL];

        // Break it into an array of strings
        NSArray *names = [nameString componentsSeparatedByString:@"\n"];

        // Go through the array one string at a time
        for (NSString *n in names) {

            // Look for the string "aa" in a case-insensitive manner
            NSRange r = [n rangeOfString:@"AA" options:NSCaseInsensitiveSearch];

            // Was it found?
            if (r.location != NSNotFound) {
                NSLog(@"%@", n);
            }
        }

    }
    return 0;
}
```

The file /usr/share/dict/propernames came pre-installed on your Mac. It contains common proper names. The file/usr/share/dict/words contains regular words *and* proper names. In the word files, proper names are capitalized.

Write a program based on the one above that finds common proper names that are also regular words; words present in the proper names list that are also present (lowercase) in the regular words list.

For example, if you only had these lists:

```
(words)          (names)
woldy            Wilson
Wolf             Win
wolf             Winnie
wolfachite       Winston
wolfberry        Wolf
wolfdom          Wolfgang
wolfen           Woody
wolfer           Yvonne
Wolffia
Wolffian
Wolffianism
Wolfgang
wolfhood
```

then the solution would have only one pair that matches our criteria: "wolf" (the canine) in the words list would match "Wolf" (the common last name) in the names list.

18

Your First Class

So far, you have only used classes created by Apple. Now you get to write your own class. Remember that a class describes objects in two ways: instance variables within each instance of the class and methods implemented by the class.

You are going to write a **BNRPerson** class, which will be similar to the `struct Person` you wrote in Chapter 11. This class, like all Objective-C classes, will be defined in two files:

- BNRPerson.h is the class's *header* and will contain the declarations of instance variables and methods.

- BNRPerson.m is the *implementation file*. This is where you write out the code for, or *implement*, each method.

First, create a new project: a Foundation Command Line Tool named BMITime.

To create a new class, select File → New → File.... From the OS X section on the left, select Cocoa. Choose the Objective-C class template and click Next.

Figure 18.1 Creating a new class

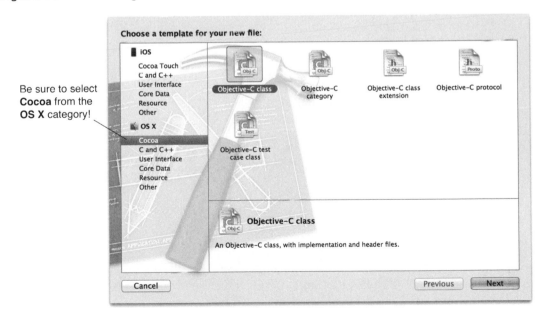

Name your class **BNRPerson** and make it a subclass of **NSObject**. (You will learn about subclasses and **NSObject** in Chapter 20.)

Figure 18.2 Naming your new class

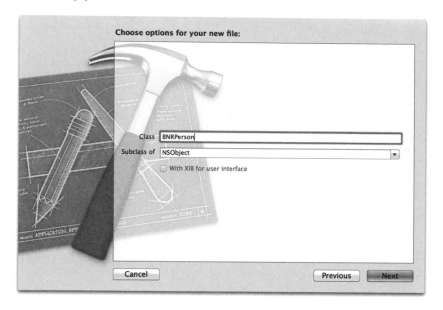

Click Next. Finally, make sure the BMITime target is checked and then click Create.

Find BNRPerson.h and BNRPerson.m in the project navigator. Open BNRPerson.h and declare two instance variables:

```
#import <Foundation/Foundation.h>

@interface BNRPerson : NSObject

{
    // BNRPerson has two instance variables
    float _heightInMeters;
    int _weightInKilos;
}

@end
```

A header file starts with @interface and finishes off with @end. Notice that you declared the instance variables first and inside of curly braces.

By convention, instance variable names start with an underscore ("_"). Using the underscore prefix lets you easily tell instance variables from local variables when reading code. The underscore does not mean anything special to the compiler; it is simply the first character in the instance variable's name.

Next, declare five instance methods after the instance variables and outside of the curly braces:

```
#import <Foundation/Foundation.h>

@interface BNRPerson : NSObject

{
    // BNRPerson has two instance variables
    float _heightInMeters;
    int _weightInKilos;
}

// BNRPerson has methods to read and set its instance variables
- (float)heightInMeters;
- (void)setHeightInMeters:(float)h;
- (int)weightInKilos;
- (void)setWeightInKilos:(int)w;

// BNRPerson has a method that calculates the Body Mass Index
- (float)bodyMassIndex;

@end
```

To return to BNRPerson.m, use the keyboard shortcut Control-Command-up arrow. This shortcut moves you back and forth between the header and implementation files of a class.

Implement the methods that you declared in BNRPerson.h. The methods that you implement must exactly match the ones that you declared in the header. In Xcode, this is easy; when you start typing a method in the implementation file, Xcode will suggest names of methods that you have already declared.

```
#import "BNRPerson.h"

@implementation BNRPerson

- (float)heightInMeters
{
    return _heightInMeters;
}

- (void)setHeightInMeters:(float)h
{
    _heightInMeters = h;
}

- (int)weightInKilos
{
    return _weightInKilos;
}

- (void)setWeightInKilos:(int)w
{
    _weightInKilos = w;
}

- (float)bodyMassIndex
{
    return _weightInKilos / (_heightInMeters * _heightInMeters);
}

@end
```

Now that you have implemented the methods that you declared in BNRPerson.h, the **BNRPerson** class is complete and you can use it in a program.

Open main.m and import BNRPerson.h so that **main()** can see the declarations in the **BNRPerson** class header:

```
#import <Foundation/Foundation.h>
#import "BNRPerson.h"

int main(int argc, const char * argv[])
{
    ...
}
```

Why is Foundation.h inside angled brackets and BNRPerson.h inside quotation marks? The angled brackets tell the compiler that Foundation/Foundation.h is a precompiled header found in Apple's libraries. The quotation marks tell the compiler to look for BNRPerson.h within the current project.

Next, add code to **main()** that uses the **BNRPerson** class:

```
int main(int argc, const char * argv[])
{
    @autoreleasepool {

        // Create an instance of BNRPerson
        BNRPerson *mikey = [[BNRPerson alloc] init];

        // Give the instance variables interesting values using setters
        [mikey setWeightInKilos:96];
        [mikey setHeightInMeters:1.8];

        // Log the instance variables using the getters
        float height = [mikey heightInMeters];
        int weight = [mikey weightInKilos];
        NSLog(@"mikey is %.2f meters tall and weighs %d kilograms", height, weight);

        // Log some values using custom methods
        float bmi = [mikey bodyMassIndex];
        NSLog(@"mikey has a BMI of %f", bmi);

    }
    return 0;
}
```

Build and run the program.

Figure 18.3 Object diagram for BMITime

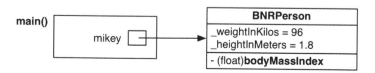

Accessor methods

When you created struct Person back in Chapter 11, you accessed the data members of the structure directly in **main()**:

```
mikey.weightInKilos = 96;
mikey.heightInMeters = 1.8;
```

In object-oriented thinking, however, code that is outside of a class should not directly read or write to the instance variables of an instance of that class. Only code within the class can do that.

Instead, a class will provide methods that let external code (like in **main()**) access the instance variables of an instance. This is what you have done in **BNRPerson**. In **main()**, you send messages to the **BNRPerson** instance to read the values of its instance variables:

```
int weight = [mikey weightInKilos];
float height = [mikey heightInMeters];
```

The **heightInMeters** and **weightInKilos** methods are *getter methods*. A getter method, or *getter*, allows code outside of a class to read, or get, the value of an instance variable.

BNRPerson also has the methods **setHeightInMeters:** and **setWeightInKilos:**. These are *setter methods*. A setter method, or *setter*, allows code outside of a class to change, or set, the value of an instance variable.

Setter and getter methods are collectively known as *accessor methods*, or simply *accessors*.

Accessor naming conventions

In declaring accessor methods for **BNRPerson**, you followed important Objective-C naming conventions. Getter methods are given the name of the instance variable minus the underscore.

```
// Instance variable declarations
{
    float _heightInMeters;
    int _weightInKilos;
}

// Getter method declarations
- (float)heightInMeters;
- (int)weightInKilos;
```

Setter methods start with **set** followed by the name of the instance variable minus the underscore. Notice that the case of the setter's name adjusts to preserve the camel-casing. Thus, the first letter of the instance variable name is uppercase in the setter's name.

```
// Setter method declarations - notice difference in casing!
- (void)setHeightInMeters:(float)h;
- (void)setWeightInKilos:(int)w;
```

Learning these conventions is important. In the next chapter, you will learn a shortcut where the compiler creates accessor methods for you. The compiler will name the accessors according to these conventions.

self

Inside any method, you have access to the implicit local variable self. self is a pointer to the object that is running the method. It is used when an object wants to send a message to itself.

For example, many Objective-C programmers are quite religious about never reading or writing to an instance variable directly. They even call accessors within implementations of other methods in the same class.

Currently, your implementation of **bodyMassIndex** accesses the instance variables directly. In BNRPerson.m, update **bodyMassIndex** to use the accessor methods instead:

```
- (float)bodyMassIndex
{
    return _weightInKilos / (_heightInMeters * _heightInMeters);
    float h = [self heightInMeters];
    return [self weightInKilos] / (h * h);
}
```

You can also pass self as an argument to let other objects know where the current object is. For example, your **BNRPerson** class might have a method **addYourselfToArray:** that would look like this:

```
- (void)addYourselfToArray:(NSMutableArray *)theArray
{
    [theArray addObject:self];
}
```

Here you use self to tell the array where the instance of **BNRPerson** lives. It is literally the **BNRPerson** instance's address.

Multiple files

Notice that your project now has executable code in two files: main.m and BNRPerson.m. (BNRPerson.h is a declaration of a class and has no executable code in it.) When you build the project, these files are compiled separately and then linked together. It is not uncommon that a real-world project will consist of hundreds of files of C and Objective-C code.

When Xcode builds your project, it compiles each of the .m and .c files into machine code. Then, it links those files together with any libraries into the executable file. What libraries? In this section of the book, all of your executables have been link to the Foundation framework.

There are many libraries of reusable code downloadable from the internet. A lot are free, some are not.

Class prefixes

Objective-C is not namespaced. This means that if you write a program with a class called **Person** in it, and you link in a library of someone else's code that also declares a **Person** class, then the compiler will not be able to tell these two classes apart, and you will get a compiler error.

To prevent name collisions like this, Apple recommends that you prefix each of your class names with three or more letters, to make your class names more unique and less likely to collide with someone else's class name. Most developers use either their company's or their project's initials. In this book, we use the **BNR** class prefix.

Challenge

Create a new Foundation Command Line Tool called Stocks. Then create a class called **BNRStockHolding** to represent a stock that you have purchased. It will be a subclass of **NSObject**. For instance variables, it will have two `floats` named `_purchaseSharePrice` and `_currentSharePrice` and one `int` named `_numberOfShares`. Use properties to create accessor methods and instance variables. Create two other instance methods:

```
- (float)costInDollars;   // purchaseSharePrice * numberOfShares
- (float)valueInDollars;  // currentSharePrice * numberOfShares
```

In **main()**, fill an array with three instances of **BNRStockHolding**. Then iterate through the array printing out the value of each.

Figure 18.4 An array of **BNRStockHolding** objects

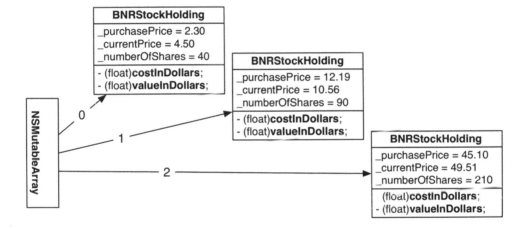

19

Properties

Objective-C has a convenient shortcut called *properties* that lets you skip declaring instance variables and declaring and implementing accessor methods. Using properties simplifies your class's code.

Declaring properties

In BNRPerson.h, remove the instance variable and accessor method declarations and replace them with two properties: heightInMeters and weightInKilos.

```
#import <Foundation/Foundation.h>

@interface BNRPerson : NSObject

// BNRPerson has two properties
@property (nonatomic) float heightInMeters;
@property (nonatomic) int weightInKilos;

{
    // BNRPerson has two instance variables
    float _heightInMeters;
    int _weightInKilos;
}

// BNRPerson has methods to read and set its instance variables
- (float)heightInMeters;
- (void)setHeightInMeters:(float)h;
- (int)weightInKilos;
- (void)setWeightInKilos:(int)w;

// BNRPerson has a method that calculates the Body Mass Index
- (float)bodyMassIndex;

@end
```

A property declaration begins with @property and includes the type of the property and its name. Ignore the (nonatomic) for now. This is a property attribute, which we will discuss later in the chapter.

Declaring properties makes your header file short and sweet. In the future, declaring properties will save you a few lines of typing. But wait, there's more. When you declare a property, the compiler not only declares your accessors for you, it also implements them based on the property's declaration.

This means you no longer need the accessor implementations that you wrote in BNRPerson.m. Open BNRPerson.m and delete them:

```
@implementation BNRPerson

- (float)heightInMeters
{
    return _heightInMeters;
}

- (void)setHeightInMeters:(float)h
{
    _heightInMeters = h;
}

- (int)weightInKilos
{
    return _weightInKilos;
}

- (void)setWeightInKilos:(int)w
{
    _weightInKilos = w;
}

- (float)bodyMassIndex
{
    float h = [self heightInMeters];
    return [self weightInKilos] / (h * h);
}

@end
```

Build and run your program. It should work exactly as before. By using properties, you have not changed this class at all. You did not have to make any changes in main.m because **BNRPerson** still has all the same accessor methods with all the same names. They are simply written using a terser (and more stylish) syntax.

What about the instance variables? The compiler created instance variables named _heightInMeters and _weightInKilos. However, you do not see these variables in your code because there are no longer any explicit accessor implementations. When using properties, you rarely need to use instance variables directly and can rely on the accessors that the compiler created.

From here on out, you will almost always use properties when creating a class. Apple recommends using properties, and so do we.

So why did you need to learn about instance variables and accessors methods first? There are some exceptions that you will learn about later where you need to adjust the property declaration or implement accessor methods yourself. It is much easier to work with properties when you understand what they are doing for you in the first place.

Property attributes

A property declaration can have one or more *property attributes*. Property attributes give the compiler more information about how the property should behave. Property attributes appear in a comma-delimited list in parentheses after the @property annotation.

In **BNRPerson**, the properties are declared as `nonatomic`.

```
@property (nonatomic) float heightInMeters;
@property (nonatomic) int weightInKilos;
```

Properties are either `atomic` or `nonatomic`. The difference has to do with multithreading, which is a topic beyond the scope of this book. All of the properties that you will declare in this book will be `nonatomic`.

Let's consider another property attribute. Sometimes a class needs a "read-only" property – a property whose value can be read but not changed. A property like this should have a getter method but no setter method. You can instruct the compiler to create only a getter method by including a `readonly` value in the list of property attributes.

```
@property (nonatomic, readonly) double circumferenceOfEarth;
```

When the compiler sees this declaration, it will create a **circumferenceOfEarth** getter method but not a **setCircumferenceOfEarth:** setter method.

Properties are either `readonly` or `readwrite`.

```
@property (nonatomic, readwrite) double humanPopulation;
```

Based on this declaration, the compiler will create a **humanPopulation** getter method and a **setHumanPopulation:** setter method.

Both **BNRPerson** properties are `readwrite` properties. However, you did not have to include the `readwrite` attribute because `readwrite` is the default value. Default values are optional in declarations.

Sadly, `atomic` is the default value for the atomic/nonatomic attribute, so you must include the `nonatomic` value in all of your property declarations.

Another attribute that you will see shortly is `copy`. Practically speaking, whenever you declare a property that points to an **NSString** or an **NSArray**, you should include the `copy` attribute. You will find out why in Chapter 34.

There are other property attributes and values that you will learn about as you continue through the book.

Dot notation

Objective-C programmers call accessor methods a lot. When properties were introduced, Apple also introduced a shorthand *dot notation* for calling those accessors.

Many Objective-C programmers prefer dot notation because it is easier to type. In `main.m`, try out dot notation:

```
int main(int argc, const char * argv[])
{
    @autoreleasepool {

        // Create an instance of BNRPerson
        BNRPerson *mikey = [[BNRPerson alloc] init];

        // Give the instance variables interesting values using setters
        [mikey setWeightInKilos:96];
        [mikey setHeightInMeters:1.8];
        mikey.weightInKilos = 96;
        mikey.heightInMeters = 1.8;

        // Log the instance variables using the getters
        float height = [mikey heightInMeters];
        int weight = [mikey weightInKilos];
        float height = mikey.heightInMeters;
        int weight = mikey.weightInKilos;
        NSLog(@"mikey is %.2f meters tall and weighs %d kilos", height, weight);

        // Log some values using custom methods
        float bmi = [mikey bodyMassIndex];
        NSLog(@"mikey has a BMI of %.2f", bmi);

    }
    return 0;
}
```

This notation looks just like the notation used for accessing the members of a struct. It is critical to remember, however, that when using dot notation with an object, a message is being sent.

These two lines do the exact same thing:

```
mikey.weightInKilos = 96;
[mikey setWeightInKilos:96];
```

and these two lines do the exact same thing:

```
float w = mikey.weightInKilos;
float w = [mikey weightInKilos];
```

Notice that mikey.weightInKilos sends one of two possible messages, depending on the context in which it is being used. That is, it calls either the getter method (**weightInKilos**) or the setter method (**setWeightInKilos:**) depending on whether it is being used to get or set mikey's _weightInKilos.

20

Inheritance

When you created the **BNRPerson** class, you declared it to be a subclass of **NSObject**. This means that every instance of **BNRPerson** will have the instance variables and methods defined in **NSObject** as well as the instance variables and methods defined in **BNRPerson**. We say that **BNRPerson** *inherits* the instance variables and methods from **NSObject**.

In this chapter, you are going to create a new class named **BNREmployee**. **BNREmployee** will be a subclass of **BNRPerson**.

Figure 20.1 **BNREmployee** inherits from **BNRPerson**

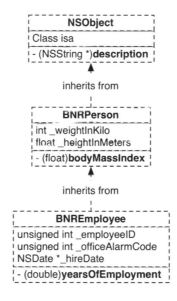

Makes sense, right? Employees are people. They have heights and weights. But not all people are employees; employees can have characteristics specific to being an employee. Your **BNREmployee** class adds two **BNREmployee**-specific characteristics – an employee ID and a hire date.

Open up the BMITime project and create a new file: an Objective-C class. Name the class **BNREmployee** and leave its superclass as **NSObject** for now.

Open BNREmployee.h. Import BNRPerson.h and change the superclass from **NSObject** to **BNRPerson**:

```
#import "BNRPerson.h"

@interface BNREmployee : BNRPerson

@end
```

BNREmployee is now a subclass of **BNRPerson**.

The **main** function of BMITime will need to access the employee ID and the hire date. Each employee also has an alarm code to get into the office. Thus, you need three new properties, and you need to add them in BNREmployee.h. Also declare a method that will calculate the years of employment based on the employee's hire date.

```
#import "BNRPerson.h"

@interface BNREmployee : BNRPerson

@property (nonatomic) unsigned int employeeID;
@property (nonatomic) unsigned int officeAlarmCode;
@property (nonatomic) NSDate *hireDate;
- (double)yearsOfEmployment;

@end
```

The hireDate property is the first property you have declared that points to another object. When a property points to an object, there are memory management implications that you will learn about in later chapters.

For now, recognize that you have declared a property named hireDate that is a pointer to an **NSDate**. You tell the compiler that this property is to be nonatomic, like all the other properties.

Figure 20.2 **BNREmployee** has a pointer to an **NSDate**

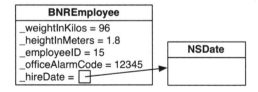

And, like with your primitive type properties, by default you get an instance variable. This variable is named _hireDate and is a pointer to an **NSDate**. The compiler also synthesizes two accessor methods:

```
- (void)setHireDate:(NSDate *)d;
- (NSDate *)hireDate;
```

In BNREmployee.m, implement the **yearsOfEmployment** method:

```
@implementation BNREmployee

- (double)yearsOfEmployment
{
    // Do I have a non-nil hireDate?
    if (self.hireDate) {
        // NSTimeInterval is the same as double
        NSDate *now = [NSDate date];
        NSTimeInterval secs = [now timeIntervalSinceDate:self.hireDate];
        return secs / 31557600.0;  // Seconds per year
    } else {
        return 0;
    }
}

@end
```

To try out the **BNREmployee** class, open main.m and make two changes: import BNREmployee.h and create an instance of **BNREmployee** instead of a **BNRPerson**. Leave the person variable declared as a pointer to a **BNRPerson** for now:

```
#import <Foundation/Foundation.h>
#import "BNRPerson.h"
#import "BNREmployee.h"

int main(int argc, const char * argv[])
{
    @autoreleasepool {

        // Create an instance of BNREmployee
        BNRPerson *mikey = [[BNREmployee alloc] init];

        // Give properties interesting values using setter methods
        mikey.weightInKilos = 96;
        mikey.heightInMeters = 1.8;

        // Log some properties using getter methods
        NSLog(@"mikey has a weight of %d", mikey.weightInKilos);
        NSLog(@"mikey has a height of %f", mikey.heightInMeters);

        // Log the body mass index
        float bmi = [mikey bodyMassIndex];
        NSLog(@"mikey has a BMI of %f", bmi);

    }
    return 0;
}
```

Think this will cause a problem? Build and run the program to see.

The program works fine, and nothing in the output has changed. *An employee is a person* – it can do anything a person can. An instance of **BNREmployee** can respond to methods from **BNRPerson** (like **setWeightInKilos:**). You can use an instance of **BNREmployee** anywhere that the program expects an instance of **BNRPerson**. A instance of a subclass can stand in for an instance of the superclass without problems because it inherits everything in the superclass.

Also note that you do not need to import BNRPerson.h. The compiler will find the #import "BNRPerson.h" statement in the BNREmployee.h file, so including it in here would be redundant.

Now make the following changes in main.m to make fuller use of the **BNREmployee** class. Give mikey an employee ID and set the hire date to the current date.

```
#import <Foundation/Foundation.h>
#import "BNREmployee.h"

int main(int argc, const char * argv[])
{
    @autoreleasepool {

        // Create an instance of BNREmployee
        BNREmployee *mikey = [[BNREmployee alloc] init];

        // Give the instance variables interesting values using setter methods
        mikey.weightInKilos = 96;
        mikey.heightInMeters = 1.8;
        mikey.employeeID = 12;
        mikey.hireDate = [NSDate dateWithNaturalLanguageString:@"Aug 2nd, 2010"];

        // Log the instance variables using the getters
        float height = mikey.heightInMeters;
        int weight = mikey.weightInKilos;
        NSLog(@"mikey is %.2f meters tall and weighs %d kilos", height, weight);
        NSLog(@"Employee %lu hired on %@", mikey.employeeID, mikey.hireDate);

        // Log the body mass index using the bodyMassIndex method
        float bmi = [mikey bodyMassIndex];
        double years = [mikey yearsOfEmployment];
        NSLog(@"BMI of %.2f, has worked with us for %.2f years", bmi, years);
    }
    return 0;
}
```

Build and run the program and see your new output.

Overriding methods

Usually, a subclass needs to do something differently than its superclass. Let's say, for example, that, unlike people in general, employees always have a BMI of 19. In this case, you would *override* the **bodyMassIndex** method in **BNREmployee**.

You override an inherited method by writing a new implementation.

In BNREmployee.m, override **bodyMassIndex**:

```
#import "BNREmployee.h"
@implementation BNREmployee

- (double)yearsOfEmployment
{
    // Do I have a non-nil hireDate?
    if (self.hireDate) {
        // NSTimeInterval is the same as double
        NSTimeInterval secs = [self.hireDate timeIntervalSinceNow];
        return secs / 31557600.0;  // Seconds per year
    } else {
        return 0;
    }
}

- (float)bodyMassIndex
{
    return 19.0;
}

@end
```

Because **BNREmployee** inherits from **BNRPerson**, everyone already knows that instances of **BNREmployee** will respond to a **bodyMassIndex** message. There is no need to advertise it again, so you do not declare it in BNREmployee.h.

This also means that, when you override a method, you can only change its implementation. You cannot change how it is declared; the method's name, return type, and argument types must stay the same.

Build and run the program. Confirm that **BNREmployee**'s implementation of **bodyMassIndex** is the one that gets executed – not the implementation from **BNRPerson**.

super

When overriding a method, a subclass can build on the implementation of its superclass rather than replacing it wholesale. What if you decided that employees get 10% off their BMI as calculated in **BNRPerson**'s implementation? It would be convenient to call **BNRPerson**'s version of **bodyMassIndex** and then multiply the result by 0.9. To do this, you use the super directive. Try it in BNREmployee.m:

```
- (float)bodyMassIndex
{
    return 19.0;
    float normalBMI = [super bodyMassIndex];
    return normalBMI * 0.9;
}
```

Build and run the program.

Inheritance hierarchy

All objects inherit (either directly or indirectly) from **NSObject**:

Figure 20.3 Inheritance diagram of some classes you know

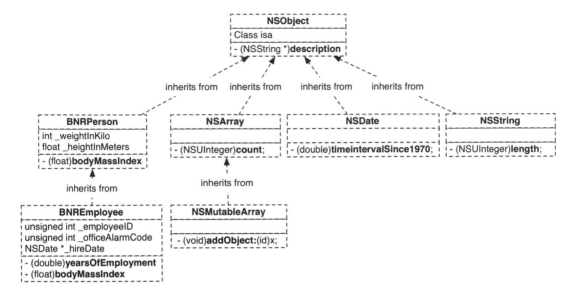

NSObject has many methods but only one instance variable: the isa pointer. Every object's isa pointer points at the class that created it. (Get it? When you have a **BNRPerson** instance, that object "is a" **BNRPerson**. When you have an **NSString** instance, that object "is a[n]" **NSString**.)

Figure 20.4 Every object knows which class created it

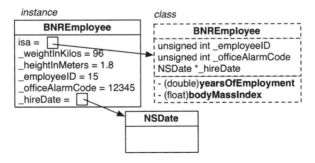

When you send a message to an object, you kick off a search for a method of that name. The search follows the object's isa pointer to start looking for the method in the object's class. If there is no method of that name there, then it is on to the superclass. The hunt stops when the method is found or when the top of the hierarchy (**NSObject**) is reached.

Let's say that you send the message **fido** to an object. To respond to this message, the object uses the isa pointer to find its class and ask, "Do you declare an instance method named **fido**?"

If the class has a method named **fido**, it gets executed. If the class does not have a **fido** method, it asks its superclass, "Do you declare an instance method named **fido**?"

And up, up the hierarchy it goes on the hunt for the implementation of a method named **fido**. The hunt stops when the method is found or when the top of the hierarchy is reached.

Figure 20.5 Object diagram for BMITime

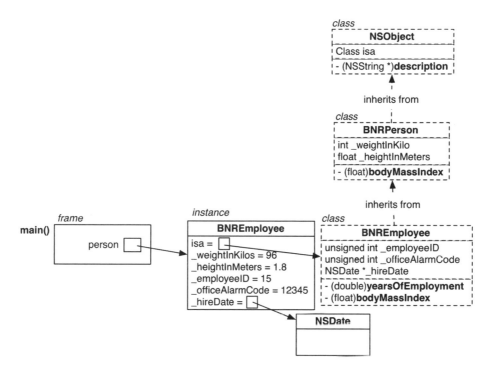

At the top of the hierarchy, **NSObject** says, "Nope, no **fido** method." At this point, you get an error message that says something like, `-[BNREmployee fido]: unrecognized selector sent to instance 0x100106e102`. This can be translated as, "There is no instance method of this name defined anywhere in this object's inheritance hierarchy."

The first implementation that is found is the one that gets executed. **BNREmployee** and **BNRPerson** both have implementations of **bodyMassIndex**, but if a **BNREmployee** is sent the **bodyMassIndex** message, the implementation in **BNREmployee** will be found first and executed. The hunt ends before reaching the **BNRPerson** class.

When you use the super directive, you are sending a message to the current object but saying, "Run a method with this name, but start the search for its implementation at your superclass."

description and %@

In calls to **NSLog()**, you have been using the token %@ to get an object to describe itself. The %@ token sends a **description** message to the object pointed to by the corresponding variable.

The **description** method returns a string that is a useful description of an instance of the class. It is an **NSObject** method, so every object implements it. The default **NSObject** implementation returns the object's address in memory as a string.

However, a memory address is often not the most useful way to describe an instance. A class can override **description**:. For example, **NSDate** overrides **description** to return the date/time that the instance holds. **NSString** overrides **description** to return the string itself.

In BNREmployee.m, override **description** to return a string that describes an instance of **BNREmployee**:

```
@implementation BNREmployee

...

- (NSString *)description
{
    return [NSString stringWithFormat:@"<Employee %d>", self.employeeID];
}

@end
```

Modify main.m to use **BNREmployee**'s implementation of **description**.

```
int main(int argc, const char * argv[])
{
    @autoreleasepool {

        // Create an instance of BNREmployee
        BNREmployee *mikey = [[BNREmployee alloc] init];

        ...

        NSLog(@"mikey is %.2f meters tall and weighs %d kilos", height, weight);
        NSDate *date = mikey.hireDate;
        NSLog(@"%@ hired on %@", mikey, date);

        // Log some values using custom methods
        float bmi = [mikey bodyMassIndex];
        double years = [mikey yearsOfEmployment];
        NSLog(@"BMI of %.2f, has worked with us for %.2f years", bmi, years);
    }
    return 0;
}
```

Challenge

This challenge builds on the challenge from the previous chapter.

Create a subclass of **BNRStockHolding** called **BNRForeignStockHolding**. Give **BNRForeignStockHolding** an additional property: conversionRate, which will be a float. (The conversion rate is what you need to multiply the local price by to get a price in US dollars. Assume the purchasePrice and currentPrice are in the local currency.) Override **costInDollars** and **valueInDollars** to do the right thing.

In **main()**, add a few instances of **BNRForeignStockHolding** to your array.

Figure 20.6 **BNRStockHolding** and **BNRForeignStockHolding** objects

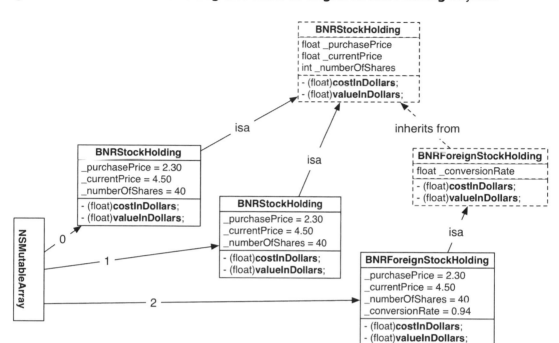

21

Object Instance Variables and Properties

Thus far, the instance variables of your objects have been mostly simple C types like int or float. It is far more common for instance variables to be pointers to other objects, like _hireDate. An object instance variable points to another object and describes a relationship between the two objects. Usually, object instance variables fall into one of three categories:

- *Object-type attributes*: a pointer to a simple, value-like object like an **NSString** or an **NSDate**. For example, an employee's last name would be stored in an **NSString**. Thus, an instance of **BNREmployee** would have an instance variable that would be a pointer to an instance of **NSString**. We recommend that you always declare these as a property with an implicit instance variable; you typically will not need to explicitly create accessors.

- *To-one relationships*: a pointer to a single complex object. For example, an employee might have a spouse. Thus, an instance of **BNREmployee** would have an instance variable that would be a pointer to an instance of **BNRPerson**. Once again, we will recommend that you always declare these as a property with an implicit instance variable; you typically will not need to explicitly create accessors.

- *To-many relationships*: a pointer to an instance of a collection class, such as an **NSMutableArray**. (You will see other examples of collections in Chapter 24.) For example, an employee might have children. In this case, the instance of **BNREmployee** would have an instance variable that would be a pointer to an instance of **NSMutableArray**. The **NSMutableArray** would hold a list of pointers to one or more **BNRPerson** objects. To-many relationships are trickier than attributes or to-one relationships. You will often end up explicitly creating instance variables, accessors, and methods for adding or removing objects from the relationship.

Figure 21.1 A **BNREmployee** with object instance variables

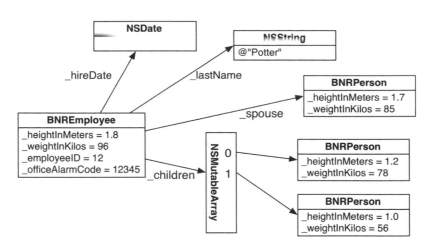

Notice that, as in other diagrams, pointers are represented by arrows. In addition, those pointers are named. So a **BNREmployee** would have three new instance variables: _lastName, _spouse, and _children. The declaration of **BNREmployee**'s properties might look like this:

```
@interface BNREmployee : BNRPerson

@property (nonatomic) unsigned int employeeID;
@property (nonatomic) unsigned int officeAlarmCode;
@property (nonatomic) NSDate *hireDate;
@property (nonatomic) NSString *lastName;
@property (nonatomic) BNRPerson *spouse;
@property (nonatomic) NSMutableArray *children;
```

With the exception of employeeID and officeAlarmCode, these properties are all pointers. For example, the variable spouse is a pointer to another object that lives on the heap. The pointer named spouse is inside the **BNREmployee** object, but the **BNRPerson** object that spouse points to is not. Objects do not live inside other objects. The employee object contains its employee ID (the variable and the value itself), but it only knows where its spouse lives in memory.

There are two important side-effects to objects pointing to – rather than containing – other objects:

- One object can take on several roles. For example, it is likely that the employee's spouse is also listed as the emergency contact for the children:

Figure 21.2 One object, multiple roles

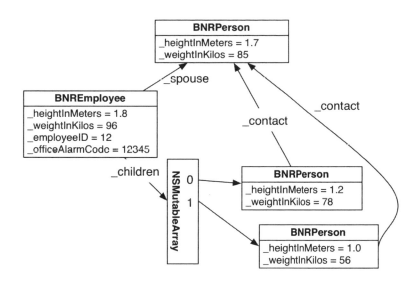

- You end up with a lot of distinct objects using up your program's memory. You need the objects being used to stay around, but you want the unnecessary ones to be deallocated (have their memory returned to the heap) so that their memory can be reused.

Object ownership and ARC

To manage these issues, we have the idea of *object ownership*. When an object has an object instance variable, the object with the pointer is said to *own* the object that is being pointed to.

From the other end of things, because of ARC (discussed briefly in Chapter 15), an object knows how many *owners* it currently has. For instance, in the diagram above, the instance of **BNRPerson** has three owners: the **BNREmployee** object and the two **Child** objects. When an object has zero owners, it figures no one needs it around anymore and deallocates itself. Before ARC was introduced in Xcode 4.2, we managed ownership manually and spent a lot of time and effort doing so. (There is more about manual reference counting and how it worked in the final section of Chapter 23. All the code in this book, however, assumes that you are using ARC.)

Let's expand the BMITime project to see how ownership works in practice. It is not uncommon for a company to keep track of what assets have been issued to which employee. You are going to create an **BNRAsset** class, and each **BNREmployee** will have an array containing his or her assets.

Figure 21.3 Employees and assets

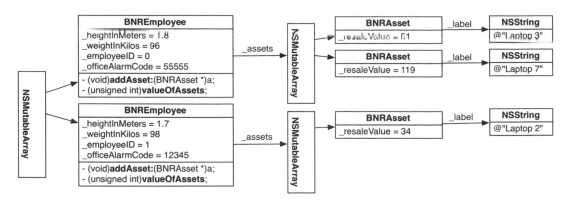

This is often called a "parent-child" relationship: The parent (an instance of **BNREmployee**) has a collection of children (an **NSMutableArray** of **BNRAsset** objects).

Creating the BNRAsset class

Create a new file: an Objective-C subclass of **NSObject**. Name it **BNRAsset**. Open BNRAsset.h and declare two properties:

```
#import <Foundation/Foundation.h>

@interface BNRAsset : NSObject

@property (nonatomic, copy) NSString *label;
@property (nonatomic) unsigned int resaleValue;

@end
```

Remember that when an object has no owners, it is deallocated. There is an **NSObject** method named **dealloc**. If a class overrides **dealloc**, then this method will be executed when an instance of the class is deallocated. You are going to override **dealloc** in **BNRAsset** to see when instances of **BNRAsset** are being deallocated.

To make it clear which particular instance of **BNRAsset** is being deallocated, you will also override **description** to return a string that includes the instance's label and resaleValue.

Open BNRAsset.m. Override **description** and **dealloc**.

```
#import "BNRAsset.h"

@implementation BNRAsset


- (NSString *)description
{
    return [NSString stringWithFormat:@"<%@: $%d>", self.label, self.resaleValue];
}

- (void)dealloc
{
    NSLog(@"deallocating %@", self);
}

@end
```

Try building what you have so far to see if you made any errors typing it in. You can build your program without running it by using the keyboard shortcut Command-B. This is useful for testing your code without taking the time to run the program or when you know the program is not ready to run yet. Plus, it is always a good idea to build after making changes so that if you have introduced a syntax error you can find and fix it right away. If you wait, you will not be as sure what changes are responsible for your "new" bug.

Adding a to-many relationship to BNREmployee

Now you are going to add a to-many relationship to the **BNREmployee** class. Recall that a to-many relationship includes a collection object (like an array) and the objects contained in the collection. There are two other important things to know about collections and ownership:

- When an object is added to the collection, the collection establishes a pointer to the object, and the object gains an owner.

- When an object is removed from a collection, the collection gets rid of its pointer to the object, and the object loses an owner.

To set up the to-many relationship in **BNREmployee**, you will need a new instance variable to hold a pointer to the mutable array of assets. You will also need a couple of methods. Open BNREmployee.h and add them:

```
#import "BNRPerson.h"
@class BNRAsset;

@interface BNREmployee : BNRPerson
{
    NSMutableArray *_assets;
}

@property (nonatomic) unsigned int employeeID;
@property (nonatomic) unsigned int officeAlarmCode;
@property (nonatomic) NSDate *hireDate;
@property (nonatomic, copy) NSArray *assets;
- (double)yearsOfEmployment;
- (void)addAsset:(BNRAsset *)a;
- (unsigned int)valueOfAssets;

@end
```

Notice the line that says @class BNRAsset;. As the compiler is reading this file, it will come across the class name **BNRAsset**. If it does not know about the class, it will throw an error. The @class BNRAsset; line tells the compiler "There is a class called **BNRAsset**. Do not panic when you see it in this file. That is all you need to know for now."

Using @class instead of #import gives the compiler less information, but makes the processing of this particular file faster. You can use @class with BNREmployee.h and other header files because the compiler does not need to know a lot to process a file of declarations.

The property has type **NSArray**, which tells other classes, "If you ask for my assets, you are going to get something that is not mutable." However, behind the scenes, the assets array is actually an instance of **NSMutableArray** so that you can add and remove items in BNREmployee.m. That is why you are declaring a property and an instance variable: in this case, the type of the property and the type of the instance variable are not the same.

Now turn your attention to BNREmployee.m. With a to-many relationship, you need to create the collection object (an array, in this case) before you put anything in it. You can do this when the original object (an employee) is first created, or you can be lazy and wait until the collection is needed. Let's be lazy.

```
#import "BNREmployee.h"
#import "BNRAsset.h"

@implementation BNREmployee

// Accessors for assets properties
- (void)setAssets:(NSArray *)a
{
    _assets = [a mutableCopy];
}

- (NSArray *)assets
{
    return [_assets copy];
}

- (void)addAsset:(BNRAsset *)a
{
    // Is assets nil?
    if (!_assets) {

        // Create the array
        _assets = [[NSMutableArray alloc] init];
    }
    [_assets addObject:a];
}

- (unsigned int)valueOfAssets
{
    // Sum up the resale value of the assets
    unsigned int sum = 0;
    for (BNRAsset *a in _assets) {
        sum += [a resaleValue];
    }
    return sum;
}
```

```
- (double)yearsOfEmployment
{
    ...
```

To process the BNREmployee.m file, the compiler needs to know a lot about the **BNRAsset** class. Thus, you imported BNRAsset.h instead of using @class.

To track the deallocation of **BNREmployee** instances, modify the implementation of **description** and implement **dealloc** in BNREmployee.m.

```
...

- (float)bodyMassIndex
{
    float normalBMI = [super bodyMassIndex];
    return normalBMI * 0.9;
}

- (NSString *)description
{
    return [NSString stringWithFormat:@"<Employee %d>", self.employeeID];
    return [NSString stringWithFormat:@"<Employee %d: $%d in assets>",
                                        self.employeeID, self.valueOfAssets];
}

- (void)dealloc
{
    NSLog(@"deallocating %@", self);
}

@end
```

Build the project to see if you have made any mistakes.

Now you need to create some assets and assign them to employees. Replace the contents of main.m:

```
#import <Foundation/Foundation.h>
#import "BNREmployee.h"
#import "BNRAsset.h"

int main(int argc, const char * argv[])
{
    @autoreleasepool {

        // Create an array of BNREmployee objects
        NSMutableArray *employees = [[NSMutableArray alloc] init];

        for (int i = 0; i < 10; i++) {
            // Create an instance of BNREmployee
            BNREmployee *mikey = [[BNREmployee alloc] init];

            // Give the instance variables interesting values
            mikey.weightInKilos = 90 + i;
            mikey.heightInMeters = 1.8 - i/10.0;
            mikey.employeeID = i;

            // Put the employee in the employees array
            [employees addObject:mikey];
        }

        // Create 10 assets
        for (int i = 0; i < 10; i++) {
            // Create an asset
            BNRAsset *asset = [[BNRAsset alloc] init];

            // Give it an interesting label
            NSString *currentLabel = [NSString stringWithFormat:@"Laptop %d", i];
            asset.label = currentLabel;
            asset.resaleValue = 350 + i * 17;

            // Get a random number between 0 and 9 inclusive
            NSUInteger randomIndex = random() % [employees count];

            // Find that employee
            BNREmployee *randomEmployee = [employees objectAtIndex:randomIndex];

            // Assign the asset to the employee
            [randomEmployee addAsset:asset];
        }

        NSLog(@"Employees: %@", employees);

        NSLog(@"Giving up ownership of one employee");

        [employees removeObjectAtIndex:5];

        NSLog(@"Giving up ownership of arrays");

        employees = nil;

    }
    return 0;
}
```

Build and run the program. You should see something like this:

```
Employees: (
    "<Employee 0: $0 in assets>",
    "<Employee 1: $153 in assets>",
    "<Employee 2: $119 in assets>",
    "<Employee 3: $68 in assets>",
    "<Employee 4: $0 in assets>",
    "<Employee 5: $136 in assets>",
    "<Employee 6: $119 in assets>",
    "<Employee 7: $34 in assets>",
    "<Employee 8: $0 in assets>",
    "<Employee 9: $136 in assets>"
)
Giving up ownership of one employee
deallocating <Employee 5: $136 in assets>
deallocating <Laptop 3: $51 >
deallocating <Laptop 5: $85  >
Giving up ownership of arrays
deallocating <Employee 0: $0 in assets>
deallocating <Employee 1: $153 in assets>
deallocating <Laptop 9: $153 >
...
deallocating <Employee 9: $136 in assets>
deallocating <Laptop 8: $136 >
```

When Employee 5 is removed from the array, it is deallocated because it has no owner. Then its assets are deallocated because they have no owner. (And you will have to trust us on this: the labels (instances of **NSString**) of the deallocated assets are also deallocated once they have no owner.)

When employees is set to nil, the array no longer has an owner. So it is deallocated, which sets up an even larger chain reaction of memory clean-up and deallocation when, suddenly, none of the employees has an owner.

Tidy, right? As the objects become unnecessary, they are being deallocated. This is good. When unnecessary objects do not get deallocated, you are said to have a *memory leak*. Typically, a memory leak causes more and more objects to linger unnecessarily over time, which will cause your application to run low on memory.

Challenge: holding portfolio

Using the **BNRStockHolding** class from a previous challenge, make a tool that creates an instance of a **BNRPortfolio** class and fills it with stock holdings. A portfolio can tell you what its current value is.

Also, add a symbol property to **BNRStockHolding** that holds the stock ticker symbol as an **NSString**.

Figure 21.4 Create a **BNRPortfolio** class

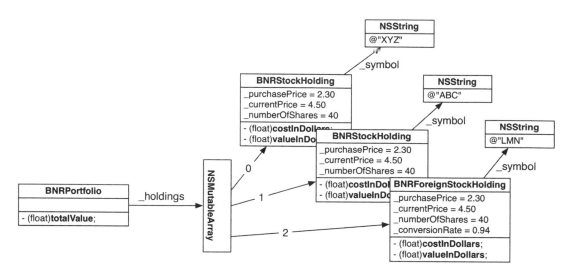

Challenge: removing assets

Your **BNREmployee** class has an **addAsset:** method. Give it a working **removeAsset:** method and test it in **main()**.

22
Class Extensions

So far, you have declared all of your properties, instance variables, and methods in the class header file. The header is where a class advertises its properties and methods so that other objects will know how to interact with it.

However, not every property or method should be advertised in a class's header. Some properties or methods may only be intended for use by the class or instances of the class. Such internal details are better declared in a *class extension*. A class extension is a set of declarations that is private. Only the class or instances of the class are able to use the properties, instance variables, or methods declared in a class extension.

For example, the officeAlarmCode property of **BNREmployee** should be private. The employee object needs to be able to access its alarm code, while non-employee objects do not need access to the alarm code and should not have it. You can make this happen by moving the declaration of officeAlarmCode from the header (BNREmployee.h) to a class extension.

Typically, class extensions are added to the class implementation file above the @implementation block where methods are implemented. In BNREmployee.m, create a class extension. Then declare the officeAlarmCode property there:

```
#import "BNREmployee.h"


// A class extension
@interface BNREmployee ()

@property (nonatomic) unsigned int officeAlarmCode;

@end


@implementation BNREmployee

...
```

A class extension starts with @interface and finishes off with @end. In fact, an extension looks a lot like a header, and both are known as "interfaces." However, in an extension, instead of the colon and the superclass name found in the header, there is a pair of empty parentheses.

In BNREmployee.h, remove the officeAlarmCode declaration:

```
#import "BNRPerson.h"
@class DNNAsset;

@interface BNREmployee : BNRPerson
{
    NSMutableArray *_assets
}
@property (nonatomic) unsigned int employeeID;
@property (nonatomic) unsigned int officeAlarmCode;
@property (nonatomic) NSDate *hireDate;
@property (nonatomic, copy) NSArray *assets;
- (void)addAsset:(BNRAsset *)a;
- (unsigned int)valueOfAssets;

@end
```

Build and run the program. Its behavior has not changed. However, moving the officeAlarmCode declaration to a class extension has two related effects:

First, objects that are not instances of **BNREmployee** can no longer see this property. For instance, a non-**BNREmployee** object could attempt to access an employee's alarm code like this:

```
BNREmployee *mikey = [[BNREmployee alloc] init];
unsigned int mikeysCode = mikey.officeAlarmCode;
```

This attempt would result in a compiler error that reads "No visible @interface declares the instance method officeAlarmCode". The only interface that is visible to a non-**BNREmployee** object is the **BNREmployee** header. And because the officeAlarmCode property is declared in a class extension rather than in the header, it is not visible (and as such, is unavailable) to non-**BNREmployee** objects.

Second, the **BNREmployee** header has one less declaration and thus is a little bit simpler. This is a good thing. The header is intended to be a billboard; its job is to advertise what other developers need to know to make your class work in the code that they write. Too much information makes a header difficult to for other developers to read and use.

Hiding mutability

Now let's look at a slightly different case for putting a declaration in a class extension instead of the class's header. In BNREmployee.h, you declared an assets property that is an **NSArray**, an **addAsset:** method, and an _assets instance variable that is an **NSMutableArray**. A developer will see both the property and the instance variable advertised in the header and will be uncertain which you intended outsiders to use.

Now that you know about class extensions, the solution is simple: move the _assets instance variable to **BNREmployee**'s class extension. In BNREmployee.m, add this declaration:

```
#import "BNREmployee.h"

// A class extension
@interface BNREmployee ()
{
    NSMutableArray *_assets;
}

@property (nonatomic) unsigned int officeAlarmCode;

@end

@implementation BNREmployee

...
```

In BNREmployee.h, remove the _assets declaration:

```
#import "BNRPerson.h"
@class BNRAsset;

@interface BNREmployee : BNRPerson
{
    NSMutableArray *_assets
}
@property (nonatomic) unsigned int employeeID;
@property (nonatomic) NSDate *hireDate;
@property (nonatomic, copy) NSArray *assets;
- (void)addAsset:(BNRAsset *)a;
- (unsigned int)valueOfAssets;

@end
```

Now the array of assets is only advertised as an immutable array, so non-**BNREmployee** objects will need to use the **addAsset:** method to manipulate this array. The fact that there is an **NSMutableArray** instance backing the assets property is a private implementation detail of the **BNREmployee** class.

Headers and inheritance

A subclass has no access to its superclass's class extensions. **BNREmployee** is a subclass of **BNRPerson** and imports its superclass's header file, BNRPerson.h. Thus, **BNREmployee** knows about what is declared in **BNRPerson**'s header but knows nothing about anything that **BNRPerson** may have declared in a class extension.

For example, if you implemented a **hasDriversLicense** method in BNRPerson.m but declared it in a class extension rather than BNRPerson.h, then **BNREmployee** would not know that this method existed. If you tried to call it in BNREmployee.m:

```
BOOL canDriveCompanyVan = [self hasDriversLicense];
```

you would get an error from the compiler: "No visible @interface declares the instance method hasDriversLicense".

Headers and generated instance variables

When a class declares a property in its header, only the accessors for this property are visible to other objects. Non-**BNREmployee** objects (including subclasses) cannot directly access the instance variables generated by property declarations.

For example, imagine that BNRPerson.h declares this property:

```
@property (nonatomic) NSMutableArray *friends;
```

In BNREmployee.m, even though **BNREmployee** is a subclass of **BNRPerson**, you cannot access the _friends instance variable:

```
[_friends addObject:@"Susan"]; // Error!
```

However, you can use the accessor:

```
[self.friends addObject:@"Susan"];
```

Challenge

Re-open your project from the Chapter 21 challenge.

No one other than you (the creator of the **BNRPortfolio** class) needs to know that you are using an **NSMutableArray** to hold the **BNRStockHolding** instances.

Move the property declaration for the array into a class extension in BNRPortfolio.m and add methods to **BNRPortfolio** to allow the addition and removal of stock holdings.

23

Preventing Memory Leaks

It is pretty common to have relationships that go in two directions. For example, maybe an asset should know which employee is currently holding it. Let's add that relationship. The new object diagram would look like this:

Figure 23.1 Adding holder relationship

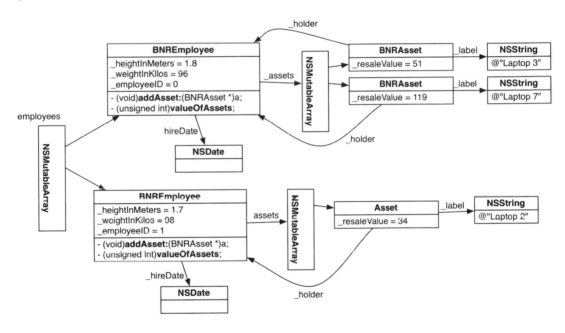

From a design standpoint, you would say that you are adding a pointer from the child (an instance of **BNRAsset**) back to its parent (the instance of **BNREmployee** that is holding it).

In BNRAsset.h, add a pointer instance variable to hold on to the holding employee:

```
#import <Foundation/Foundation.h>
@class BNREmployee;

@interface BNRAsset : NSObject
@property (nonatomic, copy) NSString *label;
@property (nonatomic) BNREmployee *holder;
@property (nonatomic) unsigned int resaleValue;

@end
```

In BNRAsset.m, extend the **description** method to display the holder:

```
#import "BNRAsset.h"
#import "BNREmployee.h"

@implementation BNRAsset

- (NSString *)description
{
    return [NSString stringWithFormat:@"<%@: $%d>", self.label, self.resaleValue];
    // Is holder non-nil?
    if (self.holder) {
        return [NSString stringWithFormat:@"<%@: $%d, assigned to %@>",
                self.label, self.resaleValue, self.holder];
    } else {
        return [NSString stringWithFormat:@"<%@: $%d unassigned>",
                self.label, self.resaleValue];
    }
}

- (void)dealloc
{
    NSLog(@"deallocating %@", self);
}

@end
```

This brings us to a style question: When people use the **BNRAsset** class and **BNREmployee** class together, how do you make sure that the two relationships are consistent? That is, an asset should appear in an employee's assets array if and only if the employee is the asset's holder. There are three options:

- Set both relationships explicitly:

  ```
  [vicePresident addAsset:townCar];
  [townCar setHolder:vicePresident];
  ```

- In the method that sets the child's pointer, add the child to the parent's collection.

  ```
  - (void)setHolder:(BNREmployee *)e
  {
      holder = e;
      [e addAsset:self];
  }
  ```

  (This approach is not at all common.)

- In the method that adds the child to the parent's collection, set the child's pointer.

In this exercise, you will take this last option. In BNREmployee.m, extend the **addAsset:** method to also set holder:

```
- (void)addAsset:(BNRAsset *)a
{
    // Is assets nil?
    if (!assets) {
        // Create the array
        assets = [[NSMutableArray alloc] init];
    }
    [assets addObject:a];
    a.holder = self;
}
```

(For an entertaining bug, have both accessors automatically call the other. This creates an infinite loop: **addAsset:** calls **setHolder:** which calls **addAsset:** which calls **setHolder:** which....)

Build and run the program. You should see something like this:

```
Employees: (
    "<Employee 0: $0 in assets>",
    "<Employee 1: $153 in assets>",
    "<Employee 2: $119 in assets>",
    "<Employee 3: $68 in assets>",
    "<Employee 4: $0 in assets>",
    "<Employee 5: $136 in assets>",
    "<Employee 6: $119 in assets>",
    "<Employee 7: $34 in assets>",
    "<Employee 8: $0 in assets>",
    "<Employee 9: $136 in assets>"
)
Giving up ownership of one employee
Giving up ownership of arrays
deallocating <Employee 0: $0 in assets>
deallocating <Employee 4: $0 in assets>
deallocating <Employee 8: $0 in assets>
```

Notice that now none of the employees with assets are getting deallocated properly. Also, none of the assets are being deallocated, either. Why?

Strong reference cycles

The asset owns the employee, the employee owns the assets array, and the assets array owns the asset. It is an island of garbage created by this circle of ownership. These objects should be getting deallocated to free up memory, but they are not. This is known as a *strong reference cycle*. Strong reference cycles are a very common source of memory leaks.

Figure 23.2 Every object owned by some other object

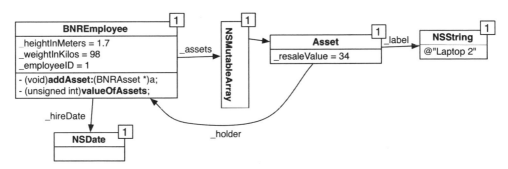

To find strong reference cycles in your program, you can use Apple's profiling tool, Instruments. When you *profile* a program, you monitor it while it runs to see what is happening behind the scenes with your code and the system. However, your program runs and exits very, very quickly. To give you time to profile, put in a hundred seconds of `sleep()` at the end of your `main()` function:

```
    ...
    }
    sleep(100);
    return 0;
}
```

In Xcode, choose Product → Profile in the menu. Instruments will launch. When the list of possible profiling instruments appears, choose Leaks:

Figure 23.3 Picking a profiler

As your program runs, you can browse the state of things. You have two instruments to choose from on the lefthand side of the window (Figure 23.4). Clicking on the Allocations instrument will let you see a bar graph of everything that has been allocated in your heap:

Figure 23.4 Allocations instrument

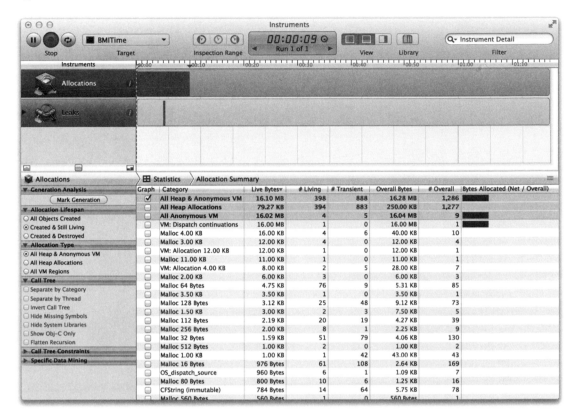

To look for strong reference cycles, click **Leaks** on the menu bar above the table and choose **Cycles & Roots** from the drop-down menu. Select a particular cycle to see an object graph of it:

Figure 23.5 Leaks instrument

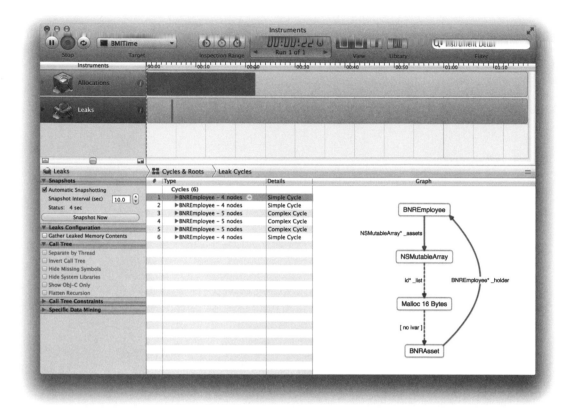

Weak references

How do you fix a strong reference cycle? Use a weak reference. A *weak reference* is a pointer that *does not* imply ownership. To fix our strong reference cycle, an asset should not own its holder. Edit BNRAsset.h to make holder a weak reference:

```
#import <Foundation/Foundation.h>
@class BNREmployee;

@interface BNRAsset : NSObject

@property (nonatomic, copy) NSString *label;
@property (nonatomic, weak) BNREmployee *holder;
@property (nonatomic) unsigned int resaleValue;
@end
```

Build and run the program. Note that all the objects are now being deallocated correctly.

In a parent-child relationship, the general rule for preventing this type of strong reference cycle is the parent owns the child, but the child should not own the parent.

Zeroing of weak references

To see weak references in action, let's add another array to the mix. What if you wanted an array of all assets – even ones that have not been assigned to a particular employee? You could add the assets to an array as they are created. Add a few lines of code to main.m:

```
#import <Foundation/Foundation.h>
#import "BNREmployee.h"
#import "BNRAsset.h"

int main(int argc, const char * argv[])
{
    @autoreleasepool {

        // Create an array of Employee objects
        NSMutableArray *employees = [[NSMutableArray alloc] init];

        for (int i = 0; i < 10; i++) {

            // Create an instance of BNREmployee
            BNREmployee *mikey = [[BNREmployee alloc] init];

            // Give the instance variables interesting values
            [mikey setWeightInKilos:90 + i];
            [mikey setHeightInMeters:1.8 - i/10.0];
            [mikey setEmployeeID:i];

            // Put the employee in the employees array
            [employees addObject:person];
        }

        NSMutableArray *allAssets = [[NSMutableArray alloc] init];

        // Create 10 assets
        for (int i = 0; i < 10; i++) {

            // Create an asset
            BNRAsset *asset = [[BNRAsset alloc] init];

            // Give it an interesting label
            NSString *currentLabel = [NSString stringWithFormat:@"Laptop %d", i];
            asset.label = currentLabel;
            asset.resaleValue = i * 17;

            // Get a random number between 0 and 9 inclusive
            NSUInteger randomIndex = random() % [employees count];

            // Find that employee
            BNREmployee *randomEmployee = [employees objectAtIndex:randomIndex];

            // Assign the asset to the employee
            [randomEmployee addAsset:asset];

            [allAssets addObject:asset];
        }

        NSLog(@"Employees: %@", employees);
```

```
        NSLog(@"Giving up ownership of one employee");

        [employees removeObjectAtIndex:5];

        NSLog(@"allAssets: %@", allAssets);

        NSLog(@"Giving up ownership of arrays");

        allAssets = nil;
        employees = nil;
    }
    sleep(100);
    return 0;
}
```

Before you build and run your program, think about what you expect your output to look like. You will see the contents of the allAssets array – after Employee 5 has been deallocated. What will the status of Employee 5's assets be at this point? These assets lose one owner (Employee 5), but they are still owned by allAssets, so they will not be deallocated.

What about the holder for the assets previously owned by Employee 5? When the object that a weak reference points to is deallocated, the pointer variable is *zeroed*, or set to nil. So Employee 5's assets will not be deallocated, and their holder variables will be automatically set to nil.

Now build and run the program and check your output:

```
Employees: (
    "<Employee 0: $0 in assets>",
...
    "<Employee 9: $136 in assets>"
)
Giving up ownership of one employee
deallocating <Employee 5: $136 in assets>
allAssets: (
    "<Laptop 0: $0, assigned to <Employee 3: $68 in assets>>",
    "<Laptop 1: $17, assigned to <Employee 6: $119 in assets>>",
    "<Laptop 2: $34, assigned to <Employee 7: $34 in assets>>",
    "<Laptop 3: $51 unassigned>",
    "<Laptop 4: $68, assigned to <Employee 3: $68 in assets>>",
    "<Laptop 5: $85 unassigned>",
    "<Laptop 6: $102, assigned to <Employee 6: $119 in assets>>",
    "<Laptop 7: $119, assigned to <Employee 2: $119 in assets>>",
    "<Laptop 8: $136, assigned to <Employee 9: $136 in assets>>",
    "<Laptop 9: $153, assigned to <Employee 1: $153 in assets>>"
)
Giving up ownership of arrays
deallocating <Laptop 3: $51 unassigned>
...
deallocating <Laptop 8: $136 unassigned>
```

Here is a quick summary: A strong reference will keep the object it points to from being deallocated. A weak reference will not. Thus instance variables and properties that are marked as weak are pointing at objects that might go away. If this happens, that instance variable or property will be set to nil, instead of continuing to point to where the object used to live.

If you are explicitly declaring a pointer variable that should be weak, mark it with __weak like this:

```
__weak BNRPerson *parent;
```

For the More Curious: manual reference counting and ARC history

As mentioned at the beginning of Chapter 21, before automatic reference counting (ARC) was added to Objective-C, you had *manual reference counting*, which used *retain counts*. With manual reference counting, ownership changes only happened when you sent an explicit message to an object that decremented or incremented the retain count.

```
[anObject release]; // anObject loses an owner
[anObject retain]; // anObject gains an owner
```

You would see these sorts of calls primarily in accessor methods (where the new value was retained and the old value was released) and in **dealloc** methods (where all the previously retained objects were released). The **setHolder:** method for **BNRAsset** would have looked like this:

```
- (void)setHolder:(BNREmployee *)newEmp
{
    // Take ownership of the new holder
    [newEmp retain];

    // Give up ownership of the old holder
    [holder release];

    // Set the pointer to point to the new holder
    holder = newEmp;
}
```

The **dealloc** method would have looked like this:

```
- (void)dealloc
{
    // You're dying, so give up ownership of all objects you used to own
    [label release];
    [holder release];
    [super dealloc];
}
```

What about the **description** method? It creates and returns a string. Should **BNRAsset** claim ownership of it? That would not make sense; the asset is giving away the string it created. When you **autorelease** an object, you are marking it to be sent **release** in the future. Before ARC, the **description** method for **BNRAsset** would look like this:

```
- (NSString *)description
{
    NSString *result = [[NSString alloc] initWithFormat:@"<%@: $%d >",
                                    [self label], [self resaleValue]];
    [result autorelease];
    return result;
}
```

When would it be sent **release**? When the current autorelease pool was drained:

```
// Create the autorelease pool
NSAutoreleasePool *arp = [[NSAutoreleasePool alloc] init];
BNRAsset *asset = [[BNRAsset alloc] init];

NSString *d = [asset description];
// The string that d points to is in the autorelease pool

NSLog(@"The asset is %@", d);

[arp drain]; // The string is sent the message release
```

ARC *uses* the autorelease pool automatically, but you must create and drain the pool. When ARC was created, we also got a new syntax for creating an autorelease pool. The code above now looks like this:

```
// Create the autorelease pool
@autoreleasepool {
    BNRAsset *asset = [[BNRAsset alloc] init];

    NSString *d = [asset description];
    // The string that d points to is in the autorelease pool

} // The pool is drained
```

Retain count rules

There are a set of memory management conventions that all Objective-C programmers follow. If you are using ARC, it is following these conventions behind the scenes.

In these rules, we use the word "you" to mean "an instance of whatever class you are currently working on." It is a useful form of empathy: you imagine that you are the object you are writing. So, for example, "If you retain the string, it will not be deallocated." really means "If an instance of the class that you are currently working on retains the string, it will not be deallocated."

Here, then, are the rules. (Implementation details are in parentheses.)

- If you create an object using a method whose name starts with **alloc** or **new** or contains **copy**, then you have taken ownership of it. (That is, assume that the new object has a retain count of 1 and is *not* in the autorelease pool.) You have a responsibility to release the object when you no longer need it. Here are some of the common methods that convey ownership: **alloc** (which is always followed by an **init** method), **copy**, and **mutableCopy**.

- An object created through *any* other means is *not* owned by you. (That is, assume it has a retain count of one and is already in the autorelease pool, and thus is doomed unless it is retained before the autorelease pool is drained.)

- If you do not own an object and you want to ensure its continued existence, take ownership by sending it the message **retain**. (This increments the retain count.)

- When you own an object and no longer need it, give up ownership by sending it the message **release** or **autorelease**. (**release** decrements the retain count immediately. **autorelease** causes the message **release** to be sent when the autorelease pool is drained.)

- As long as an object has at least one owner, it will continue to exist. (When its retain count goes to zero, it is sent the message **dealloc**.)

One of the tricks to understanding memory management is to think locally. The **BNRAsset** class does not need to know anything about other objects that also care about its label. As long as a **BNRAsset** instance retains objects it wants to keep, you will not have any problems. Programmers new to the language sometimes make the mistake of trying to keep tabs on objects throughout an application. Do not do this. If you follow these rules and always think local to a class, you never have to worry what the rest of an application is doing with an object.

Following the idea of ownership, now it becomes clear why you need to autorelease the string in your **description** method: The employee object created the string, but it does not want to own it. It wants to give it away.

24

Collection Classes

A *collection class* is one whose instances hold pointers to other objects. You have already used two collection classes: **NSArray** and its subclass **NSMutableArray**. In this chapter, you will delve deeper into arrays and learn about some other collection classes: **NSSet/NSMutableSet** and **NSDictionary/NSMutableDictionary**.

NSSet/NSMutableSet

A *set* is a collection that has no sense of order, and a particular object can only appear in a set once.

Sets are primarily useful for asking the question "Is it in there?" For example, you might have a set of URLs that are not child-appropriate. Before displaying any web page to a child, you would do a quick check to see if the URL is in the set. Sets are faster at testing object membership than arrays are.

Like arrays, sets come in immutable and mutable flavors: An **NSSet** is immutable — you cannot add or remove objects after the set has been created. **NSMutableSet** is the subclass that adds the ability to add and remove objects from a set.

In this section, you are going to change your program so that the employee-asset relationship uses an **NSMutableSet** instead of an **NSMutableArray**.

NSMutableSet is a good choice to describe the employee-asset relationship: an employee's `assets` have no inherent order, and an asset should never appear twice in the same employee's `assets` collection.

Figure 24.1 Using **NSMutableSet** for assets

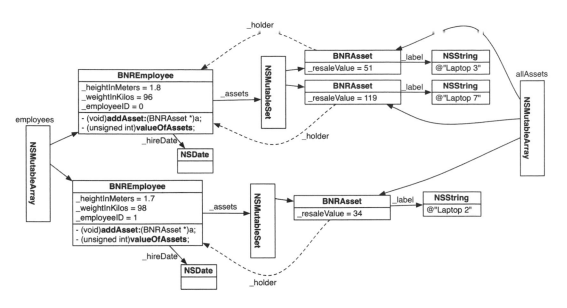

In BNREmployee.h, change the property's declaration:

```
#import "BNRPerson.h"
@class BNRAsset;

@interface BNREmployee : BNRPerson

@property (nonatomic) unsigned int employeeID;
@property (nonatomic) NSDate *hireDate;
@property (nonatomic, copy) NSSet *assets;
- (void)addAsset:(BNRAsset *)a;
- (unsigned int)valueOfAssets;

@end
```

In BNREmployee.m, update the instance variable declaration and make sure that you create an instance of the correct class:

```
// A class extension
@interface BNREmployee ()
{
    NSMutableSet *_assets;
}
@property (nonatomic) unsigned int officeAlarmCode;
@end

@implementation BNREmployee

   ...

- (void)addAsset:(BNRAsset *)a
{
    if (!_assets) {
        _assets = [[NSMutableSet alloc] init];
    }
    [_assets addObject:a];
    a.holder = self;
}

   ...
```

Build and run the program. It should function the same.

You cannot access an object in a set by index because there is no sense of order in a set. Instead, all you can do is ask "Is there one of these in there?" You ask this question with the following **NSSet** method:

```
- (BOOL)containsObject:(id)x;
```

When you send this message to a set, it goes through its collection of objects looking for an object equal to x. If it finds one, it returns YES; otherwise it returns NO.

This brings us to a rather deep question: what does *equal* mean? The class **NSObject** defines a method called **isEqual:**. To check if two objects are equal, you use the **isEqual:** method:

```
if ([myDoctor isEqual:yourTennisPartner]) {
    NSLog(@"my doctor is equal to your tennis partner");
}
```

NSObject has a simple implementation of **isEqual:**. It looks like this:

```
- (BOOL)isEqual:(id)other
{
    return (self == other);
}
```

Thus, if you have not overridden **isEqual:**, the code snippet is equivalent to:

```
if (myDoctor == yourTennisPartner) {
    NSLog(@"my doctor is equal to your tennis partner");
}
```

Some classes override **isEqual:**. For example, in **NSString**, **isEqual:** is overridden to compare the characters in the string. For these classes, there is a difference between *equal* and *identical*. Consider a situation in which you might have four **NSString** pointers:

Figure 24.2 Equal vs. identical

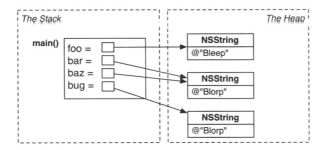

You could describe the relationships between these pointers multiple ways:

- foo is not equal or identical to any of the others.

- bar and baz are *equal and identical* because the objects they point to have the same letters in the same order, and in fact they point to the same object.

- baz and bug are *equal*, but they are *not identical*.

Thus, identical objects are always equal. Equal objects are not always identical.

Does this difference matter? Yes. For example, **NSMutableArray** has two methods:

- (NSUInteger)**indexOfObject:**(id)anObject;

- (NSUInteger)**indexOfObjectIdenticalTo:**(id)anObject;

The first steps through the collection asking each object "isEqual:anObject?" The second steps through the collection asking each object "== anObject"?

NSDictionary/NSMutableDictionary

A *dictionary* is a collection of *key-value pairs*. The *key* is typically a string, and the *value* can be any sort of object. Dictionaries are indexed by key: you provide a key and get back the value (an object) associated with that particular key. Keys in a dictionary are unique and a dictionary's key-value pairs are not kept in any particular order.

Like arrays and sets, dictionaries can be mutable (**NSMutableDictionary**) or immutable (**NSDictionary**). Like **NSArray**, **NSDictionary** has a shorthand you can use when creating an immutable dictionary. The dictionary literal syntax is formed with the @ symbol and curly braces. Within the curly braces, you provide a comma-delimited list of the key-value pairs and separate each key from its value with a colon.

For example, say you wanted a place to keep the number of moons for each planet in the solar system. Here is how you would create an **NSDictionary** with planet names as keys and number of moons as values.

```
NSDictionary *numberOfMoons = @{ @"Mercury" : @0,
                                 @"Venus"   : @0,
                                 @"Earth"   : @1,
                                 @"Mars"    : @2,
                                 @"Jupiter" : @67,
                                 @"Saturn"  : @62,
                                 @"Uranus"  : @27,
                                 @"Neptune" : @13, };
```

The keys are **NSString** objects, and the values are **NSNumber** objects. Both are created on the spot using literal syntax.

Here is how you would access an item from this dictionary:

```
NSString *marsMoonCount = numberOfMoons[@"Mars"];
```

This is similar to how you access an item in an array except, within the square brackets, you give the item's key rather than its integer index.

Sometimes it is useful to *nest* collections. For example, here is an **NSDictionary** instance whose values are **NSArray** instances.

```
NSDictionary *innerPlanetsMoons = @{
    @"Mercury"  : @[], // @[] is an empty array, equivalent to [NSArray array]
    @"Venus"    : @[],
    @"Earth"    : @[ @"Luna" ],
    @"Mars"     : @[ @"Deimos", @"Phobos" ]
};
```

Now you are going to add a mutable dictionary of executives to the BMITime project. The key will be an executive title, and the value will be an instance of **BNREmployee**. The first employee in the employees array will be put in the dictionary under @"CEO"; the second under @"CTO".

Figure 24.3 Two instances of **BNREmployee** in an **NSMutableDictionary**

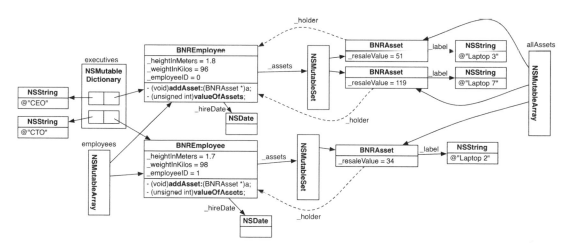

This dictionary will be an **NSMutableDictionary**, so you will use **alloc** and **init** to create it and not the literal syntax shown above.

Change main.m to create and populate an **NSMutableDictionary**. Print out some executive information and then set the pointer to the dictionary to nil so that you can see the dictionary being deallocated.

```
        // Create an array of BNREmployee objects
        NSMutableArray *employees = [[NSMutableArray alloc] init];

        // Create a dictionary of executives
        NSMutableDictionary *executives = [[NSMutableDictionary alloc] init];

        for (int i = 0; i < 10; i++) {

            // Create an instance of BNREmployee
            BNREmployee *mikey = [[BNREmployee alloc] init];

            // Give the instance variables interesting values
            [mikey setWeightInKilos:90 + i];
            [mikey setHeightInMeters:1.8 - i/10.0];
            [mikey setEmployeeID:i];

            // Put the employee in the employees array
            [employees addObject:mikey];

            // Is this the first employee?
            if (i == 0) {
                [executives setObject:mikey forKey:@"CEO"];
            }

            // Is this the second employee?
            if (i == 1) {
                [executives setObject:mikey forKey:@"CTO"];
            }

        }

        ...

        NSLog(@"allAssets: %@", allAssets);

        // Print out the entire dictionary
        NSLog(@"executives: %@", executives);

        // Print out the CEO's information
        NSLog(@"CEO: %@", executives[@"CEO"]);
        executives = nil;

        NSLog(@"Giving up ownership of arrays");

        allAssets = nil;
        employees = nil;
    }
    return 0;
}
```

Build and run the program. The executives dictionary should log itself out:

```
executives = {
    CEO = "<Employee 0: $0 in assets>";
    CTO = "<Employee 1: $153 in assets>";
}

CEO: "<Employee 0: $0 in assets>"
```

Before Objective-C had subscripting, we used methods instead of square bracket:

```
NSMutableDictionary *dict = [[NSMutableDictionary alloc] init];
[dict setObject:@"Hola" forKey:@"Hello"];
NSString *greeting = [dict objectForKey:@"Hello"];
```

The keys in a dictionary are unique. If you try to add a second object under an existing key, the first key-value pair gets replaced.

```
// Create a dictionary
NSMutableDictionary *friends = [NSMutableDictionary dictionary];

// Put an object under key "bestFriend"
[friends setObject:betty forKey:@"bestFriend"];

// Replace that object with a new best friend
[friends setObject:jane forKey:@"bestFriend"];
```

Now friends has only one key-value pair (bestFriend => jane).

Immutable objects

Most beginning programmers are surprised by the immutability of **NSArray**, **NSSet**, and **NSDictionary**. Why would anyone want a list that cannot be changed? The reasons are performance and security:

You do not trust the people you work with. That is, you want to let them look at an array, but you do not want them to be able change it. A gentler approach is to give them an **NSMutableArray** but tell them it is an **NSArray**. For example, consider the following method:

```
// Returns an array of 30 odd numbers
- (NSArray *)odds
{
    NSMutableArray *oddsArray = [[NSMutableArray alloc] init];
    int i = 1;
    while ([oddsArray count] < 30) {
        [oddsArray addObject:[NSNumber numberWithInt:i];
        i += 2;
    }
    return oddsArray;
}
```

Anyone calling this method assumes from its declaration

```
    - (NSArray *)odds;
```

that it is returning an immutable **NSArray**. If the caller tries to add or remove items from the returned array, the compiler will issue a warning – even though, it is, in fact, an instance of **NSMutableArray**.

Using an immutable collection conserves memory and improves performance because that collection never needs to be copied. With a mutable object, there is the possibility that some other code might change the object behind your back while you are in the middle of using it. To avoid this situation, you would have to make a private copy of the collection. And so would everyone else, which leads to multiple copies of a potentially large object.

With immutable objects, making a copy is unnecessary. In fact, where the **copy** method of **NSMutableArray** makes a copy of itself and returns a pointer to the new array, the **copy** method of **NSArray** does nothing – it just quietly returns a pointer to itself.

Immutable objects are fairly common in Objective-C programming. In Foundation, there are many classes that create immutable instances: **NSArray**, **NSString**, **NSAttributedString**, **NSData**, **NSCharacterSet**, **NSDictionary**, **NSSet**, **NSIndexSet**, and **NSURLRequest**.

All of these have mutable subclasses: **NSMutableArray**, **NSMutableString**, **NSMutableAttributedString**, etc.

NSDate and **NSNumber** are immutable but do not have mutable subclasses. If you need a new date or number, then you must create a new object.

Sorting arrays

Arrays often require sorting. Immutable arrays cannot be sorted, but mutable ones can. There are several ways to sort an **NSMutableArray**. The most common is using the **NSMutableArray** method:

```
- (void)sortUsingDescriptors:(NSArray *)sortDescriptors;
```

The argument is an array of **NSSortDescriptor** objects. A *sort descriptor* has the name of a property of the objects contained in the array and whether that property should be sorted in ascending or descending order. Imagine you had a list of doctors. If you wanted to sort the list by last name in ascending (A-Z) order, then you would create the following sort descriptor:

```
NSSortDescriptor *lastAsc = [NSSortDescriptor sortDescriptorWithKey:@"lastName"
                                                          ascending:YES];
```

The property you sort on can be any instance variable or the result of any method of the object.

Why do you pass an array of sort descriptors? What if two doctors have the same last name? You can specify "Sort by last name ascending, and if the last names are the same, sort by first name ascending, and if the first and last names are the same, sort by zip code."

Figure 24.4 Sort by `lastName`, then `firstName`, then `zipCode`

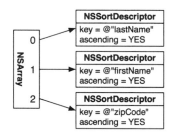

Let's return to the BMITime project to see sorting in practice. In **main()**, just before logging the employees array, sort it by **valueOfAssets**. If two employees are holding assets of the same value, sort them by employeeID. Edit main.m:

```
    ...

    [allAssets addObject:asset];
}

NSSortDescriptor *voa = [NSSortDescriptor sortDescriptorWithKey:@"valueOfAssets"
                                                      ascending:YES];
NSSortDescriptor *eid = [NSSortDescriptor sortDescriptorWithKey:@"employeeID"
                                                      ascending:YES];
[employees sortUsingDescriptors: @[voa, eid]];

NSLog(@"Employees: %@", employees);

    ...
```

Build and run the program. You should see the employees list ordered correctly:

```
Employees: (
    "<Employee 0: $0 in assets>",
    "<Employee 4: $0 in assets>",
    "<Employee 8: $0 in assets>",
    "<Employee 7: $34 in assets>",
    "<Employee 3: $68 in assets>",
    "<Employee 2: $119 in assets>",
    "<Employee 6: $119 in assets>",
    "<Employee 5: $136 in assets>",
    "<Employee 9: $136 in assets>",
    "<Employee 1: $153 in assets>"
```

Sets and dictionaries are unordered by nature, so they are not typically sorted.

Filtering

When you filter a collection, you compare its objects to a logical statement to get a resultant collection that only contains objects for which the statement is true.

A *predicate* contains a statement that might be true, like "The employeeID is greater than 75." There is a class called **NSPredicate**. **NSMutableArray** has a handy method for discarding all the objects that do not satisfy the predicate:

```
- (void)filterUsingPredicate:(NSPredicate *)predicate;
```

With **NSArray**, you cannot remove objects that do not match the predicate. Instead, **NSArray** has a method that creates a new array that contains all the objects that satisfy the predicate:

```
- (NSArray *)filteredArrayUsingPredicate:(NSPredicate *)predicate;
```

Imagine that you are going to reclaim all the assets given to employees who currently hold assets worth more than $70 total. Add the code near the end of main.m:

```
        ...

        // Print out the CEO's information
        NSLog(@"CEO: %@", executives[@"CEO"]);
        executives = nil;

        NSPredicate *predicate = [NSPredicate predicateWithFormat:
                                            @"holder.valueOfAssets > 70"];
        NSArray *toBeReclaimed = [allAssets filteredArrayUsingPredicate:predicate];
        NSLog(@"toBeReclaimed: %@", toBeReclaimed);
        toBeReclaimed = nil;

        NSLog(@"Giving up ownership of arrays");

        allAssets = nil;
        employees = nil;
    }
    return 0;
}
```

Build and run the program. You should see a list of assets:

```
toBeReclaimed: (
    "<Laptop 1: $17, assigned to <Employee 6: $119 in assets>>",
    "<Laptop 3: $51, assigned to <Employee 5: $136 in assets>>",
    "<Laptop 5: $85, assigned to <Employee 5: $136 in assets>>",
    "<Laptop 6: $102, assigned to <Employee 6: $119 in assets>>",
    "<Laptop 8: $136, assigned to <Employee 9: $136 in assets>>",
    "<Laptop 9: $153, assigned to <Employee 1: $153 in assets>>"
)
```

The format string used to create the predicate can be very complex. If you do a lot of filtering of collections, be sure to read Apple's *Predicate Programming Guide*.

Filtering can be done with sets as well as arrays. **NSSet** has the method:

```
- (NSSet *)filteredSetUsingPredicate:(NSPredicate *)predicate;
```

and **NSMutableSet** has the method:

```
- (void)filterUsingPredicate:(NSPredicate *)predicate;
```

Collections and ownership

When you add an object to a collection, the collection claims ownership of it. When you remove the object from the collection, the collection gives up ownership. This is true for **NSMutableArray**, **NSMutableSet**, and **NSMutableDictionary**. (An immutable collection also claims ownership of its objects, but the immutability of the collection means that all the objects in the collection are owned when the collection is created and disowned when the collection is deallocated.)

C primitive types

The collections covered in this chapter only hold objects. What if you want a collection of floats or ints? You can wrap common C number types using **NSNumber**.

You can create a literal **NSNumber** instance using the @ symbol – similar to how you create literal **NSString** instances. For instance, if you wanted to put the numbers 4 and 5.6 into an array, you would create the instance of **NSNumber** and then add the **NSNumber** object to the array:

```
NSMutableArray *list = [[NSMutableArray alloc] init];
[list addObject:@4];
[list addObject:@5.6];
```

Note that you cannot do math directly with an **NSNumber**, only with primitives. You must first extract the primitive value using one of several **NSNumber** methods, do the math, and then re-wrap the result into an **NSNumber**. You can find the methods for extracting and rewrapping primitive values in the **NSNumber** class reference.

What about structs? You can wrap a pointer to a struct in an instance of another wrapper class – **NSValue** (the superclass of **NSNumber**). Commonly-used structs such as NSPoint (which contains the x and y values of a coordinate) can be boxed using instances of **NSValue**:

```
NSPoint somePoint = NSMakePoint(100, 100);
NSValue *pointValue = [NSValue valueWithPoint:somePoint];
[list addObject:pointValue];
```

NSValue instances can be used to hold just about any scalar value. Read the **NSValue** class reference to learn more.

Collections and nil

You are not allowed to add nil to any of the collection classes we have covered. What if you need to put that idea of nothingness, a "hole," into a collection? There is a class called **NSNull**. There is exactly one instance of **NSNull**, and it is an object that represents nothingness. Here is an example:

```
NSMutableArray *hotel = [[NSMutableArray alloc] init];

// Lobby on the ground floor
[hotel addObject:lobby];

// Pool on the second
[hotel addObject:pool];

// The third floor has not been built out
[hotel addObject:[NSNull null]];

// Bedrooms on fourth floor
[hotel addObject:bedrooms];
```

Challenge: reading up

Explore the class references for **NSArray**, **NSMutableArray**, **NSDictionary**, and **NSMutableDictionary**. You will use these classes every day.

Challenge: top holdings

This challenge and the next one build on the challenge from Chapter 22. Add a method to the **BNRPortfolio** class that returns an **NSArray** of only the top three most valuable holdings, sorted by current value in dollars. Test it in **main()**.

Challenge: sorted holdings

Add another method to **BNRPortfolio** that returns an **NSArray** of all of its stock holdings, sorted alphabetically by symbol. Test this method in **main()** as well.

25
Constants

We have spent a lot of time discussing variables, which, as the name indicates, change their values as the program runs. There are, however, pieces of information that *do not* change value. For example, the mathematical constant π never changes. We call these things *constants*, and there are two common ways that Objective-C programmers define them: #define and global variables.

In Xcode, create a new Foundation Command Line Tool called Constants.

In the standard C libraries, constants are defined using the #define preprocessor directive. The math part of the standard C library is declared in the file math.h. One of the constants defined there is M_PI. Use it in main.m:

```
#import <Foundation/Foundation.h>

int main (int argc, const char * argv[])
{
    @autoreleasepool {

        NSLog(@"\u03c0 is %f", M_PI);

    }
    return 0;
}
```

When you build and run it, you should see:

π is 3.141593

To the definition for the M_PI constant, press the Command key and then click on M_PI in your code.

Figure 25.1 Definition for M_PI

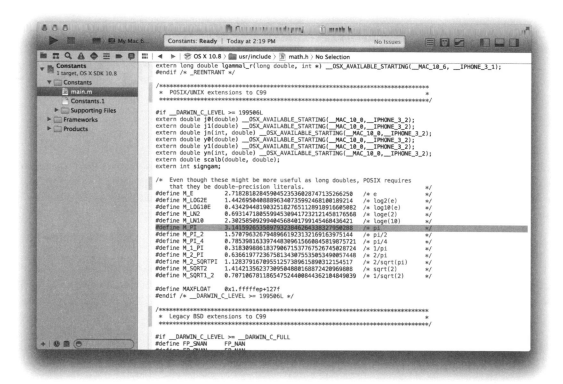

Where are you? If you look at the navigation bar at the top of the editor area, you will see that you are now in math.h.

Command-clicking is useful whenever you need to see how something is defined. You can use it with constants, functions, classes, methods, types, and more.

To get back to main.m, click the ◀ button to the left of the navigation bar at the top of the editor area. Or select main.m in the project navigator.

You may be wondering why you did not have to explicitly include math.h in main.m to use M_PI. When you created a new Foundation command-line tool, the template imported Foundation/Foundation.h for you. Foundation/Foundation.h includes CoreFoundation/CoreFoundation.h, which includes math.h.

Preprocessor directives

Compiling a file of C, C++, or Objective-C code is done in two passes. First, the *preprocessor* runs through the file. The output from the preprocessor then goes into the real compiler. Preprocessor directives start with #, and the three most popular are #include, #import, and #define.

#include and #import

#include and #import do essentially the same thing: request that the preprocessor read a file and add it to its output. Usually, you are including a file of declarations (a .h file), and those declarations are used by the compiler to understand the code it is compiling.

What is the difference between #include and #import? #import ensures that the preprocessor only includes a file once. #include will allow you to include the same file many times. C programmers tend to use #include. Objective-C programmers tend to use #import.

When specifying the name of the file to be imported, you can wrap the filename in quotes or angle brackets. Quotes indicate that the header is in your project directory. Angle brackets indicate that the header is in one of the standard locations that the preprocessor knows about. (<math.h>, for example, is /Applications/Xcode46-DP3.app/Contents/Developer/Platforms/MacOSX.platform/Developer/SDKs/MacOSX10.8.sdk/usr/include/math.h.) Here are two examples of #import directives:

```
// Include the headers I wrote for Pet Store operations
#import "PetStore.h"

// Include the headers for the OpenLDAP libraries
#import <ldap.h>
```

In a project, it used to be pretty common to include a collection of headers in *every* file of code. This led to clutter at the beginning of your file and made compiles take longer. To make life easier and compiles faster, most Xcode projects have a file that lists headers to be precompiled and included in every file. In your Constants project, this file is called Constants-Prefix.pch.

So, how did a constant from math.h get included when main.m was compiled? Your main.m file has the following line:

```
#import <Foundation/Foundation.h>
```

The file Foundation.h has this line:

```
#include <CoreFoundation/CoreFoundation.h>
```

And the file CoreFoundation.h has this line:

```
#include <math.h>
```

#define

#define tells the preprocessor, "Whenever you encounter A, replace it with B before the compiler sees it." Look at the line from math.h again:

```
#define M_PI        3.14159265358979323846264338327950288
```

In the #define directive, you just separate the two parts (the token and its replacement) with whitespace.

#define can be used to make something like a function. In main.m, print the larger of two numbers:

```
#import <Foundation/Foundation.h>

int main (int argc, const char * argv[])
{
    @autoreleasepool {

        NSLog(@"\u03c0 is %f", M_PI);
        NSLog(@"%d is larger", MAX(10, 12));

    }
    return 0;
}
```

MAX is not a function; it is a #define. The most basic C version of MAX is:

```
#define MAX(A,B)    ((A) > (B) ? (A) : (B))
```

So, by the time the compiler saw the line you just added, it looked like this:

```
NSLog(@"%d is larger", ((10) > (12) ? (10) : (12)));
```

When you use #define to do function-like stuff instead of simply substituting a value, you are creating a *macro*.

Global variables

Instead of using #define, Objective-C programmers commonly use global variables to hold constant values.

Let's add to your program to explain. First, there is a class named **NSLocale** that stores information about different geographical locations. You can get an instance of the user's current locale and then ask it questions. For instance, if you wanted to know what the currency is in the user's locale, you could ask for it like this:

```
#import <Foundation/Foundation.h>

int main (int argc, const char * argv[])
{
    @autoreleasepool {

        NSLog(@"\u03c0 is %f", M_PI);
        NSLog(@"%d is larger", MAX(10, 12));

        NSLocale *here = [NSLocale currentLocale];
        NSString *currency = [here objectForKey:@"currency"];
        NSLog(@"Money is %@", currency);

    }
    return 0;
}
```

Build and run it. Depending on where you are, you should see something like

```
Money is USD
```

If, however, you mistype the key as @"Kuruncy", you will not get anything back. To prevent this problem, the Foundation framework defines a global variable called NSLocaleCurrencyCode. It is no easier to type, but if you do mistype it, the compiler will complain. Also, code completion in Xcode works properly for a global variable, but not for the string @"currency". Change your code to use the constant:

```
#import <Foundation/Foundation.h>

int main (int argc, const char * argv[])
{
    @autoreleasepool {

        NSLog(@"\u03c0 is %f", M_PI);
        NSLog(@"%d is larger", MAX(10, 12));

        NSLocale *here = [NSLocale currentLocale];
        NSString *currency = [here objectForKey:NSLocaleCurrencyCode];
        NSLog(@"Money is %@", currency);

    }
    return 0;
}
```

When the class **NSLocale** was written, this global variable appeared in two places. In NSLocale.h, the variable was declared something like this:

```
extern NSString * const NSLocaleCurrencyCode;
```

The const means that this pointer will not change for the entire life of the program. The extern means "I promise this exists, but it will be defined in some other file." In the file NSLocale.m (which lives in a vault at Apple), there is certainly a line like this:

```
NSString * const NSLocaleCurrencyCode = @"currency";
```

enum

Often you will need to define a set of constants. For example, imagine that you were developing a blender with five speeds: Stir, Chop, Liquefy, Pulse, and Ice Crush. Your class **Blender** would have a method called **setSpeed:**. It would be best if the type indicated that only one of the five speeds was allowed. To do this, you would define an enumeration:

```
enum BlenderSpeed {
    BlenderSpeedStir = 1,
    BlenderSpeedChop = 2,
    BlenderSpeedLiquify = 5,
    BlenderSpeedPulse = 9,
    BlenderSpeedIceCrush = 15
};

@interface Blender : NSObject
{
    // speed must be one of the five speeds
    enum BlenderSpeed speed;
}

// setSpeed: expects one of the five speeds
- (void)setSpeed:(enum BlenderSpeed)x;
@end
```

Developers get tired of typing enum `BlenderSpeed`, so they often use `typedef` to create a shorthand for it:

```
typedef enum {
    BlenderSpeedStir = 1,
    BlenderSpeedChop = 2,
    BlenderSpeedLiquify = 5,
    BlenderSpeedPulse = 9,
    BlenderSpeedIceCrush = 15
} BlenderSpeed;

@interface Blender : NSObject
{
    // speed must be one of the five speeds
    BlenderSpeed speed;
}

// setSpeed: expects one of the five speeds
- (void)setSpeed:(BlenderSpeed)x;
@end
```

Often you will not care what numbers the five speeds represent – only that they are different from each other. You can leave out the values, and the compiler will make up values for you:

```
typedef enum {
    BlenderSpeedStir,
    BlenderSpeedChop,
    BlenderSpeedLiquify,
    BlenderSpeedPulse,
    BlenderSpeedIceCrush
} BlenderSpeed;
```

Starting with OS X 10.8 and iOS 6, Apple introduced a new enum declaration syntax: `NS_ENUM()`. Here is what your enum looks like using this syntax:

```
typedef NS_ENUM(int, BlenderSpeed) {
    BlenderSpeedStir,
    BlenderSpeedChop,
    BlenderSpeedLiquify,
    BlenderSpeedPulse,
    BlenderSpeedIceCrush
};
```

`NS_ENUM()` is actually a preprocessor macro that takes two arguments: a data type and a name.

Apple has adopted `NS_ENUM()` for enum declarations. The most important advantage of `NS_ENUM()` over the other syntax is the ability to declare the integral data type that the enum will represent (`short`, `unsigned long`, etc.).

With the old syntax, the compiler would choose an appropriate data type for the enum, usually `int`. If your enum will only have four options whose values do not matter, you do not need four bytes to store it; one byte will represent integral numbers up to 255 just fine. Recalling from Chapter 3 that a `char` is a one-byte integer, you can declare a space-saving enum:

```
typedef NS_ENUM(char, BlenderSpeed) {
    BlenderSpeedStir,
    BlenderSpeedChop,
    BlenderSpeedLiquify,
    BlenderSpeedPulse,
    BlenderSpeedIceCrush
};
```

#define vs. global variables

Given that you can define a constant using #define or a global variable (which includes the use of enum), why do Objective-C programmers tend to use global variables? In some cases, there are performance advantages to using global variables. For example, you can use == instead of **isEqual:** to compare strings if you consistently use the global variable (a pointer comparison is faster than a message send and scanning two strings character-by-character). Also, global variables are easier to work with when you are in the debugger.

In general, you should use global variables and enum for constants, not #define.

26

Writing Files with NSString and NSData

The Foundation framework gives the developer a few easy ways to read from and write to files. In this chapter, you will try a few of them out.

Writing an NSString to a file

First, let's see how you would take the contents of an **NSString** and put it into a file. When you write a string to a file, you need to specify which *string encoding* you are using. A string encoding describes how each character is stored as an array of bytes. ASCII is a string encoding that defines the letter 'A' as being stored as 01000001. In UTF-16, the letter 'A' is stored as 0000000001000001.

The Foundation framework supports about 20 different string encodings, but we end up using UTF a lot because it can handle an incredible collection of writing systems. It comes in two flavors: UTF-16, which uses two or more bytes for every character, and UTF-8, which uses one byte for the first 128 ASCII characters and two or more for other characters. For most purposes, UTF-8 is a good fit.

Create a new project: a Foundation Command Line Tool called Stringz. In **main()**, use methods from the **NSString** class to create a string and write it to the filesystem:

```
#import <Foundation/Foundation.h>

int main (int argc, const char * argv[])    {
    @autoreleasepool {

        NSMutableString *str = [[NSMutableString alloc] init];
        for (int i = 0; i < 10; i++) {
            [str appendString:@"Aaron is cool!\n"];
        }
        [str writeToFile:@"/tmp/cool.txt"
               atomically:YES
                 encoding:NSUTF8StringEncoding
                    error:NULL];
        NSLog(@"done writing /tmp/cool.txt");

    }
    return 0;
}
```

This program will create a text file that you can read and edit in any text editor. The string /tmp/cool.txt is known as the file path.

File paths can be absolute or relative: absolute paths start with a / that represents the top of the file system, whereas relative paths start at the working directory of the program. Relative paths do not start with a /. In Objective-C programming, you will find that you nearly always use absolute paths because you typically do not know what the working directory of the program is.

Build and run the program. (To find the /tmp directory in Finder, use the Go → Go to Folder menu item.)

NSError

As you might imagine, all sorts of things can go wrong when you try to write a string to a file. For example, the user may not have write-access to the directory where the file would go. Or the directory may not exist at all. Or the filesystem may be full. For situations like these, where an operation may be impossible to complete, the method needs a way to return a description of what went wrong in addition to the boolean value for success or failure.

Recall from Chapter 10 that when you need a function to return something in addition to its return value, you can use pass-by-reference. You pass the function (or method) a reference to a variable where it can directly store or manipulate a value. The reference is the memory address for that variable.

For error handling, many methods take an **NSError** pointer by reference. Add error handling to Stringz:

```
#import <Foundation/Foundation.h>

int main (int argc, const char * argv[])     {
    @autoreleasepool {

        NSMutableString *str = [[NSMutableString alloc] init];
        for (int i = 0; i < 10; i++) {
            [str appendString:@"Aaron is cool!\n"];
        }


        // Declare a pointer to an NSError object, but do not instantiate it.
        // The NSError instance will only be created if there is, in fact, an error.
        NSError *error;

        // Pass the NSError pointer by reference to the NSString method
        BOOL success = [str writeToFile:@"/tmp/cool.txt"
                            atomically:YES
                              encoding:NSUTF8StringEncoding
                                 error:&error];

        // Test the returned BOOL, and query the NSError if the write failed
        if (success) {
            NSLog(@"done writing /tmp/cool.txt");
        } else {
            NSLog(@"writing /tmp/cool.txt failed: %@", [error localizedDescription]);
        }

    }
    return 0;
}
```

Build and run it. Now change the code to pass the write method a file path that does not exist, like @"/too/darned/bad.txt". You should get a friendly error message.

Notice that you declare a pointer to an instance of **NSError** in this code, but you do not create, or *instantiate*, an **NSError** object to assign to that pointer.

Why not? You want to avoid creating an unnecessary error object if there is no error. If there is an error, **writeToFile:atomically:encoding:error:** will be responsible for creating a new **NSError** instance and then modifying the error pointer you declared to point to the new error object. Then you can ask that object what went wrong via your error pointer.

This conditional creation of the **NSError** requires you to pass a reference to error (&error) because there is no object yet to pass. However, unlike the passing by reference you did in Chapter 10, where you passed the reference of a primitive C variable, here you are passing the address of a pointer variable. In essence, you are passing the address of another address (which may become the address of an **NSError** object).

Figure 26.1 Errors are passed by reference

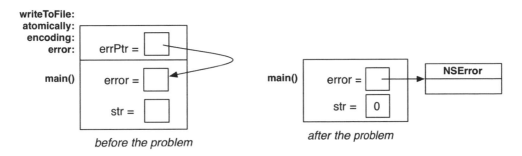

before the problem   *after the problem*

To revisit our international espionage analogy from Chapter 10, you might tell your spy, "If anything goes wrong, make a complete report (much too large to put in the steel pipe) and hide it in a book at the library. I need to know where you hid it, so put the call number of the book in the steel pipe." That is, you are giving the spy a location where she can put the address of an error report she created.

Here is a look inside the **NSString** class where **writeToFile:atomically:encoding:error:** is declared:

```
- (BOOL)writeToFile:(NSString *)path
         atomically:(BOOL)useAuxiliaryFile
           encoding:(NSStringEncoding)enc
              error:(NSError **)error
```

Notice the double asterisk. Many programmers would say "The method expects a pointer to a pointer to an **NSError**." However, that sounds more confusing than it needs to be. In our opinion, this is more descriptive: "The method expects an address where it can put a pointer to an instance of **NSError**."

Methods that pass an **NSError** by reference always return a value that indicates whether there was an error or not. This method, for example, returns NO if there is an error. Do not try to access the **NSError** unless the return value indicates that an error occurred; if the **NSError** object does not actually exist, trying to access it will crash your program.

Reading files with NSString

Reading a file into a string is very similar:

```
#import <Foundation/Foundation.h>

int main (int argc, const char * argv[])    {
    @autoreleasepool {

        NSError *error;
        NSString *str = [[NSString alloc] initWithContentsOfFile:@"/etc/resolv.conf"
                                                 encoding:NSASCIIStringEncoding
                                                    error:&error];

        if (!str) {
            NSLog(@"read failed: %@", [error localizedDescription]);
        } else {
            NSLog(@"resolv.conf looks like this: %@", str);
        }

    }
    return 0;
}
```

Here you are creating a new string by reading in the contents of a file as ASCII text. If the read fails (for example, if you did not have permission to read the file), then the method returns nil. In that case, you print out the error's localized description.

Writing an NSData object to a file

An **NSData** object represents a buffer of bytes. For example, if you fetch some data from a URL, you get an instance of **NSData**. And you can ask an **NSData** to write itself to a file. Create a new Foundation Command Line Tool named ImageFetch that fetches an image from the Google website into an instance of **NSData**. Then ask the **NSData** to write its buffer of bytes to a file:

```objc
#import <Foundation/Foundation.h>

int main (int argc, const char * argv[])
{
    @autoreleasepool {

        NSURL *url = [NSURL URLWithString:
                             @"http://www.google.com/images/logos/ps_logo2.png"];
        NSURLRequest *request = [NSURLRequest requestWithURL:url];
        NSError *error = nil;
        NSData *data = [NSURLConnection sendSynchronousRequest:request
                                             returningResponse:NULL
                                                         error:&error];

        if (!data) {
            NSLog(@"fetch failed: %@", [error localizedDescription]);
            return 1;
        }

        NSLog(@"The file is %lu bytes", (unsigned long)[data length]);


        BOOL written = [data writeToFile:@"/tmp/google.png"
                                 options:0
                                   error:&error];

        if (!written) {
            NSLog(@"write failed: %@", [error localizedDescription]);
            return 1;
        }

        NSLog(@"Success!");

    }
    return 0;
}
```

Build and run the program. Open the resulting image file in Preview.

Note that the **writeToFile:options:error:** method takes a number that indicates options to be used in the saving process. The most common option is NSDataWritingAtomic. Let's say that you have already fetched an image and you are just re-fetching and replacing it with a newer version. While the new image is being written, the power goes off. A half-written file is worthless. In cases where a half-written file is worse than no file at all, you can make the writing atomic. Add this option:

```objc
NSLog(@"The file is %lu bytes", (unsigned long)[data length]);


BOOL written = [data writeToFile:@"/tmp/google.png"
                         options:NSDataWritingAtomic
                           error:&error];

if (!written) {
    NSLog(@"write failed: %@", [error localizedDescription]);
    return 1;
}
```

Now, the data will be written out to a temporary file, and, when the writing is done, the file is renamed the correct name. This way, you either get the whole file or nothing. (Note that this nothing to do with atomic/nonatomic properties.)

Reading an NSData from a file

o You can also create an instance of **NSData** from the contents of a file. Add two lines to your program:

```
#import <Foundation/Foundation.h>

int main (int argc, const char * argv[])
{
    @autoreleasepool {

        NSURL *url = [NSURL URLWithString:
                            @"http://www.google.com/images/logos/ps_logo2.png"];
        NSURLRequest *request = [NSURLRequest requestWithURL:url];
        NSError *error;

        // This method will block until all the data has been fetched
        NSData *data = [NSURLConnection sendSynchronousRequest:request
                                            returningResponse:NULL
                                                        error:&error];

        if (!data) {
            NSLog(@"fetch failed: %@", [error localizedDescription]);
            return 1;
        }

        NSLog(@"The file is %lu bytes", (unsigned long)[data length]);


        BOOL written = [data writeToFile:@"/tmp/google.png"
                                 options:NSDataWritingAtomic
                                   error:&error];

        if (!written) {
            NSLog(@"write failed: %@", [error localizedDescription]);
            return 1;
        }

        NSLog(@"Success!");

        NSData *readData = [NSData dataWithContentsOfFile:@"/tmp/google.png"];
        NSLog(@"The file read from the disk has %lu bytes",
                                        (unsigned long)[readData length]);

    }
    return 0;
}
```

Build and run the program.

Finding special directories

Users expect files to be saved to specific directories. For example, my browser, by default, will download files to /Users/aaron/Downloads/. To make it easy for the programmer to do the right thing, Apple has created a function that will tell you the right directories for the appropriate purpose. For example, this piece of code will get you the path for the user's Desktop directory:

```
// The function returns an array of paths
NSArray *desktops =
     NSSearchPathForDirectoriesInDomains(NSDesktopDirectory, NSUserDomainMask, YES);

// But I know the user has exactly one desktop directory
NSString *desktopPath = desktops[0];
```

What other special directories are there? Here are the commonly used constants:

- NSApplicationDirectory

- NSLibraryDirectory

- NSUserDirectory

- NSDocumentDirectory

- NSDesktopDirectory

- NSCachesDirectory

- NSApplicationSupportDirectory

- NSDownloadsDirectory

- NSMoviesDirectory

- NSMusicDirectory

- NSPicturesDirectory

- NSTrashDirectory

27

Callbacks

Thus far, your code has been the boss. It has been sending messages to standard Foundation objects, like instances of **NSString** and **NSArray**, and telling them what to do. When your code has finished executing, the program ends.

In this chapter, you are going to create a program that does not just start, execute, and end. Instead, this program is *event-driven*. It will start and wait for an event. When that event happens, the program will execute code in response. This program will not end by itself; it will keep sitting and waiting for the next event until you tell it to stop.

The events that can happen on a Mac or an iOS device are many and varied. Here are a few examples: the user clicks the mouse or taps a button, some period of time elapses, the device runs low on memory, the system connects to the network, the user closes a window.

A *callback* lets you write a piece of code and then associate that code with a particular event. When the event happens, your code is executed.

In Objective-C, there are four forms that a callback can take:

- *Target-action:* Before the wait begins, you say "When this event happens, send this message to this object." The object receiving the message is the *target*. The selector for the message is the *action*.

- *Helper objects:* Before the wait begins, you say "Here is an object that will take on a role that helps another object do its job. When one of the events related to this role occurs, send a message to the helper object." Helper objects are often known as *delegates* or *data sources*.

- *Notifications:* There is an object called the notification center. When an event happens, a notification associated with that event will be posted to the notification center. Before the wait begins, you tell the notification center "This object is interested in this kind of notification. When one is posted, send this message to the object."

- *Blocks:* A block is a just a chunk of code to be executed. Before the wait begins, you say "Here is a block. When this event happens, execute this block."

In this chapter, you will implement the first three types of callbacks and learn which to employ in what circumstances. Blocks will be covered in Chapter 28.

The run loop

In an event-driven program, there needs to be an object that does the sitting and waiting for events. In OS X and iOS, this object is an instance of **NSRunLoop**. We say that when an event happens, the run loop causes a callback to occur.

Create a new project: a Foundation Command Line Tool named Callbacks. First, you are just going to get a run loop and start it running. Edit main.m:

```
#import <Foundation/Foundation.h>

int main (int argc, const char * argv[])
{
    @autoreleasepool {

        [[NSRunLoop currentRunLoop] run];

    }
    return 0;
}
```

Build and run the program. Notice that the **run** method never returns. The console does not report the familiar Program ended with exit code: 0. The run loop is waiting for something to happen. Choose Product → Stop to stop the program.

Now that you have a run loop, you can start implementing callbacks.

Target-action

Timers use a target-action mechanism. You create a timer with a time interval, a target, and an action. After the interval has elapsed, the timer sends the action message to its target.

You are going to add an instance of **NSTimer** to your program. Every two seconds, the timer will send the action message to its target. You will also create a class named **BNRLogger**. An instance of that class will be the timer's target.

Figure 27.1 **BNRLogger** is the target of the **NSTimer**

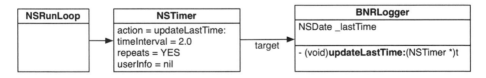

Create a new file: an Objective-C class called **BNRLogger** that is a subclass of **NSObject**.

In BNRLogger.h, declare a property that holds a date, a method that returns the date as a string, and the action method to be triggered by the timer:

```
#import <Foundation/Foundation.h>

@interface BNRLogger : NSObject
@property (nonatomic) NSDate *lastTime;
- (NSString *)lastTimeString;
- (void)updateLastTime:(NSTimer *)t;
@end
```

Action methods always take one argument – the object that is sending the action message. In this case, it is the timer object.

In BNRLogger.m, implement the methods:

```
#import "BNRLogger.h"

@implementation BNRLogger


- (NSString *)lastTimeString
{
    static NSDateFormatter *dateFormatter = nil;
    if (!dateFormatter)
    {
        dateFormatter = [[NSDateFormatter alloc] init];
        [dateFormatter setTimeStyle:NSDateFormatterMediumStyle];
        [dateFormatter setDateStyle:NSDateFormatterMediumStyle];
        NSLog(@"created dateFormatter");
    }
    return [dateFormatter stringFromDate:self.lastTime];
}

- (void)updateLastTime:(NSTimer *)t
{
    NSDate *now = [NSDate date];
    [self setLastTime:now];
    NSLog(@"Just set time to %@", self.lastTimeString);
}


@end
```

This may be the first time you have seen the static modifier used this way. If you have a thousand instances of **BNRLogger** and all of them format their strings the same way, you want all of the instances of **BNRLogger** to share a single instance of **NSDateFormatter**. Many object-oriented languages have class variables (rather than instance variables) for this sort of thing. Objective-C just uses static variables, which were discussed in Chapter 5.

In main.m, create an instance of **BNRLogger** and make it the target of an instance of **NSTimer**. Set the action to be **updateLastTime:**.

```
#import <Foundation/Foundation.h>
#import "BNRLogger.h"

int main (int argc, const char * argv[])
{
    @autoreleasepool {

        BNRLogger *logger = [[BNRLogger alloc] init];

        NSTimer *timer =
                    [NSTimer scheduledTimerWithTimeInterval:2.0
                                                     target:logger
                                                   selector:@selector(updateLastTime:)
                                                   userInfo:nil
                                                    repeats:YES];

        [[NSRunLoop currentRunLoop] run];

    }
    return 0;
}
```

Notice the @selector syntax that you use to pass the name of the action message to this method. This is required for this argument; you cannot simply pass the method's name. There is more about @selector and passing selectors at the end of this chapter.

Build and run the program. (You will get an unused variable warning. Ignore it for now.) The log statement with the current date and time will appear in the console every 2 seconds.

Now look at the unused variable warning from the compiler. It is saying, "Hey, you created this timer variable, but you never use it. That might be a problem." In some settings, like this one, it is not a problem, and you can flag a variable as purposefully unused to silence this warning. This is done with the __unused modifier.

In main.m, flag the timer variable as unused:

```
    __unused NSTimer *timer =
                    [NSTimer scheduledTimerWithTimeInterval:2.0
                                                     target:logger
                                                   selector:@selector(updateLastTime:)
                                                   userInfo:nil
                                                    repeats:YES];
```

Build again, and the warning will go away.

Timers are simple. They only do one thing: fire. Thus, target-action is a good fit. A lot of simple user interface controls, like buttons and sliders, use the target-action mechanism. What about something more complex?

Helper objects

In Chapter 26, you used an **NSURLConnection** to fetch data from a web server. This connection was synchronous – all the data was delivered at one time. It worked fine, but there are two problems with a synchronous connection:

- It blocks the main thread while waiting for all the data to arrive. If you use this type of connection in an interactive application, the user interface will be unresponsive while the data was fetched.

- It has no way to call back if, for example, the web server asks for a username and password.

For these reasons, it is more common to use an **NSURLConnection** asynchronously. In an asynchronous connection, the data comes in chunks rather than all at once. This means that there are connection-related events that you must be ready to respond to. Some examples of connection-related events are a chunk of data arrives, the web server demands credentials, and the connection fails.

To manage this more complex connection, you must give it a helper object. In the helper object, you implement the methods to be executed in response to different connection-related events.

In your Callbacks program, you are going to use an asynchronous **NSURLConnection** to fetch data from a website. The instance of **BNRLogger** will serve as the **NSURLConnection**'s helper object. More specifically, the **BNRLogger** will be the delegate of the **NSURLConnection**.

Figure 27.2 **BNRLogger** is the delegate of the **NSURLConnection**

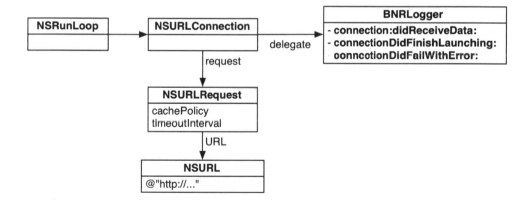

In main.m, create an **NSURL** and an **NSURLRequest** like you did in Chapter 26. Then create an
NSURLConnection and set the instance of **BNRLogger** to be its delegate:

```
#import <Foundation/Foundation.h>
#import "BNRLogger.h"

int main (int argc, const char * argv[])
{
    @autoreleasepool {

        BNRLogger *logger = [[BNRLogger alloc] init];

        NSURL *url = [NSURL URLWithString:
                            @"http://www.gutenberg.org/cache/epub/205/pg205.txt"];

        NSURLRequest *request = [NSURLRequest requestWithURL:url];

        __unused NSURLConnection *fetchConn =
                            [[NSURLConnection alloc] initWithRequest:request
                                                           delegate:logger
                                                    startImmediately:YES];

        __unused NSTimer *timer =
                    [NSTimer scheduledTimerWithTimeInterval:2.0
                                                     target:logger
                                                   selector:@selector(updateLastTime:)
                                                   userInfo:nil
                                                    repeats:YES];

        [[NSRunLoop currentRunLoop] run];

    }
    return 0;
}
```

Now, in **BNRLogger**, you need to implement the callback methods – the methods to be executed in
response to specific events.

You do not come up with or declare these methods yourself. They have already been declared
in a *protocol*. A protocol is a list of method declarations. You will learn more about protocols in
Chapter 29, but for now, think of a protocol as a prearranged set of messages that an object can send its
helper object.

In BNRLogger.h, declare that **BNRLogger** will implement methods from the NSURLConnectionDelegate
and NSURLConnectionDataDelegate protocols:

```
#import <Foundation/Foundation.h>

@interface BNRLogger : NSObject
     <NSURLConnectionDelegate, NSURLConnectionDataDelegate>

@property (nonatomic) NSDate *lastTime;
- (NSString *)lastTimeString;
- (void)updateLastTime:(NSTimer *)t;
@end
```

There are three messages that **BNRLogger** will need to respond to as the delegate of the **NSURLConnection**. Two are from the NSURLConnectionDataDelegate protocol:

```
- (void)connection:(NSURLConnection *)connection
    didReceiveData:(NSData *)data;
```

```
- (void)connectionDidFinishLoading:(NSURLConnection *)connection;
```

The other is from the NSURLConnectionDelegate protocol:

```
- (void)connection:(NSURLConnection *)connection
  didFailWithError:(NSError *)error;
```

(How do you know what methods a protocol has and which ones you should implement? Go to the developer documentation. Protocols have references, similar to class references, with information about their methods. You will also learn more about protocols and their methods in Chapter 29.)

Before you get to implementing these methods, **BNRLogger** needs a new instance variable. When you created a synchronous **NSURLConnection** in Chapter 26, you used an instance of **NSData** to hold the bytes coming from the server. In an asynchronous connection, you need an instance of **NSMutableData**. As the chunks of data arrive, you will add them to this object.

In BNRLogger.h, add an **NSMutableData** instance variable:

```
#import <Foundation/Foundation.h>

@interface BNRLogger : NSObject
      <NSURLConnectionDelegate, NSURLConnectionDataDelegate>

{
    NSMutableData *incomingData;
}
@property (nonatomic) NSDate *lastTime;
- (NSString *)lastTimeString;
- (void)updateLastTime:(NSTimer *)t;
@end
```

In BNRLogger.m, implement the three protocol methods:

```
#import "BNRLogger.h"

@implementation BNRLogger

    . . .

// Called each time a chunk of data arrives
- (void)connection:(NSURLConnection *)connection
    didReceiveData:(NSData *)data
{
    NSLog(@"received %lu bytes", [data length]);

    // Create a mutable data if it does not already exist
    if (!incomingData) {
        incomingData = [[NSMutableData alloc] init];
    }

    [incomingData appendData:data];
}

// Called when the last chunk has been processed
- (void)connectionDidFinishLoading:(NSURLConnection *)connection
{
    NSLog(@"Got it all!");
    NSString *string = [[NSString alloc] initWithData:incomingData
                                             encoding:NSUTF8StringEncoding];
    incomingData = nil;
    NSLog(@"string has %lu characters", [string length]);

    // Uncomment the next line to see the entire fetched file
    // NSLog(@"The whole string is %@", string);

}

// Called if the fetch fails
- (void)connection:(NSURLConnection *)connection
  didFailWithError:(NSError *)error
{
    NSLog(@"connection failed: %@", [error localizedDescription]);
    incomingData = nil;
}
@end
```

Build and run the program. You will see the data coming from the web server in chunks. Eventually, the **BNRLogger** will be informed that the fetch is complete.

Here are the rules, so far, for callbacks: When sending one callback to one object, Apple uses target-action. When sending an assortment of callbacks to one object, Apple uses a helper object with a protocol. These helper objects are typically called delegates or data sources.

What if the callback needs to go to multiple objects?

Notifications

Imagine the user changes the time zone on a Mac. Many objects in your program might want to know that this event has happened. Each of them can register as an observer with the notification center.

When the time zone is changed, the notification NSSystemTimeZoneDidChangeNotification will be posted to the center, and the center will forward it to all the relevant observers.

In main.m, register the instance of **BNRLogger** to receive a notification when the time zone changes:

```
#import <Foundation/Foundation.h>
#import "BNRLogger.h"

int main (int argc, const char * argv[])
{
    @autoreleasepool {

        BNRLogger *logger = [[BNRLogger alloc] init];

        [[NSNotificationCenter defaultCenter]
                            addObserver:logger
                               selector:@selector(zoneChange:)
                                   name:NSSystemTimeZoneDidChangeNotification
                                 object:nil];

        NSURL *url = [NSURL URLWithString:
                            @"http://www.gutenberg.org/cache/epub/205/pg205.txt"];
        NSURLRequest *request = [NSURLRequest requestWithURL:url];

        __unused NSURLConnection *fetchConn =
                                [[NSURLConnection alloc] initWithRequest:request
                                                               delegate:logger
                                                        startImmediately:YES];

        __unused NSTimer *timer =
                [NSTimer scheduledTimerWithTimeInterval:2.0
                                                 target:logger
                                               selector:@selector(updateLastTime:)
                                               userInfo:nil
                                                repeats:YES];

        [[NSRunLoop currentRunLoop] run];

    }
    return 0;
}
```

Now implement the method that will get called in BNRLogger.m:

```
- (void)zoneChange:(NSNotification *)note
{
    NSLog(@"The system time zone has changed!");
}
```

Build and run the program. While it is running, open System Preferences and change the time zone for your system. You should see that your **zoneChange:** method gets called. (On some systems, it seems to get called twice. This is not cause for concern.)

Many of the classes that Apple has written post notifications when interesting things happen. You can find out what notifications a class posts in its reference in the developer documentation.

When you register as an observer with the notification center, you can specify the name of the notification (for example, NSWindowDidResizeNotification) and which posters of this notification you care about ("I only want to hear about the resize notification from this particular window."). For either of these parameters, you can supply nil, which works as the wild card. If you supply nil for both, you will receive every notification posted by every object in your program. On a desktop application, this is a *lot* of notifications.

Which to use?

In this chapter, you have seen three kinds of callbacks. How does Apple decide which one to use in any particular situation?

* Objects that do just one thing (like **NSTimer**) use target-action.

* Objects that have more complicated lives (like an **NSURLConnection**) use helper objects, and the most common type of helper object is the delegate.

* Objects that might need to trigger callbacks in several other objects (like **NSTimeZone**) use notifications.

Callbacks and object ownership

Inherent in any of these callback schemes is the risk of strong reference cycles. Often the object you create has a pointer to the object that is going to call back. And it has a pointer to the object you created. If they each have strong references to each other, you end up with a strong reference cycle – neither of them will ever get deallocated.

Figure 27.3 Strong reference cycle

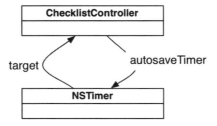

Thus, it was decided that:

* *Notification centers do not own their observers.* If an object is an observer, it will typically remove itself from the notification center in its **dealloc** method:

```
- (void)dealloc
{
    [[NSNotificationCenter defaultCenter] removeObserver:self];
}
```

* *Objects do not own their delegates or data sources.* If you create an object that is a delegate or data source, your object should "excuse" itself in its **dealloc** method:

```
- (void)dealloc
{
    [windowThatBossesMeAround setDelegate:nil];
    [tableViewThatBegsForData setDataSource:nil];
}
```

- *Objects do not own their targets.* If you create an object that is a target, your object should zero the target pointer in its **dealloc** method:

```
- (void)dealloc
{
    [buttonThatKeepsSendingMeMessages setTarget:nil];
}
```

None of these issues exist in this program because your **BNRLogger** object will not be deallocated before the program terminates. (Also, in a bit of a fluke, in this exercise you happen to have used two well-documented exceptions to the rules: an **NSURLConnection** *does* own its delegate while the connection is running, and an **NSTimer** *does* own its target while the timer is valid.)

For the more curious: how selectors work

You learned in Chapter 20 that when you send a message to an object, the object's class is asked if it has a method with that name. The search goes up the inheritance hierarchy until a class responds with "Yeah, I have a method with that name."

Figure 27.4 The search for a method with the right name

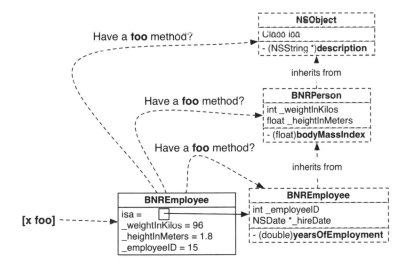

As you can imagine, this search needs to happen very, very quickly. If the compiler used the actual name of the method (which could be very long), method lookup would be really slow. To speed things up, the compiler assigns a unique number to each method name it encounters. At runtime, it uses that number instead of the method name.

Figure 27.5 How it really works

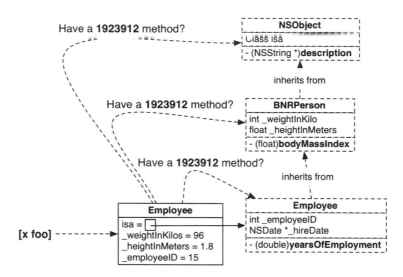

Thus, a selector is the unique number that represents a particular method name. When a method expects a selector as an argument (like `scheduledTimerWithTimeInterval:target:selector:userInfo:repeats:` does), it is expecting this number. You use the `@selector` compiler directive to tell the compiler to look up the selector for the given method name.

28
Blocks

A *block* is a chunk of code. Here is a block:

```
^{
    NSLog(@"This is an instruction within a block.");
}
```

It looks like a C function; it is a set of instructions inside curly braces. It does not, however, have a name. Instead, the caret (^) identifies this bit of code as a block.

Like a function, a block can take arguments and return values. Here is another block:

```
^(double dividend, double divisor) {
    double quotient = dividend / divisor;
    return quotient;
}
```

This block takes two doubles as arguments and returns a double.

You can pass a block as an argument to a method that accepts a block. Many of Apple's classes have methods that accept blocks as arguments.

For instance, **NSArray**, **NSDictionary**, and **NSSet** allow block-based enumeration: Each class has at least one method that accepts a block. When one of these methods is called, it will execute the code within the passed-in block once for each object in the collection. In this chapter, you are going to use **NSArray**'s **enumerateObjectsUsingBlock:** method.

(If you have a background in another programming language, you might know blocks as anonymous functions, closures, or lambdas. If you are familiar with function pointers, blocks may seem similar, but blocks allow for more elegant code than can be written with function pointers.)

Create a new Foundation Command Line Tool and call it VowelMovement. This program will iterate through an array of strings, remove the vowels from each string, and store the "devowelized" strings in a new array.

In main.m, set up three arrays: one for the original strings, one for the devowelized strings, and a third for a list of vowels.

```
int main (int argc, const char * argv[])
{
    @autoreleasepool {

        // Create array of strings and a container for devowelized ones
        NSArray *originalStrings = @[@"Sauerkraut", @"Raygun",
                                     @"Big Nerd Ranch", @"Mississippi"];

        NSLog(@"original strings: %@", originalStrings);

        NSMutableArray *devowelizedStrings = [NSMutableArray array];

        // Create a list of characters to be removed from the string
        NSArray *vowels = @[@"a", @"e", @"i", @"o", @"u"];

    }
    return 0;
}
```

Nothing new here; you are just setting up arrays. Build your program, and ignore the warnings about unused variables for now.

Using blocks

Soon you will compose your first block. This block will make a copy of a given string, remove the vowels from the copied string, and then add this string to the devowelizedStrings array.

You are going to send the originalStrings array the **enumerateObjectsUsingBlock:** message with your devowelizing block as its argument. But first, there is some more block syntax to learn.

Declaring a block variable

A block can be stored in a variable. In main.m, type in the following block variable declaration.

```
int main (int argc, const char * argv[])
{
    @autoreleasepool {
        // Create array of strings and a container for devowelized ones
        NSArray *originalStrings = @[@"Sauerkraut", @"Raygun",
                                     @"Big Nerd Ranch", @"Mississippi"];

        NSLog(@"original strings: %@", originalStrings);

        NSMutableArray *devowelizedStrings = [NSMutableArray array];

        // Create a list of characters to be removed from the string
        NSArray *vowels = @[@"a", @"e", @"i", @"o", @"u"];

        // Declare the block variable
        void (^devowelizer)(id, NSUInteger, BOOL *);

    }
    return 0;
}
```

Let's break down this declaration. The name of the block variable (devowelizer) is in a set of parentheses right after the caret. The declaration includes the block's return type (void) and the types of its arguments (id, NSUInteger, BOOL *), just like in a function declaration.

Figure 28.1 Block variable declaration

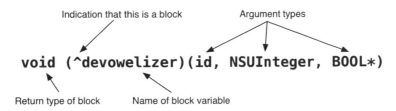

What is the type of this block variable? It is not simply "block." Its type is "a block that takes an object, an integer, and a BOOL pointer, and returns nothing." This is the type of block that **enumerateObjectsUsingBlock:** expects. You will learn what each of these arguments is used for shortly.

Composing a block

Now you need to compose a block of the declared type and assign it to the new variable. In main.m, compose a block that makes a mutable copy of the original string, removes its vowels, and then adds the new string to the array of devowelized strings and assigns it to devowelizer:

```
int main (int argc, const char * argv[])
{
    @autoreleasepool {
        ...

        // Declare the block variable
        void (^devowelizer)(id, NSUInteger, BOOL *);

        // Compose a block and assign it to the variable
        devowelizer = ^(id string, NSUInteger i, BOOL *stop) {

            NSMutableString *newString = [NSMutableString stringWithString:string];

            // Iterate over the array of vowels, replacing occurrences of each
            // with an empty string
            for (NSString *s in vowels) {
                NSRange fullRange = NSMakeRange(0, [newString length]);
                [newString replaceOccurrencesOfString:s
                                           withString:@""
                                              options:NSCaseInsensitiveSearch
                                                range:fullRange];
            }

            [devowelizedStrings addObject:newString];

        }; // End of block assignment

    }
    return 0;
}
```

Notice that the block assignment ends with a semi-colon just like any variable assignment would. Build your program to check your typing. The warnings about unused variables should disappear.

As with any variable, you can perform the declaration and assignment of devowelizer in one or two steps. Here is what it would look like in one step:

```
void (^devowelizer)(id, NSUInteger, BOOL *) = ^(id string, NSUInteger i, BOOL *stop) {

    NSMutableString *newString = [NSMutableString stringWithString:string];

    // Iterate over the array of vowels, replacing occurrences of each
    // with an empty string.
    for (NSString *s in vowels) {
        NSRange fullRange = NSMakeRange(0, [newString length]);
        [newString replaceOccurrencesOfString:s
                                   withString:@""
                                      options:NSCaseInsensitiveSearch
                                        range:fullRange];
    }

    [devowelizedStrings addObject:newString];
};
```

Passing in a block

In main.m, send the **enumerateObjectsUsingBlock:** message with devowelizer to the array of original strings and then print out the devowelized strings.

```
int main (int argc, const char * argv[])
{
    @autoreleasepool {

        ...

        // Declare the block variable
        void (^devowelizer)(id, NSUInteger, BOOL *);

        // Assign a block to the variable
        devowelizer = ^(id string, NSUInteger i, BOOL *stop) {

            NSMutableString *newString = [NSMutableString stringWithString:string];

            // Iterate over the array of vowels, replacing occurrences of each
            // with an empty string.
            for (NSString *s in vowels) {
                NSRange fullRange = NSMakeRange(0, [newString length]);
                [newString replaceOccurrencesOfString:s
                                           withString:@""
                                              options:NSCaseInsensitiveSearch
                                                range:fullRange];
            }

            [devowelizedStrings addObject:newString];

        }; // End of block assignment

        // Iterate over the array with your block
        [originalStrings enumerateObjectsUsingBlock:devowelizer];
        NSLog(@"devowelized strings: %@", devowelizedStrings);


    }
    return 0;
}
```

Build and run your program. You will see two arrays logged to the console.

```
2011-09-03 10:27:02.617 VowelMovement[787:707] original strings: (
    Sauerkraut,
    Raygun,
    "Big Nerd Ranch",
    Mississippi
)
2011-09-03 10:27:02.618 VowelMovement[787:707] new strings: (
    Srkrt,
    Rygn,
    "Bg Nrd Rnch",
    Msssspp
)
```

The three arguments of this block type are specifically designed for iterating through an array. The first is a pointer to the current object. Notice that this pointer's type is id so that it will work no matter what kind of objects the array contains. The second argument is an NSUInteger that is the index of the current object. The third argument is a pointer to a BOOL, which defaults to NO. Changing it to YES will stop executing the block after the current iteration.

Modify your block to check for an uppercase or lowercase 'y' character. If there is one, set the pointer to YES (which will prevent the block from performing any more iterations) and end the current iteration.

```
devowelizer = ^(id string, NSUInteger i, BOOL *stop){

    NSRange yRange = [string rangeOfString:@"y"
                                options:NSCaseInsensitiveSearch];

    // Did I find a y?
    if (yRange.location != NSNotFound) {
        *stop = YES; // Prevent further iterations
        return;      // End this iteration
    }

    NSMutableString *newString = [NSMutableString stringWithString:string];

    // Iterate over the array of vowels, replacing occurrences of each
    // with an empty string.
    for (NSString *s in vowels) {
        NSRange fullRange = NSMakeRange(0, [newString length]);
        [newString replaceOccurrencesOfString:s
                              withString:@""
                                  options:NSCaseInsensitiveSearch
                                    range:fullRange];
    }

    [devowelizedStrings addObject:newString];

}; // End of block assignment
```

Build and run the program. Again, two arrays are logged to the debugger output, but this time, the array enumeration was cancelled during the second iteration when the block encountered a word with the letter 'y' in it. All you get is Srkrt.

typedef

Block syntax can be confusing, but you can make it clearer using the typedef keyword that you learned about in Chapter 11. Remember that typedefs belong at the top of the file or in a header, outside of any method implementations. In main.m, add the following line of code:

```
#import <Foundation/Foundation.h>

typedef void (^ArrayEnumerationBlock)(id, NSUInteger, BOOL *);

int main (int argc, const char * argv[])
{
```

Notice that this looks identical to a block variable declaration. However, here you are defining a type rather than a variable, hence the appropriate type name next to the caret. This allows you to simplify declarations of similar blocks.

Now you can declare devowelizer using your new type:

```
int main(int argc, const char * argv[])
{

    @autoreleasepool {

        ...

        // Declare the block variable
        void (^devowelizer)(id, NSUInteger, BOOL *);
        ArrayEnumerationBlock devowelizer;

        // Compose and assign a block to the variable
        devowelizer = ^(id string, NSUInteger i, BOOL *stop) {
            ...
```

Note that the block type itself only defines the block's arguments and return types; it has no bearing on the set of instructions within a block of that type.

Blocks vs. other callbacks

In Chapter 27, you learned about the callback mechanisms helper objects and notifications. Callbacks allow other objects to call methods in your object in response to events. While perfectly functional, these approaches break up your code. Pieces of your program that you would like to be close together for clarity's sake usually are not.

The Callbacks program includes the following code that calls back to the **zoneChange:** method:

```
[[NSNotificationCenter defaultCenter]
                  addObserver:logger
                     selector:@selector(zoneChange:)
                         name:NSSystemTimeZoneDidChangeNotification
                       object:nil];
```

It is natural, then, for someone reading your code to wonder, "What does this **zoneChange:** method do?" To answer this question, the programmer must hunt down the implementation of **zoneChange:**, which could be hundreds of lines away.

Blocks, on the other hand, keep the code to be triggered by an event close by. For instance, **NSNotificationCenter** has a method **addObserverForName:object:queue:usingBlock:**. This method is similar to **addObserver:selector:name:object:**, but it accepts a block instead of a selector. That block can be defined right next to the call to **addObserverForName:object:queue:usingBlock:**. Then your curious programmer friend can see what your code does from start to finish in one place.

You will get to make this change to the Callbacks program in the second challenge at the end of this chapter.

More on blocks

Here are some other things you can do with blocks.

Return values

The block that you created for VowelMovement does not have a return value, but many blocks will. When a block returns a value, you can get the return value by calling the block variable like a function.

Let's look again at one of the sample blocks you saw at the beginning of the chapter:

```
^(double dividend, double divisor) {
    double quotient = dividend / divisor;
    return quotient;
}
```

This block takes two doubles and returns a double. To store this block in a variable, you would declare a variable of that type and assign the block to it:

```
// Declare divBlock variable
double (^divBlock)(double,double);

// Assign block to variable
divBlock = ^(double dividend, double divisor) {
    double quotient = dividend / divisor;
    return quotient;
}
```

You can then call divBlock like a function to get its return value:

```
double myQuotient = divBlock(42.0, 12.5);
```

Anonymous blocks

An *anonymous block* is a block that you pass directly to a method without assigning it to a block variable first.

Let's consider the case of an anonymous integer first. When you want to pass an integer to a method, you have three options:

```
// Option 1: Totally break it down
int i;
i = 5;
NSNumber *num = [NSNumber numberWithInt:i];

// Option 2: Declare and assign on one line
int i = 5;
NSNumber *num = [NSNumber numberWithInt:i];

// Option 3: Skip the variable entirely
NSNumber *num = [NSNumber numberWithInt:5];
```

If you take the third option, you are passing the integer anonymously. It is anonymous because it does not have a name (or a variable) associated with it.

You have the same options when you want to pass a block to a method. Currently, your code puts the block declaration, assignment, and usage on three separate lines of code. But it is more common to pass blocks anonymously. The first challenge at the end of this chapter is to modify the VowelMovement program to use an anonymous block.

External variables

A block typically uses other variables (both primitive variables and pointers to objects) that were created outside of the block. These are called *external variables*. To make sure that they will be available for as long as the block needs them, these variables are *captured* by the block.

For primitive variables, the values are copied and stored as local variables within the block. For pointers, the block will keep a strong reference to the objects it references. This means that any objects referred to by the block are guaranteed to live as long as the block itself. (If you have been wondering about the difference between blocks and function pointers, it is right here. Let's see a function pointer do that!)

Using self in blocks

If you need to write a block that uses self, you must take a couple of extra steps to avoid a strong reference cycle. Consider an example where an instance of **BNREmployee** creates a block that will log the **BNREmployee** instance each time it executes:

```
myBlock = ^{
    NSLog(@"Employee: %@", self);
};
```

The **BNREmployee** instance has a pointer to a block (myBlock). The block captures self, so it has a pointer back to the **BNREmployee** instance. You have a strong reference cycle.

To break the strong reference cycle, you declare a __weak pointer outside the block that points to self. Then you can use this pointer inside the block instead of self:

```
__weak BNREmployee *weakSelf = self; // a weak reference
myBlock = ^{
    NSLog(@"Employee: %@", weakSelf);
};
```

The block's reference to the **BNREmployee** instance is now a weak one, and the strong reference cycle is broken.

However, because the reference is weak, the object that self points to could be deallocated while the block is executing.

You can eliminate this risk by creating a strong local reference to self inside the block:

```
__weak BNREmployee *weakSelf = self; // a weak reference
myBlock = ^{
    BNREmployee *innerSelf = weakSelf; // a block-local strong reference
    NSLog(@"Employee: %@", innerSelf);
};
```

By creating the strong innerSelf reference, you have again created a strong reference cycle between the block and the **BNREmployee** instance. But because the innerSelf reference is local to the scope of the block, the strong reference cycle will only exist while the block is executing and will be broken automatically when the block ends.

This is good programming practice whenever you write a block that must reference self.

Unexpectedly using self in blocks

If you use an instance variable directly within a block, the block will capture self instead of the instance variable. This is because of a little-known nuance of instance variables. Consider this code that accesses an instance variable directly:

```
__weak BNREmployee *weakSelf = self;
myBlock = ^{
    BNREmployee *innerSelf = weakSelf; // a block-local strong reference
    NSLog(@"Employee: %@", innerSelf);
    NSLog(@"Employee ID: %d", _employeeID);
};
```

The compiler interprets the direct variable access like this:

```
__weak BNREmployee *weakSelf = self;
myBlock = ^{
    BNREmployee *innerSelf = weakSelf; // a block-local strong reference
    NSLog(@"Employee: %@", innerSelf);
    NSLog(@"Employee ID: %d", self->_employeeID);
};
```

Does the -> syntax look familiar? It is the syntax for accessing the member of a struct on the heap. At their deepest darkest cores, objects are actually structs.

Because the compiler reads _employeeID as self->_employeeID, self is unexpectedly captured by the block. This will cause the same strong reference cycle that you avoided with the use of weakSelf and innerSelf.

The fix? Don't access instance variables directly. Use your accessors!

```
__weak BNREmployee *weakSelf = self;
myBlock = ^{
    BNREmployee *innerSelf = weakSelf; // a block-local strong reference
    NSLog(@"Employee: %@", innerSelf);
    NSLog(@"Employee ID: %d", innerSelf.employeeID);
};
```

Now there is no direct use of self, so there is no unintentional strong reference cycle. Problem solved.

In this situation, it is important to understand what the compiler is thinking to avoid the hidden strong reference cycle. However, you should never use the -> syntax to access an object's instance variables in your code. Doing so is dangerous for reasons beyond the scope of this book. Accessors are your friends, and you should use them.

Modifying external variables

By default, variables captured by a block are constant within the block, and you cannot change their values. If you want to be able to modify an external variable within a block, you must declare the external variable using the __block keyword.

For instance, in the following code, you increment the external variable counter within the block.

```
__block int counter = 0;
void (^counterBlock)() = ^{ counter++; };
...
counterBlock(); // Increments counter to 1
counterBlock(); // Increments counter to 2
```

Without the __block keyword, you would get a compilation error.

Challenge: an anonymous block

Modify the exercise in this chapter to pass the block anonymously as an argument to **enumerateObjectsUsingBlock:**. That is, keep the block, but get rid of the devowelizer variable.

Challenge: using a block with NSNotificationCenter

In Chapter 27, you used **NSNotificationCenter**'s **addObserver:selector:name:object:** method to register to receive callbacks via your **zoneChange:** method. Update that exercise to use the **addObserverForName:object:queue:usingBlock:** method instead.

This method takes a block as an argument and then executes the block instead of calling back to your object when the specified notification is posted. This means that your **zoneChange:** method will never be called. The code that was inside this method will instead be in the block.

The passed-in block should take a single argument (an **NSNotification** *) and return nothing, just as the **zoneChange:** method does.

Pass nil as the argument for queue:; this argument is used for concurrency, a topic we will not cover in this book.

For more important details about **addObserverForName:object:queue:usingBlock:**, check the developer documentation.

29
Protocols

At this point, we need to talk about a slightly abstract concept. Someone once said, "Who you are is different from what you do." The same is true of objects: the class of an object is different from its *role* in a working system. For example, an object may be an instance of **NSMutableArray**, but its role in an application may be as a queue of print jobs to be run.

Like the array-as-print-queue example, really great classes are more general than the role they may play in any particular application. Thus, instances of that class can be used in several different ways.

For example, in an iOS application, you frequently display data in an instance of **UITableView**. However, the **UITableView** object does not contain the data that it displays; it has to get data from a helper object. You have to tell it "Here is the object that will fill the role of your data source."

Figure 29.1 **UITableView** data source

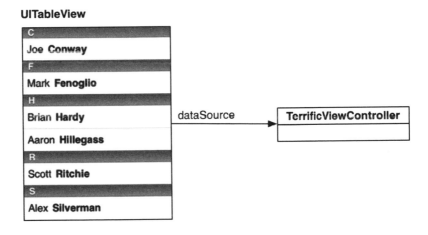

A protocol can specify a role that an object can fill. (If you are coming to Objective-C from Java or C#, protocols are called "interfaces" in those communities.)

As you learned in Chapter 27, a protocol is a list of method declarations. Some of these methods are required, and some are optional. If an object is to fill the specified role, then it must implement the required methods. It may choose to implement one or more of the optional methods.

The developer who created the **UITableView** class specified the role of **UITableView**'s data source by creating the UITableViewDataSource protocol. Here it is:

```
// Just like classes, protocols can inherit from other protocols
// This protocol inherits from the NSObject protocol
@protocol UITableViewDataSource <NSObject>

// The following methods must be implemented by any table view data source
@required

// A table view has sections, each section can have several rows
- (NSInteger)tableView:(UITableView *)tv numberOfRowsInSection:(NSInteger)section;

// This index path is two integers (a section and a row)
// The table view cell is what the user sees in that section/row
- (UITableViewCell *)tableView:(UITableView *)tv
          cellForRowAtIndexPath:(NSIndexPath *)ip;

// These methods may be implemented by a table view data source
@optional

// If data source does not implement this method, table view has only one section
- (NSInteger)numberOfSectionsInTableView:(UITableView *)tv;

// Rows can be deleted and moved
- (BOOL)tableView:(UITableView *)tv canEditRowAtIndexPath:(NSIndexPath *)ip;

- (BOOL)tableView:(UITableView *)tv canMoveRowAtIndexPath:(NSIndexPath *)ip;

- (void)tableView:(UITableView *)tv
commitEditingStyle:(UITableViewCellEditingStyle)editingStyle
 forRowAtIndexPath:(NSIndexPath *)ip;

- (void)tableView:(UITableView *)tv
moveRowAtIndexPath:(NSIndexPath *)sourceIndexPath
       toIndexPath:(NSIndexPath *)destinationIndexPath;

// To save ink and paper, we are leaving out a few optional method declarations.

@end
```

Like classes, protocols that Apple provides have reference pages in the developer documentation. You can browse a protocol's reference to see the methods that it contains.

The **UITableView** class has dataSource property. Here is its declaration:

```
@property(nonatomic, assign) id<UITableViewDataSource> dataSource;
```

So a table view's data source can be an object of any type (id), so long as the object conforms to the UITableViewDataSource protocol. The compiler considers an object to have successfully conformed to a protocol if the object has implemented all of the protocol's required methods.

When you create a class to fill the role of **UITableView**'s data source, you explicitly say, "This class conforms to the UITableViewDataSource protocol" in the header file. It looks like this:

```
@interface TerrificViewController : UIViewController <UITableViewDataSource>
...
@end
```

That is, "**TerrificViewController** is a subclass of **UIViewController** and conforms to the UITableViewDataSource protocol."

If your class conforms to several protocols, you list them within the angle brackets:

```
@interface TerrificViewController : UIViewController
    <UITableViewDataSource, UITableViewDelegate, UITextFieldDelegate>
```

Then, in the `TerrificViewController.m` file, you must implement the required methods. If you forget to implement one of the required methods, you will get a stern warning from the compiler.

Calling optional methods

In Chapter 20, you learned that if you send a message to an object and that method is not implemented by the object's class, then the program will crash. How, then, do optional methods in protocols work? For example, if a class acting as a table view's data source chooses not to implement the optional **numberOfSectionsInTableView:** protocol method, then you would expect the program to crash if the table view sends that message to its data source.

To avoid this situation, the table view asks first to see if its data source implements **numberOfSectionsInTableView:**.

You can ask an object if it implements a method using **respondsToSelector:**. This method is implemented in **NSObject**, so you can send the message to any object in your program. You pass in the selector for the method that you are asking about. The return value will be YES if the object has that method and NO if it does not.

Here is what it looks like:

```
    ...

    if ([_dataSource respondsToSelector:@selector(numberOfSectionsInTableView:)]) {
        _numberOfSections = [_dataSource numberOfSectionsInTableView:self];
    } else {
        _numberOfSections = 1; // 1 is the default number of sections
    }

    ...
```

30
Property Lists

Sometimes you need a file format that can be read by both computers and people. For example, let's say that you want to keep a description of your stock portfolio in a file. As you add new stocks, it would be nice to be able to edit that file easily by hand. But, it might also be handy for one of your programs to be able to read it. When facing this problem, most Objective-C programmers use a *property list*.

A property list is a combination of any of the following things:

- **NSArray**

- **NSDictionary**

- **NSString**

- **NSData**

- **NSDate**

- **NSNumber** (integer, float, or Boolean)

For example, an array of dictionaries with string keys and date objects is a property list (or just a "P-list").

Reading and writing a property list to a file is really easy. In Xcode, create a new project: a Foundation Command Line Tool named Stockz. In main.m, add the following code:

```
#import <Foundation/Foundation.h>

int main(int argc, const char * argv[])
{
    @autoreleasepool {

        NSMutableArray *stocks = [[NSMutableArray alloc] init];

        NSMutableDictionary *stock;

        stock = [NSMutableDictionary dictionary];
        [stock setObject:@"AAPL"
                forKey:@"symbol"];
        [stock setObject:[NSNumber numberWithInt:200]
                forKey:@"shares"];
        [stocks addObject:stock];

        stock = [NSMutableDictionary dictionary];
        [stock setObject:@"GOOG"
                forKey:@"symbol"];
        [stock setObject:[NSNumber numberWithInt:160]
                forKey:@"shares"];
        [stocks addObject:stock];

        [stocks writeToFile:@"/tmp/stocks.plist"
                atomically:YES];

    }
    return 0;
}
```

(Notice that you reuse the stock pointer. You use it to point to the first dictionary and then to the second.)

Figure 30.1 An array of dictionaries

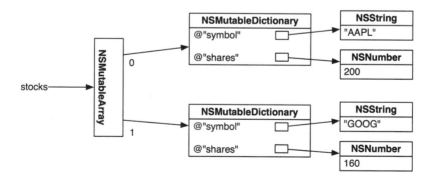

When you run the program, you will get a file: stocks.plist. If you open it in a text editor, it looks like this:

```xml
<?xml version="1.0" encoding="UTF-8"?>
<!DOCTYPE plist PUBLIC
  "-//Apple//DTD PLIST 1.0//EN" "http://www.apple.com/DTDs/PropertyList-1.0.dtd">
<plist version="1.0">
<array>
    <dict>
        <key>shares</key>
        <integer>200</integer>
        <key>symbol</key>
        <string>AAPL</string>
    </dict>
    <dict>
        <key>shares</key>
        <integer>160</integer>
        <key>symbol</key>
        <string>GOOG</string>
    </dict>
</array>
</plist>
```

Nice, eh? Human-readable. XML. One line of code.

If you find yourself creating property lists by hand, you should know that Xcode has a built-in editor specifically for property lists.

Now add the code that reads the file in:

```
int main(int argc, const char * argv[])
{
    @autoreleasepool {

        NSMutableArray *stocks = [[NSMutableArray alloc] init];

        NSMutableDictionary *stock;

        stock = [NSMutableDictionary dictionary];
        [stock setObject:@"AAPL"
                forKey:@"symbol"];
        [stock setObject:[NSNumber numberWithInt:200]
                forKey:@"shares"];
        [stocks addObject:stock];

        stock = [NSMutableDictionary dictionary];
        [stock setObject:@"GOOG"
                forKey:@"symbol"];
        [stock setObject:[NSNumber numberWithInt:160]
                forKey:@"shares"];
        [stocks addObject:stock];

        [stocks writeToFile:@"/tmp/stocks.plist"
                atomically:YES];

        NSArray *stockList = [NSArray arrayWithContentsOfFile:@"/tmp/stocks.plist"];

        for (NSDictionary *d in stockList) {
            NSLog(@"I have %@ shares of %@",
                    [d objectForKey:@"shares"], [d objectForKey:@"symbol"]);
        }

    }
    return 0;
}
```

Build and run the program.

Challenge

Write a tool that creates a property list that has all 8 types in it: array, dictionary, string, data, date, integer, float, and boolean.

Part IV
Event-Driven Applications

Here is where we have been heading and why you have been reading this book – writing iOS and Cocoa apps. In the next two chapters, you will get a taste of application development. Your applications will have a GUI (graphical user interface), and they will be event-driven.

First, you will write an iOS application and then a similar Cocoa application. Cocoa is the collection of frameworks written by Apple that you use to write applications on the Mac. You are already familiar with one of these frameworks – Foundation.

To write iOS apps, you use another set of frameworks called Cocoa Touch. Cocoa and Cocoa Touch have some frameworks in common, like Foundation. Others are specific to one platform or the other.

31

Your First iOS Application

In this chapter, you are going to create an iOS application: a simple to-do list application called iTahDoodle that stores its data as a property list. Here is what it will look like when you are done.

Figure 31.1 Complete iTahDoodle application

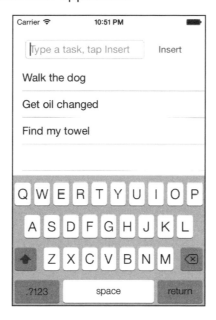

We have intentionally kept this chapter and this application very simple. It is not intended to prepare you to build iOS apps on your own, but it will give you a quick taste of iOS development. It introduces some important concepts and patterns, and we hope that it will inspire you to dive into iOS programming after you have finished this book.

GUI-based applications

None of the programs that you have written so far have had a user interface. Now you are going to write an application that has a *graphical user interface*, or GUI.

A GUI-based application is event-driven. When the application is launched, it starts a run loop that sits and waits for events. Events can be generated by the user (like a button tap) or by the system (like a low-memory warning). When an event happens, the application leaps into action to respond to the specific event. All iOS applications are event-driven applications.

Getting started with iTahDoodle

In Xcode, choose File → New → Project... Under the iOS section (not the OS X section), click Application. From the template choices that appear, select Empty Application.

Figure 31.2 Creating a new iOS application

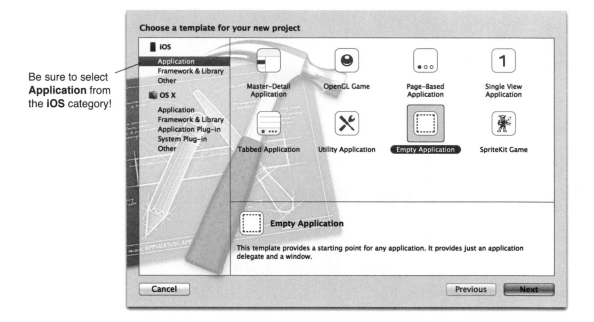

Xcode's project templates contain boilerplate code that can speed up development. However, you are using the Empty Application template, which is as close to a blank template as you can get. Allowing Xcode to generate too much boilerplate code at this point gets in the way of learning how things work.

The names of the templates often change with new Xcode releases, so do not worry if you do not see an Empty Application template. Look for the simplest-sounding template and then make changes to match your code with the book's code. If you have trouble reconciling your code or project templates, visit the Big Nerd Ranch forum for this book at forums.bignerdranch.com for help.

Click Next, and in the window that appears, name this project iTahDoodle (Figure 31.3).

Figure 31.3 Configuring the iTahDoodle project

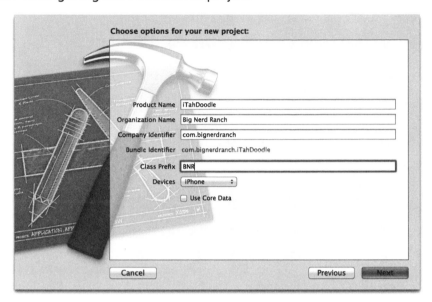

For the Company Identifier, enter com.bignerdranch. The Company Identifier is used to generate the Bundle Identifier, which uniquely identifies each app in the App Store.

The Class Prefix will be prepended to the name of the class that the template creates for you and will keep your classes distinct from classes that others have written.

Finally, make iTahDoodle an iPhone (as opposed to Universal or iPad) application. iTahDoodle will not use Core Data. Click Next and finish creating the project.

BNRAppDelegate

When Xcode created this project, it created a class named **BNRAppDelegate**. The "app delegate" is the starting point of an application, and every iOS application has one.

Open BNRAppDelegate.h. You can see that UIKit.h was imported by the template. UIKit is the framework that contains most of the iOS-specific classes, like **UITableView**, **UITextField**, and **UIButton**. Also notice that **BNRAppDelegate** is a subclass of **UIResponder** and conforms to the UIApplicationDelegate protocol.

BNRAppDelegate has one property that points to an instance of **UIWindow**. This object fills the screen of your iOS application. You add other objects (e.g., an instance of **UIButton**) to the window to create your application's user interface.

In BNRAppDelegate.h, add four properties and an instance method:

```
#import <UIKit/UIKit.h>

@interface BNRAppDelegate : UIResponder <UIApplicationDelegate>

@property (strong, nonatomic) UIWindow *window;

@property (nonatomic) UITableView *taskTable;
@property (nonatomic) UITextField *taskField;
@property (nonatomic) UIButton *insertButton;

@property (nonatomic) NSMutableArray *tasks;

- (void)addTask:(id)sender;

@end
```

The first three properties are pointers to objects that the user can see and interact with – a table view that will display all the tasks to be done, a text field where you can enter a new task, and a button that will add the new task to the table. The fourth object is a mutable array. This is where you will store the tasks as strings.

Figure 31.4 is a diagram of the six objects that will make up iTahDoodle. There is the instance of **BNRAppDelegate**, and this object has pointers to five others: instances of **UIWindow**, **UITableView**, **UITextField**, **UIButton**, and **NSMutableArray**.

Figure 31.4 Object diagram for iTahDoodle

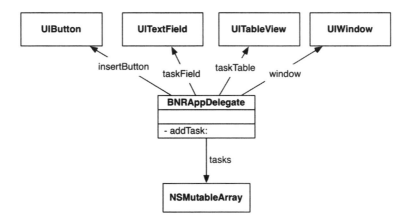

Xcode may warn you that **addTask:** has not yet been implemented. This is true, but you can ignore the warning for now. You will implement **addTask:** later in the chapter.

Before you continue work on the objects shown in Figure 31.4, let's look at some theory about objects and their relationships.

Model-View-Controller

Model-View-Controller, or MVC, is a design pattern that is based on the idea that any class that you create should fall into one of three job categories: model, view, or controller. Here is a breakdown of the division of labor:

- *Models* are responsible for storing data and making it available to other objects. Models have no knowledge of the user interface or how to draw themselves on the screen; their sole purpose is holding and managing data. **NSString**, **NSDate**, and **NSArray** are traditional model objects. In iTahDoodle, the **NSMutableArray** where tasks are stored is a model object. Later, each individual task will be described in an instance of **NSString**, and these will also be model objects.

- *Views* are the visual elements of an application. Views know how to draw themselves on the screen and how to respond to user input. Views have no knowledge of the actual data that they display or how it is structured and stored. **UIView** and its various subclasses, including **UIWindow**, are common examples of view objects. In iTahDoodle, your view objects are the instances of **UITableView**, **UITextField**, and **UIButton**. A simple rule of thumb is: if you can see it, it is a view.

- *Controllers* perform the logic necessary to connect and drive the different parts of your application. They process events and coordinate the other objects in your application. Controllers are the real workhorses of any application. While **BNRAppDelegate** is the only controller in iTahDoodle, a complex application will have many different controllers that coordinate model and view objects as well as other controllers.

Figure 31.5 shows the flow of control between objects in response to a user event, like a button tap. Notice that models and views do not talk to each other directly; controllers sit squarely in the middle of everything, receiving messages from some objects and dispatching instructions to others.

Figure 31.5 MVC flow with user input

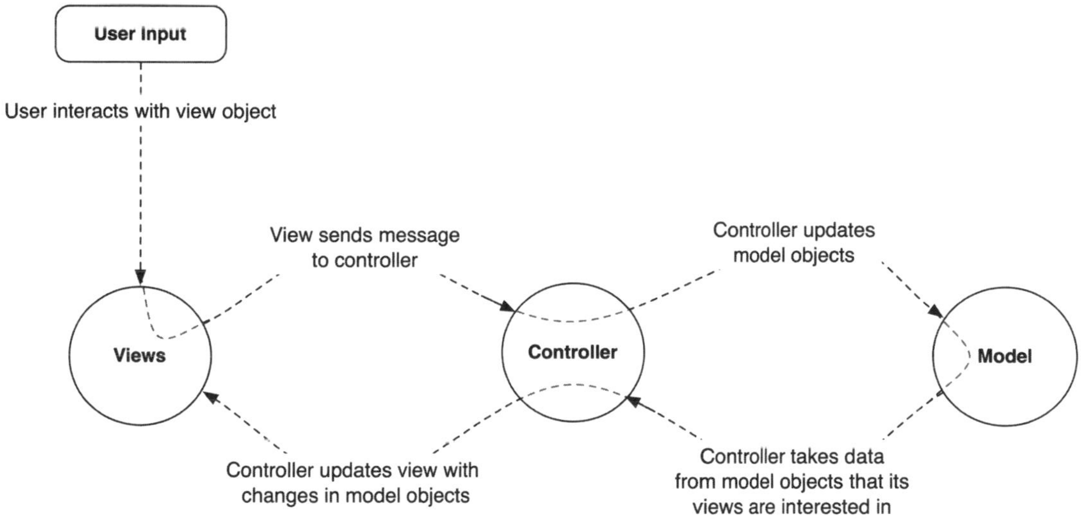

Most of the Cocoa and Cocoa Touch APIs are written with MVC in mind, and your own code should be, too. Figure 31.6 shows this division of labor in iTahDoodle.

Figure 31.6 iTahDoodle object diagram

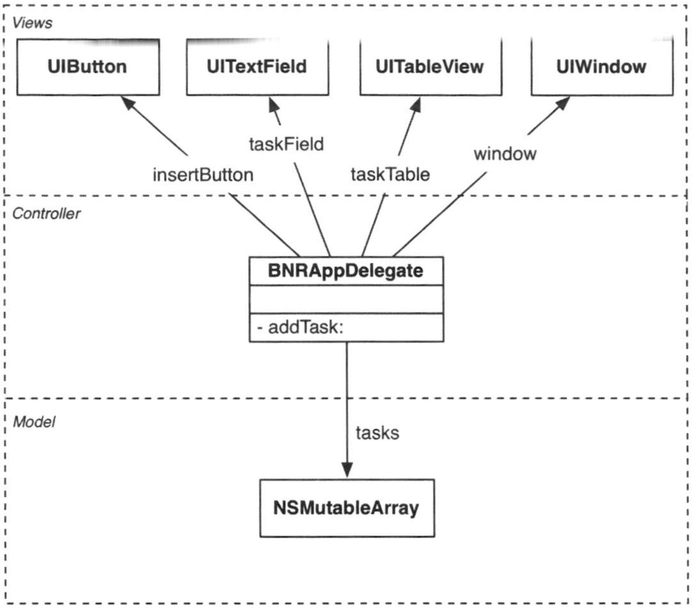

Now let's get back to your controller, the instance of **BNRAppDelegate**.

The application delegate

When an iOS application first launches, a lot of setup is happening behind the scenes. An instance of **UIApplication** is created to control the application's state and act as liaison to the operating system. An instance of **BNRAppDelegate** is also created and set as the delegate of the **UIApplication** instance (which explains the name "app delegate").

This makes **BNRAppDelegate** a busy class. In fact, all of the code that you will write for this application will be in BNRAppDelegate.m. It would be good to have a way to organize the class so that it would be easy to find methods quickly. You can use #pragma mark to group methods within a class for easier navigation.

In BNRAppDelegate.m, add a #pragma mark that identifies the existing methods as application delegate callbacks:

```
#import "BNRAppDelegate.h"

@implementation BNRAppDelegate

#pragma mark - Application delegate callbacks

- (BOOL)application:(UIApplication *)application
didFinishLaunchingWithOptions:(NSDictionary *)launchOptions
{

...
```

Next, on the navigation bar at the top of the editor area, find the item to the right of BNRAppDelegate.m. Click this item, and Xcode will show you a list of locations in this file. You can click any of the method names to be taken directly to that method's implementation. Notice that your pragma mark appears at the top.

Figure 31.7 Navigating using pragma mark

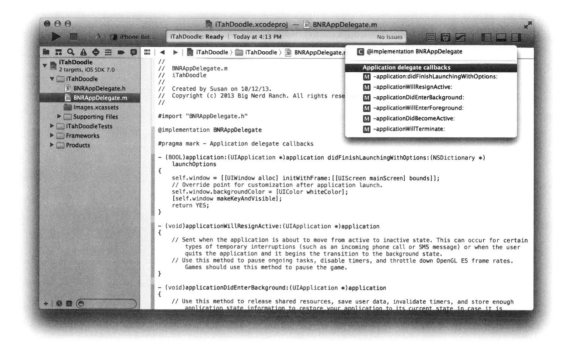

Currently, the **BNRAppDelegate** class only contains application delegate callbacks. But soon you will add methods with different roles and will use #pragma mark to group them.

The first application delegate callback under the pragma mark is **application:didFinishLaunchingWithOptions:**. This method is very important. While the application is being launched, it is not ready for work or input. When the application becomes ready, the **UIApplication** instance sends its delegate the message **application:didFinishLaunchingWithOptions:**. It is where you put everything that needs to be done before the user interacts with the application.

Setting up views

One thing that you need to do before the application is ready for the user is set up your view objects: the text field, the button, and the table view. This means creating them, configuring them, and putting them on the screen.

In iTahDoodle, you are going to set up your views programmatically in **application:didFinishLaunchingWithOptions:**. Xcode also has a visual "drag-and-drop" tool for setting up views, which you will use in Chapter 32.

The code for creating and configuring views is dense, and we are not going to cover it in detail. The detailed syntax of creating and showing views on the screen is a topic for a book specifically about iOS application programming.

Still, you can follow the gist of what is happening. First, you create each object and then configure it by setting some of its properties. Next, the configured view objects are added as *subviews* of the window object, and, finally, the window is placed on the screen.

Figure 31.8 View objects in iTahDoodle

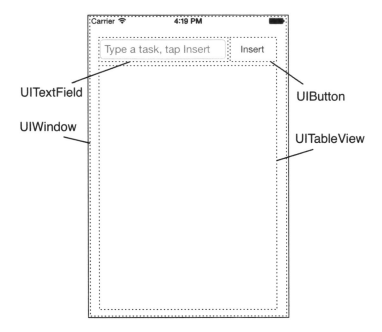

In BNRAppDelegate.m, remove any boilerplate code from **application:didFinishLaunchingWithOptions:** and replace it with the following code:

```
#pragma mark - Application delegate callbacks

- (BOOL)application:(UIApplication *)application
didFinishLaunchingWithOptions:(NSDictionary *)launchOptions
{
    // Create and configure the UIWindow instance
    // A CGRect is a struct with an origin (x,y) and a size (width,height)
    CGRect winFrame = [[UIScreen mainScreen] bounds];
    UIWindow *theWindow = [[UIWindow alloc] initWithFrame:winFrame];
    self.window = theWindow;

    // Define the frame rectangles of the three UI elements
    // CGRectMake() creates a CGRect from (x, y, width, height)
    CGRect tableFrame = CGRectMake(0, 80, winFrame.size.width,
                                            winFrame.size.height - 100);
    CGRect fieldFrame = CGRectMake(20, 40, 200, 31);
    CGRect buttonFrame = CGRectMake(228, 40, 72, 31);

    // Create and configure the UITableView instance
    self.taskTable = [[UITableView alloc] initWithFrame:tableFrame
                                            style:UITableViewStylePlain];
    self.taskTable.separatorStyle = UITableViewCellSeparatorStyleNone;

    // Tell the table view which class to instantiate whenever it
    // needs to create a new cell
    [self.taskTable registerClass:[UITableViewCell class]
            forCellReuseIdentifier:@"Cell"];

    // Create and configure the UITextField instance where new tasks will be entered
    self.taskField = [[UITextField alloc] initWithFrame:fieldFrame];
    self.taskField.borderStyle = UITextBorderStyleRoundedRect;
    self.taskField.placeholder = @"Type a task, tap Insert";

    // Create and configure the UIButton instance
    self.insertButton = [UIButton buttonWithType:UIButtonTypeRoundedRect];
    self.insertButton.frame = buttonFrame;

    // Give the button a title
    [self.insertButton setTitle:@"Insert"
                    forState:UIControlStateNormal];

    // Add our three UI elements to the window
    [self.window addSubview:self.taskTable];
    [self.window addSubview:self.taskField];
    [self.window addSubview:self.insertButton];

    // Finalize the window and put it on the screen
    self.window.backgroundColor = [UIColor whiteColor];
    [self.window makeKeyAndVisible];

    return YES;
}
```

Now that you have set up your views, you can run iTahDoodle on the iOS simulator to see them.

Running on the iOS simulator

Xcode comes with an iOS simulator that lets you run iOS applications on your Mac. The simulator is an easy way to see how your app will behave when it runs on an iOS device. In particular, you are going to simulate iTahDoodle running on an iPhone with a 3.5-inch retina display.

First, look to the right of the run and stop buttons on Xcode's toolbar. You will see iTahDoodle and then a device description.

Figure 31.9 Simulating an iPhone with a 3.5-inch retina display

If the description does not read iPhone Retina (3.5-inch), then click the description to see a drop-down menu with the available options. Choose iPhone Retina (3.5-inch) from the menu.

Build and run the application. The simulator will start up right away, but it may take a minute for iTahDoodle to come on screen for the first time.

You can see the text field and the button. By default, the table view and window have no borders or shading, which makes them hard to see. But they are there!

Figure 31.10 View objects on screen

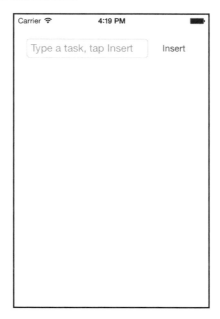

If you click the text field, the keyboard will appear and you can type text into the field. This is default behavior for an instance of **UITextField**. However, the **UIButton** does not do anything when tapped, and the **UITableView** does not display anything.

Your next step is to write code that tells these objects how to behave. Developers often refer to implementing the behavior of view objects as "wiring" or "wiring up."

Wiring up the button

A button works using target-action, like you learned about in Chapter 27. The button's action is the message that you want sent when the button is tapped. The button's target is the object to which that message should be sent.

In BNRAppDelegate.m, give the Insert button a target-action pair:

```
#pragma mark - Application delegate callbacks

- (BOOL)application:(UIApplication *)application
didFinishLaunchingWithOptions:(NSDictionary *)launchOptions
{
    ...

    // Create and configure a rounded rect Insert button
    self.insertButton = [UIButton buttonWithType:UIButtonTypeRoundedRect];
    self.insertButton.frame = buttonFrame;

    // Give the button a title
    [self.insertButton setTitle:@"Insert"
                       forState:UIControlStateNormal];

    // Set the target and action for the Insert button
    [self.insertButton addTarget:self
                          action:@selector(addTask:)
                forControlEvents:UIControlEventTouchUpInside];

    ...

    return YES;
}
```

The target is self, and the action is **addTask:**. Thus, when the Insert button is tapped, it will send the **addTask:** message to the **BNRAppDelegate**. The next step, then, is to implement the **addTask:** method in **BNRAppDelegate**.

Eventually, **addTask:** will retrieve the text entered in taskField and add it to the tasks array. The task will then appear in the table view. But because you have not yet wired up the table view, you are going to implement **addTask:** to retrieve the text from taskField and simply log it to the console.

In BNRAppDelegate.m, add an implementation of **addTask:** at the bottom of the file along with a new pragma mark:

```
@implementation BNRAppDelegate

#pragma mark - Application delegate callbacks

...

#pragma mark - Actions

- (void)addTask:(id)sender
{
    // Get the task
    NSString *text = [self.taskField text];

    // Quit here if taskField is empty
    if ([text length] == 0) {
        return;
    }

    // Log text to console
    NSLog(@"Task entered: %@", text);

    // Clear out the text field
    [self.taskField setText:@""];
    // Dismiss the keyboard
    [self.taskField resignFirstResponder];
}

@end
```

What is this **resignFirstResponder** business? Here is the short version:

Some view objects are also *controls*. A control is a view that the user can interact with. Buttons, sliders, and text fields are examples of controls. (Keep in mind that the term "control" has nothing to do with "controllers" in MVC.)

When there are controls on the screen, one of them can be the *first responder*. When a control has first responder status, it gets the first chance to handle text input from the keyboard and shake events (such as when the user shakes the device to undo the last action).

When the user interacts with a control that can accept first responder status, that control is sent the **becomeFirstResponder** message. When a control that accepts text input (like a text field) becomes the first responder, the keyboard appears on the screen. At the end of **addTask:**, you tell the text field to resign its status, which causes the keyboard to disappear.

Build and run the application. (You will need to stop the currently running instance of iTahDoodle before Xcode can build and run again.)

Once iTahDoodle is running again, enter something in the text field, click Insert, and confirm that the text is logged to the console.

You may also see a warning in the console that reads Application windows are expected to have a root view controller at the end of application launch. You can ignore this. To stick with the absolute basics, you are not implementing a "root view controller" for iTahDoodle, and this simple application will work fine without one. You will learn all about view controllers in *iOS Programming: The Big Nerd Ranch Guide* or any other book on iOS development.

Here is an updated object diagram showing the target-action pair.

Figure 31.11 Updated iTahDoodle object diagram

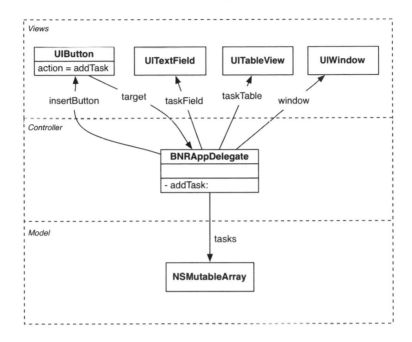

Wiring up the table view

You have a table view on the screen, but it does not display anything. As a view object, the table view does not contain anything about actual data. It needs an object to act as its *data source*. A table view's data source tells the table view what to display.

In iTahDoodle, the table view's data source will be the instance of **BNRAppDelegate**. For **BNRAppDelegate** to do this job, it must conform to the UITableViewDataSource protocol.

In BNRAppDelegate.h, declare that **BNRAppDelegate** conforms to UITableViewDataSource:

```
@interface BNRAppDelegate : UIResponder
     <UIApplicationDelegate, UITableViewDataSource>

@property (strong, nonatomic) UIWindow *window;

@property (nonatomic) UITableView *taskTable;
@property (nonatomic) UITextField *taskField;
@property (nonatomic) UIButton *insertButton;

@property (nonatomic) NSMutableArray *tasks;

- (void)addTask:(id)sender;
```

In BNRAppDelegate.m, update **application:didFinishLaunchingWithOptions:** to send a message to the table view that makes the **BNRAppDelegate** instance its data source:

```
...
// Create and configure the table view
self.taskTable = [[UITableView alloc] initWithFrame:tableFrame
                                             style:UITableViewStylePlain];
self.taskTable.separatorStyle = UITableViewCellSeparatorStyleNone;

// Make the BNRAppDelegate the table view's dataSource
self.taskTable.dataSource = self;

// Tell the table view which class to instantiate whenever it
// needs to create a new cell
[self.taskTable registerClass:[UITableViewCell class]
       forCellReuseIdentifier:@"Cell"];
...
```

The UITableViewDataSource protocol has two required methods. A table view's data source must be prepared to tell the table view:

- how many rows are in a given section of the table (**tableView:numberOfRowsInSection:**)

- what the cell in a given row should be (**tableView:cellForRowAtIndexPath:**)

In BNRAppDelegate.m, implement these callbacks:

```
@implementation BNRAppDelegate

...

#pragma mark - Table view management

- (NSInteger)tableView:(UITableView *)tableView
 numberOfRowsInSection:(NSInteger)section
{
    // Because this table view only has one section,
    // the number of rows in it is equal to the number
    // of items in the tasks array
    return [self.tasks count];
}

- (UITableViewCell *)tableView:(UITableView *)tableView
         cellForRowAtIndexPath:(NSIndexPath *)indexPath
{
    // To improve performance, this method first checks
    // for an existing cell object that we can reuse
    // If there isn't one, then a new cell is created
    UITableViewCell *c = [self.taskTable dequeueReusableCellWithIdentifier:@"Cell"];

    // Then we (re)configure the cell based on the model object,
    // in this case the tasks array, ...
    NSString *item = [self.tasks objectAtIndex:indexPath.row];
    c.textLabel.text = item;

    // ... and hand the properly configured cell back to the table view
    return c;
}

@end
```

These methods interact with the tasks array. You declared this property, but you have not yet created the array object.

In BNRAppDelegate.m, at the top of **application:didFinishLaunchingWithOptions:**, create an empty, mutable array:

```
#pragma mark - Application delegate callbacks

- (BOOL)application:(UIApplication *)application
didFinishLaunchingWithOptions:(NSDictionary *)launchOptions
{
    // Create an empty array to get us started
    self.tasks = [NSMutableArray array];

    ...

}
```

Finally, modify the implementation of **addTask:** to display the task in the table view.

```
#pragma mark - Actions

- (void)addTask:(id)sender
{
    // Get the task
    NSString *text = [self.taskField text];

    // Quit here if taskField is empty
    if ([text length] == 0) {
        return;
    }

    // Log task to console
    NSLog(@"User entered: %@", text);

    // Add it to the working array
    [self.tasks addObject:text];

    // Refresh the table so that the new item shows up
    [self.taskTable reloadData];

    // Clear out the text field
    [self.taskField setText:@""];

    // Dismiss the keyboard
    [self.taskField resignFirstResponder];
}
```

Build and run the application. Enter a few tasks for your list. Each one should appear in the table view.

Figure 31.12 iTahDoodle app, completed

Figure 31.13 shows the complete object diagram including the data source relationship that you established and the strings added to the tasks array.

Figure 31.13 Complete object diagram for iTahDoodle

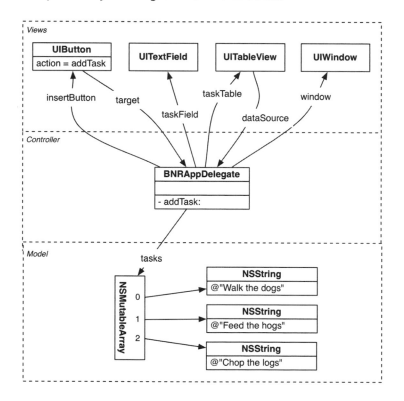

Saving and loading data

Currently, if the user force-quits iTahDoodle, or if the system terminates the application while the user is doing something else, then any changes to the task list are lost and the user will have to enter them all over again when they restart the application. This is not the user experience you want. When users quit the app, they would like their to-do lists to stick around so that they can refer them again later. In this section, you will enable iTahDoodle to save a user's tasks between runs of the application.

Adding a C helper function

To save the user's tasks between runs, iTahDoodle will store the tasks to disk as a property list – an XML file. You will need a way to get this file's location while your application is running. Thus, you are going to write a C function named **BNRDocPath** that returns that file path as an **NSString**.

In Objective-C, we usually get things done with methods. So when we do use a C function in an Objective-C application, we often refer to it as a *helper function*.

In BNRAppDelegate.h, declare **BNRDocPath()**.

```
#import <UIKit/UIKit.h>

// Declare a helper function that you will use to get a path
// to the location on disk where you can save the to-do list
NSString *BNRDocPath(void);

@interface BNRAppDelegate : UIResponder
      <UIApplicationDelegate, UITableViewDataSource>

...
```

Notice that you declare **BNRDocPath()** above the class declaration. Even though **BNRDocPath()** is declared in the file BNRAppDelegate.h, it is not part of the **BNRAppDelegate** class. In fact, this function could have its own header and implementation files in the iTahDoodle project. However, because there is just one helper function in iTahDoodle, you are putting it in the app delegate's class files to keep things simple.

In BNRAppDelegate.m, implement **BNRDocPath()**. Be sure to implement it after the #import but before the @implementation line (which is where the implementation of the **BNRDelegate** class begins).

```
#import "BNRAppDelegate.h"

// Helper function to fetch the path to our to-do data stored on disk
NSString *BNRDocPath()
{
    NSArray *pathList = NSSearchPathForDirectoriesInDomains(NSDocumentDirectory,
                                                            NSUserDomainMask,
                                                            YES);
    return [pathList[0] stringByAppendingPathComponent:@"data.td"];
}

@implementation BNRAppDelegate

...
```

Note that the **BNRDocPath()** function uses the function **NSSearchPathForDirectoriesInDomains()** that we discussed in Chapter 26.

Saving task data

When a Cocoa Touch application quits or is sent to the background, it sends its delegate a message from the UIApplicationDelegate protocol so that the delegate can take care of business and respond to these events gracefully.

In BNRAppDelegate.m, find the **applicationDidEnterBackground:** method and replace its contents with code that uses **BNRDocPath()** to save the task list when the user leaves the app:

```
- (void)applicationDidEnterBackground:(UIApplication *)application
{
    // Save our tasks array to disk
    [self.tasks writeToFile:BNRDocPath() atomically:YES];
}
```

Now any tasks that the user inserted will be written to disk for safekeeping.

Loading task data

To finish, you need to load the user's saved tasks when the application is launched.

In BNRAppDelegate.m, add the following code at the beginning of **application:didFinishLaunchingWithOptions:**.

```
#pragma mark - Application delegate callbacks

- (BOOL)application:(UIApplication *)application
didFinishLaunchingWithOptions:(NSDictionary *)launchOptions
{
    // Create an empty array to get us started
    self.tasks = [NSMutableArray array];

    // Load an existing dataset or create a new one
    NSArray *plist = [NSArray arrayWithContentsOfFile:BNRDocPath()];
    if (plist) {
        // We have a dataset; copy it into tasks
        self.tasks = [plist mutableCopy];
    } else {
        // There is no dataset; create an empty array
        self.tasks = [NSMutableArray array];
    }

    // Create and configure the UIWindow instance
    // A CGRect is a struct with an origin (x,y) and a size (width,height)
    CGRect winFrame = [[UIScreen mainScreen] bounds];
    UIWindow *theWindow = [[UIWindow alloc] initWithFrame:winFrame];
    self.window = theWindow;
    ...
}
```

Build and run the application. Insert some tasks and click the Home button. Then click iTahDoodle's icon to restart the app. Your tasks will be there waiting for you.

Note that the data will only be saved and restored when the application goes into the background or terminates gracefully. If you stop the app from Xcode while it is active, the data may not be saved.

Congratulations! You have created your first iOS app. There is much, much more out there to do and learn, and we hope you are looking forward to the challenge.

For the more curious: what about main()?

When you began learning C and Objective-C, you learned that the entry point into your program's code is the `main()` function. It is absolutely true in Cocoa and Cocoa Touch development as well, although it is extremely rare to edit this function in Cocoa and Cocoa Touch applications. Open `main.m`, and you will see why:

```
return UIApplicationMain(argc, argv, nil, NSStringFromClass([BNRAppDelegate class]));
```

Well, that was anti-climactic. Only one line of actual code.

The `UIApplicationMain` function creates the necessary objects for your application to run. First, it creates a single instance of the `UIApplication` class. Then, it creates an instance of whatever class is denoted by the fourth and final argument and sets it to be the application's delegate, so that it can send its delegate messages when memory gets low, when the application is quit or backgrounded, or when it finishes launching.

And that is the trail from `main()` to `application:didFinishLaunchingWithOptions:` and your custom code.

For the more curious: running iTahDoodle on a device

Right now, your app is running on the simulator. To run it on a device (or to publish apps to the App Store), you will need to join Apple's iOS Developer Program, which costs $99 per year. Once you are a member, you can register yourself and your devices with the developer portal. This information will be used to create a provisioning profile for your apps that will enable you to run them on your devices.

The provisioning process is complicated and a pain. To help you get through it, Apple has written an *App Distribution Guide* that describes the necessary steps in detail. Search for it on Apple's iOS developer website.

In fact, unless you can't live without seeing iTahDoodle on your iPhone, we suggest that you save this adventure until you are working through an iOS development book, like *iOS Programming: The Big Nerd Ranch Guide*.

32

Your First Cocoa Application

In this chapter, you are going to create TahDoodle, a desktop application for Mac. Like iTahDoodle, TahDoodle is a simple to-do list application that stores its data as a property list. Like the last chapter, this application is very simple; it will give you a quick taste of how Cocoa development works.

TahDoodle will be a *document-based application*. This allows users to have multiple windows (each representing a different file) open at the same time.

Figure 32.1 Complete TahDoodle application

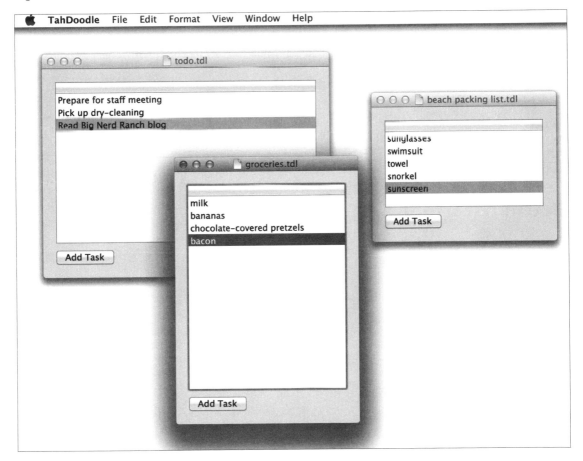

Here is an object diagram of the complete TahDoodle application.

Figure 32.2 Object diagram for TahDoodle

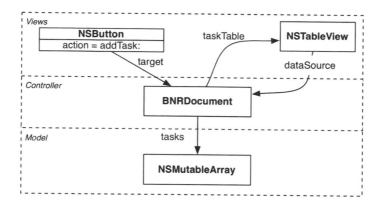

You will present the task list in an instance of **NSTableView**. An instance of **NSButton** will allow users to add a row to the table view so that a new task can be added. Any task can be edited directly in the **NSTableView**.

An instance of a class named **BNRDocument** is the controller for TahDoodle. It will connect the model object (a mutable array of strings) with two view objects. The view objects are the **NSButton** and the **NSTableView**.

The **NSButton** has a target-action pair. When it is clicked, it will send the **addTask:** message to the **BNRDocument**. The **BNRDocument** will also be the data source for the **NSTableView**.

In the last chapter, you created your view objects and made these connections programmatically. In this chapter, you are going to use Interface Builder, Xcode's drag-and-drop tool for building user interfaces.

Getting started with TahDoodle

In Xcode, choose File → New → Project... Under the OS X section (not iOS), click Application. From the template choices that appear, select Cocoa Application.

Figure 32.3 Choose Cocoa Application template

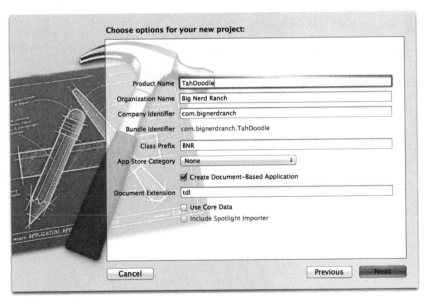

In the next window, name the project TahDoodle (Figure 32.4). Check the box to Create a Document-Based Application. For the Document Extension, enter tdl. This will be the filename extension used when TahDoodle documents (to-do lists) are saved.

Figure 32.4 Configuring TahDoodle

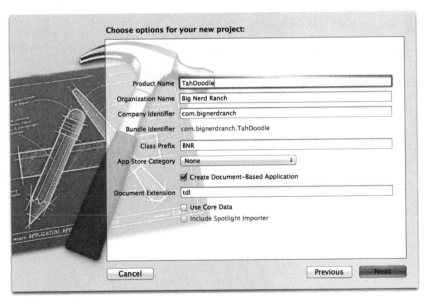

Click Next and finish creating your project.

The template created the **BNRDocument** class for you. This class is the controller for TahDoodle. For each to-do list that the user has open, there will be an instance of **BNRDocument**, which will act as the controller for that window.

Open BNRDocument.h. Add two properties and one instance method:

```
#import <Cocoa/Cocoa.h>

@interface BNRDocument : NSDocument

@property (nonatomic) NSMutableArray *tasks;

@property (nonatomic) IBOutlet NSTableView *taskTable;

- (IBAction)addTask:(id)sender;

@end
```

First, note that you have not declared a property for the **NSButton**. All the work to create and wire up this view object will be done in Interface Builder. You do not need a property for it because you will not be interacting with the button programmatically.

Second, you used two new keywords: IBOutlet and IBAction. IBOutlet tells Xcode that the taskTable pointer will be assigned in Interface Builder and not in the class's code files. IBAction tells Xcode that **addTask:** is an action method and that the associated target-action pair will be configured in Interface Builder and not in the class's code files.

Setting up views in Interface Builder

In the project navigator, find and select BNRDocument.xib. When you select a file in the project navigator that ends in .xib, Interface Builder opens in the editor area. Instead of code, you will see a layout grid displaying view objects defined in that XIB (XML Interface Builder document) file.

Right now, there are two view objects defined in BNRDocument.xib: a window and a text field. These are instances of **NSWindow** and **NSTextField**.

Figure 32.5 Current BNRDocument.xib contents

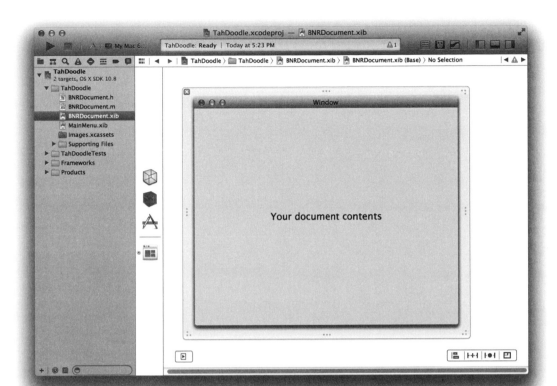

If you were to run this application now, a window would appear with the text Your document contents here centered in the window.

The window object is an instance of **NSWindow**. The template defined this object for you in the BNRDocument.xib. You simply use it as a canvas upon which you build your interface. You will not interact with it in code in TahDoodle.

In BNRDocument.xib, click the Your document contents here text to select the text field. Then press the Delete key on your keyboard to remove this object from the layout.

In the upper righthand corner of the Xcode window, click the button to reveal the utilities area.

The bottom half of the utilities area is the *library*. The library is divided into tabs. Select the ❀ tab to reveal the *object library*. The object library presents the different object types that you can drag and drop on the layout grid to build your user interface.

Setting up the button

At the bottom of the library is a search field. Search for "button." The first item, Push Button, represents an instance of the **NSButton** class.

Here is the fun part. To create an instance of **NSButton** and add it to your layout, simply drag from the Push Button item in the object library to anywhere on the window object in the layout grid.

Figure 32.6 Dragging from library to layout grid

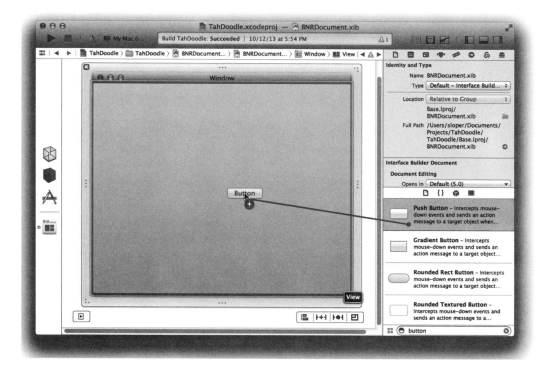

Now there is an instance of **NSButton** in TahDoodle's user interface. Not only have you created a button object, but by dragging it onto the window object, you have also added it as a subview of the window.

Being a subview of the window is important; it is what gets a view object on screen when the application is launched. In iTahDoodle, you added the button to the window in BNRAppDelegate.m:

```
- (BOOL)application:(UIApplication *)application
didFinishLaunchingWithOptions:(NSDictionary *)launchOptions
{
    ...

    [self.window addSubview:self.insertButton];

    ...
}
```

Let's get that button in the right place. Drag the button to the lower lefthand corner of the window object. When you get close to the corner, blue dashed lines will appear. Position the button just inside the lines (Figure 32.7).

Figure 32.7 Changing the button's position

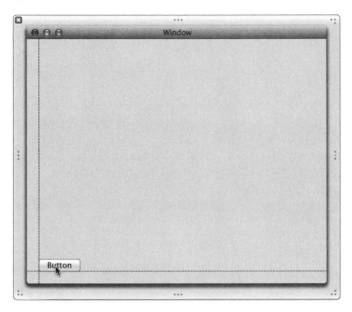

The dashed lines are from Apple's Human Interface Guidelines, or HIGs. The HIGs are a set of rules that developers should follow when designing user interfaces for the Mac. There are also HIGs for the iPhone and iPad. You can browse all of the HIGs in the developer documentation.

Now you need to change the button's title to Add Task. In iTahDoodle, you set the button's title in BNRAppDelegate.m:

```
- (BOOL)application:(UIApplication *)application
didFinishLaunchingWithOptions:(NSDictionary *)launchOptions
{
    ...

    [self.insertButton setTitle:@"Insert"
                    forState:UIControlStateNormal];
    ...
}
```

Setting the button's title in Interface Builder is even simpler: double-click the button object, type Add Task, and press Return. The object will resize itself to fit the slightly longer title.

Setting up the table view

Return to the object library and search for "table view." Select the Table View item and drag it to the upper lefthand corner of the window. Keep it just inside the dashed blue guidelines.

If you see a warning about a "misplaced view," you can ignore it; you will fix the placement of your views in the next section.

This table view object is actually a collection of nested objects: an **NSScrollView**, which contains an **NSTableView**, which, by default, contains two **NSTableColumn** instances. To get to a particular object within this collection, hold down the Control and Shift keys while clicking on the table view. You will see a list of objects and can select the object you are really interested in. Select the **NSTableView**.

Figure 32.8 Selecting **NSTableView**

Now you are going to set the table view's number of columns using another tool – the *inspector*.

The inspector is in the utilities area above the the object library. It is your one-stop shop for finding out about and configuring the object that is selected in the layout grid.

Like the object library, the inspector is organized in a set of tabs, and each tab is a different inspector.

Click the ☞ tab to get to the *attributes inspector*. The attributes inspector is where you can see and modify the object's attributes.

In the attributes inspector, find the Columns attribute of the **NSTableView**. Modify the **NSTableView** to have only one column.

Figure 32.9 Setting the number of columns

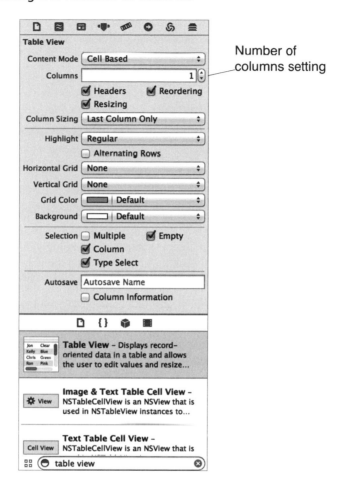

Now you need to adjust the size of the table view. This is easy to do back in the layout grid. Control-Shift-click the table view and select the **NSScrollView**, which contains the **NSTableView**. Drag the scroll view's bottom right corner so that it fills most of the window. Leave space for the button and stay inside the blue guidelines.

The objects that you have created and configured just now are described in XML in BNRDocument.xib. They will be automatically allocated and initialized at runtime when a new TahDoodle window opens and a new instance of **BNRDocument** is created.

(If you want to see the XML, right-click BNRDocument.xib in the project navigator and select Open As → Source Code.)

Build and run TahDoodle. You may need to click on the application icon in your Dock to see the window. Select File → New in TahDoodle's menu bar or use the keyboard shortcut Command-N to open a second window. Each window is a separate instance of **BNRDocument** and a separate set of view objects.

Adding autolayout constraints

To control how your user interface will appear when the window resizes, you can create several *autolayout constraints*. An autolayout constraint specifies an individual relationship between the views in your application.

In a desktop application, autolayout constraints are typically used to control how your user interface appears when the window is resized. In an iOS app, autolayout constraints are typically used to control how your user interface appears on devices with different screen sizes or font sizes.

Currently, TahDoodle's user interface does not adjust at all when the user resizes the window. The table view and button maintain their position and size no matter the user does with the window. (Try it yourself.)

It would be much better if the table view and button would maintain their positions and if the table view would resize to stretch and shrink along with the window.

Let's start with adding constraints to the table view. Recall that the table view is a nested collection of objects. The outermost object is an instance of **NSScrollView**. You are going to apply four autolayout constraints to specify the layout relationship between the scroll view and the window.

Autolayout constraints are added individually, and Control-Shift-clicking to select the scroll view in the layout grid is tiresome. Thankfully, you can also select a view object from the *document outline*.

In BNRDocument.xib, find the small black left-pointing arrow in a rounded rectangle in the bottom left corner of the editor area (Figure 32.10). Click this arrow to show the document outline. (You can click again to hide the document outline when you need more room to work in the layout grid.)

Figure 32.10 Showing and hiding the document outline

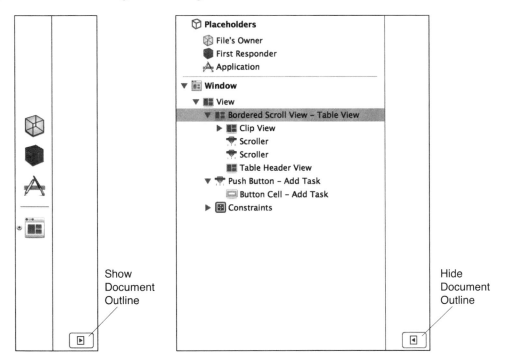

The document outline includes a hierarchical list of your view objects. Under Window, find and select the Bordered Scroll View – Table View object. This is the instance of **NSScrollView** that contains the rest of the objects that make up the table view. From Xcode's menu bar, select Editor → Pin → Leading Space to Superview.

Leading Space to Superview is an autolayout constraint. The scroll view's superview is the window object. Adding this constraint ensures that your view remains a fixed distance from the leading edge of the window regardless of the window's size.

(In most cases, "leading" will mean "lefthand." However, if your user's system is set to a language that runs right to left, then the leading edge is the righthand edge.)

You can see the new constraint listed under the Constraints heading in the document outline. Click this constraint to see it displayed in the layout grid. It will appear as a red strut between the scroll view and the window.

Select the scroll view again in the document outline and add a second autolayout constraint: Editor → Pin → Trailing Space to Superview.

Select the scroll view yet again. Notice that the two struts identifying your autolayout constraints are red. The red color tells you that the scroll view does not yet have enough constraints to ensure its position when the application is running. Let's confirm that.

Build and run TahDoodle. Drag the window's right edge to widen it. The scroll view (and the views it contains) will stretch to maintain the relationships between the window and its leading and trailing edges.

Figure 32.11 Table view resizes itself according to horizontal constraints

However, if you change the height of the window by dragging at the top or bottom, the table view's size will not change. You need constraints for the scroll view's top and bottom.

Select the scroll view and add two more constraints: from the Editor menu, pin Top Space to Superview and Bottom Space to Superview.

Now there are enough constraints to guarantee the scroll view's size and position no matter what the window does. Select the scroll view one more time, and you will see that the struts are now blue.

Figure 32.12 Scroll view's satisfactory constraints

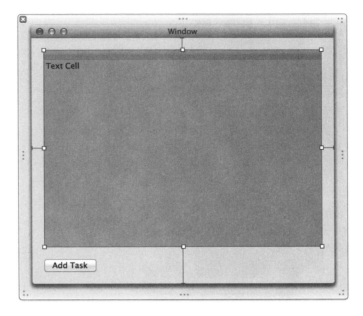

Build and run the application. The scroll view will resize itself as the window does. However, if you make the window taller, the scroll view will cover up the button. Your button needs autolayout constraints of its own to stake out its position.

In the document outline, select the Push Button and add two layout constraints: pin the leading space to the superview and pin the bottom space to the superview.

Build and run the application. The scroll view will resize with the window, and the button will maintain its position in the lower lefthand corner.

Making connections

Creating and configuring views is not all that you can do in Interface Builder. You can also connect the view objects in your XIB file to your application's code. In particular, you can set target-action pairs and assign pointers.

File's Owner

In BNRDocument.xib, find the Placeholders heading in the document outline. A *placeholder* stands in for a particular object that cannot be specified until runtime.

One of these placeholders is File's Owner. File's Owner stands in for the object that will load the XIB file as its user interface. In your case, it represents the instance of **BNRDocument**.

Setting the button's target-action pair

Recall from the object diagram at the beginning of the chapter (Figure 32.2) that the **NSButton** has a target-action pair: its target is the instance of **BNRDocument**, and its action is **addTask:**.

For iTahDoodle, you configured the target-action pair for the button in BNRAppDelegate.m:

```
- (BOOL)application:(UIApplication *)application
didFinishLaunchingWithOptions:(NSDictionary *)launchOptions
{
    ...

    [self.insertButton addTarget:self
                          action:@selector(addTask:)
                forControlEvents:UIControlEventTouchUpInside];
    ...
}
```

For TahDoodle, you are going to make this connection in Interface Builder.

In the layout grid, select the Add Task button. While pressing and holding the Control key, drag from the button to File's Owner in the document outline.

Figure 32.13 Making a connection

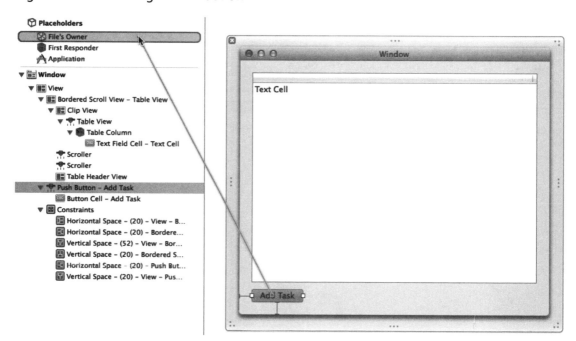

Release the mouse button, and a list of methods will appear. Select **addTask:**.

Figure 32.14 Selecting an action

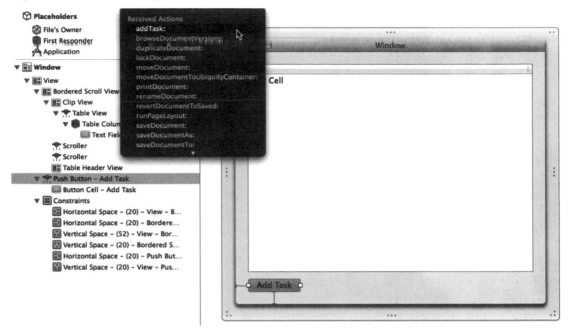

When you Control-dragged from the button to File's Owner, you set **BNRDocument** as the target of the button. When you selected **addTask:** from the list, you set this method as the action of the button.

Note that **addTask:** was only available to choose from the list of methods because you included the IBAction keyword in its declaration in BNRDocument.h:

```
- (IBAction)addTask:(id)sender;
```

IBAction is a flag for Interface Builder that says "Hey! When I try to connect a target-action pair in IB, make sure to include this method in the list of possible actions."

Here is the actual definition of IBAction:

```
#define IBAction void
```

Remember what you learned about #define in Chapter 25? This statement tells you that IBAction is replaced with void before the compiler sees it. All IBAction keywords can replaced with void because actions invoked by user interface controls are not expected to have a return value.

To run and test this connection, you must implement **addTask:**. In the project navigator, select BNRDocument.m. You are now out of Interface Builder and back in your familiar code editor.

In BNRDocument.m, first add a pragma mark to group the existing methods in **BNRDocument**:

```
#import "BNRDocument.h"

@implementation BNRDocument

#pragma mark - NSDocument Overrides

...

@end
```

Then implement **addTask:** as a stub that logs a message to the console:

```
#import "BNRDocument.h"

@implementation BNRDocument

#pragma mark - NSDocument Overrides

...

# pragma mark - Actions

- (void)addTask:(id)sender
{
    NSLog(@"Add Task button clicked!");
}

@end
```

Build and run the application. Click the Add Task button and confirm that your target-action pair is working as expected.

Connecting the table view

Earlier in the chapter, you declared the taskTable pointer in BNRDocument.h:

```
@property (nonatomic) IBOutlet NSTableView *taskTable;
```

You want to assign the **NSTableView** object in BNRDocument.xib to this pointer.

Reopen BNRDocument.xib. Control-drag from File's Owner (standing in for the **BNRDocument**) to the table view in the layout grid. When you release the mouse button, choose taskTable from the list of connections.

Figure 32.15 Making more connections

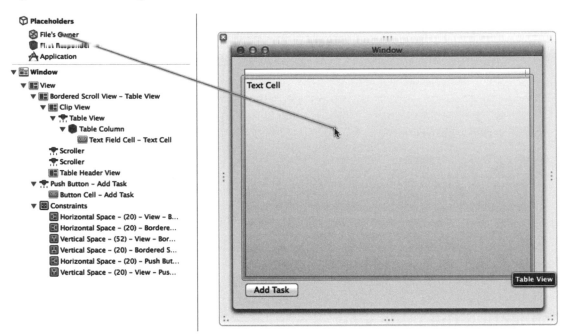

Now the `taskTable` pointer that you declared in BNRDocument.h points to the specific instance of **NSTableView** defined in BNRDocument.xib.

"Outlet" is just another word for "object pointer." Recall that you included IBOutlet when declaring the `taskTable` pointer:

```
@property (nonatomic) IBOutlet NSTableView *taskTable;
```

Unlike IBAction, IBOutlet is defined so that it will disappear completely before the compiler sees it:

```
#define IBOutlet
```

Thus, at compile time, all IBOutlet keywords get removed, leaving behind the outlets (pointers) themselves.

NSTableView has a few pointers of its own, including dataSource. You want the instance of **BNRDocument** to be assigned to the table view's dataSource pointer.

In the layout grid, Control-Shift-click on the table view to select the **NSTableView**. Then Control-drag from the table view to File's Owner. When you release the mouse button, choose dataSource from the list of connections.

Figure 32.16 Connecting the table view's data source

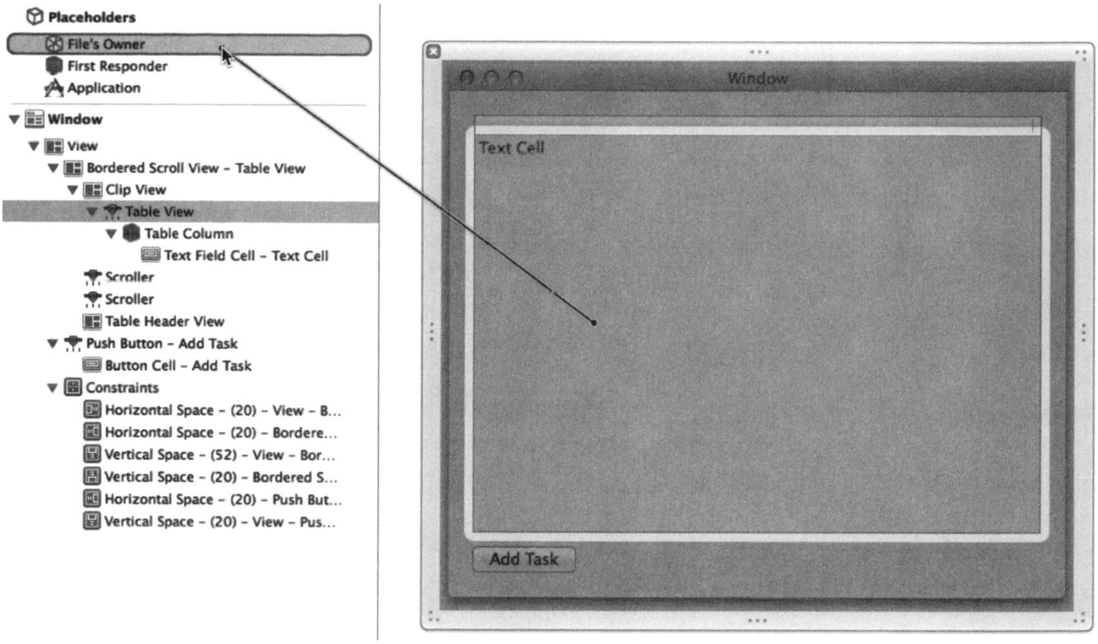

This accomplishes the same thing that you did in iTahDoodle with the following code:

```
- (BOOL)application:(UIApplication *)application
didFinishLaunchingWithOptions:(NSDictionary *)launchOptions
{
    ...

    self.taskTable.dataSource - self;

    ...
}
```

Implementing NSTableViewDataSource

Now that you have TahDoodle's user interface created, configured, and connected, the next step is to get the data source-table view relationship working. You cannot do this in Interface Builder, so it is time to go back to writing code.

Reopen BNRDocument.h and declare that **BNRDocument** conforms to the NSTableViewDataSource protocol:

```
#import <Cocoa/Cocoa.h>

@interface BNRDocument : NSDocument
    <NSTableViewDataSource>

...

@end
```

In BNRDocument.m, implement the two required NSTableViewDataSource methods:

```
#pragma mark Data Source Methods

- (NSInteger)numberOfRowsInTableView:(NSTableView *)tv
{
    // This table view displays the tasks array,
    // so the number of entries in the table view will be the same
    // as the number of objects in the array
    return [self.tasks count];
}

- (id)tableView:(NSTableView *)tableView
 objectValueForTableColumn:(NSTableColumn *)tableColumn
            row:(NSInteger)row
{
    // Return the item from tasks that corresponds to the cell
    // that the table view wants to display
    return [self.tasks objectAtIndex:row];
}

- (void)tableView:(NSTableView *)tableView
   setObjectValue:(id)object
   forTableColumn:(NSTableColumn *)tableColumn
              row:(NSInteger)row
{
    // When the user changes a task on the table view,
    // update the tasks array
    [self.tasks replaceObjectAtIndex:row withObject:object];

    // And then flag the document as having unsaved changes.
    [self updateChangeCount:NSChangeDone];
}
```

Finally, in BNRDocument.m, update the implementation of **addTask:** to actually add tasks.

```
#import "BNRDocument.h"

@implementation BNRDocument

...

#pragma mark - Actions

- (IBAction)addTask:(id)sender
{
    NSLog(@"Add Task button clicked!");
    // If there is no array yet, create one
    if (!self.tasks) {
        self.tasks = [NSMutableArray array];
    }

    [self.tasks addObject:@"New Item"];

    // -reloadData tells the table view to refresh and ask its dataSource
    // (which happens to be this BNRDocument object in this case)
    // for new data to display
    [self.taskTable reloadData];
```

```
    // -updateChangeCount: tells the application whether or not the document
    // has unsaved changes, NSChangeDone flags the document as unsaved
    [self updateChangeCount:NSChangeDone];
}
```

Build and run TahDoodle. Click the button to add a row to the table view. Double-click the row to edit its contents.

Saving and loading data

To add the ability to save and reopen a task list, you need to override two methods inherited from **BNRDocument**'s superclass, **NSDocument**:

```
- (NSData *)dataOfType:(NSString *)typeName
                error:(NSError **)outError
{
    // This method is called when our document is being saved
    // You are expected to hand the caller an NSData object wrapping our data
    // so that it can be written to disk
    // If there is no array, write out an empty array
    if (!self.tasks) {
        self.tasks = [NSMutableArray array];
    }

    // Pack the tasks array into an NSData object
    NSData *data = [NSPropertyListSerialization
                        dataWithPropertyList:self.tasks
                                      format:NSPropertyListXMLFormat_v1_0
                                     options:0
                                       error:outError];

    // Return the newly-packed NSData object
    return data;
}

- (BOOL)readFromData:(NSData *)data
              ofType:(NSString *)typeName
               error:(NSError **)outError
{
    // This method is called when a document is being loaded
    // You are handed an NSData object and expected to pull our data out of it
    // Extract the tasks
    self.tasks = [NSPropertyListSerialization
                        propertyListWithData:data
                                     options:NSPropertyListMutableContainers
                                      format:NULL
                                       error:outError];

    // return success or failure depending on success of the above call
    return (self.tasks != nil);
}
```

Notice that you are implementing a method that takes in an **NSError****. In this case, you are merely handing back the **NSError** generated by **propertyListWithData:options:format:error:**, but you could also create and hand back a new **NSError** as well, depending on the nature of the failure.

Build and run the application again. Add some tasks to the list. Save and close the list (using the familiar menu commands or keyboard shortcuts), and then reopen it. Congratulations! TahDoodle is complete.

So when should you use Interface Builder to create your user interface and when should you set up views programmatically? Under simple circumstances, either will work. iTahDoodle's interface could have been built using Interface Builder; TahDoodle's views could have been created programmatically.

In general, however, the more complex your user interface, the more sense it makes to use Interface Builder.

Now that you have seen more of Xcode, take a look at the tear-out card at the back of this book. This card contains keyboard shortcuts for navigating around Xcode. As you continue with Xcode, use this card to find shortcuts that will save you time and clicks.

Challenge

Add a Delete Selected Item button that deletes the currently-selected task.

Part V
Advanced Objective-C

You now know enough Objective-C to get started with iOS or Cocoa programming. But don't rush off just yet. These next chapters provide a gentle discussion of techniques and concepts that will be useful in your first year as an Objective-C programmer.

33
init

In the **NSObject** class, there is a method named **init**. Using **init** looks like this:

```
NSMutableArray *things = [[NSMutableArray alloc] init];
```

You send the **init** message to the new instance so that it can initialize its instance variables to usable values; **alloc** creates the space for an object, and **init** makes the object ready to work. Notice that **init** is an instance method that returns the address of the initialized object. It is the *initializer* for **NSObject**. This chapter is about how to write initializers.

Writing init methods

Create a new project: a Foundation Command Line Tool called Appliances. In this program, you are going to create two classes: **BNRAppliance** and **BNROwnedAppliance** (a subclass of **BNRAppliance**). An instance of **BNRAppliance** will have a productName and a voltage. An instance of **BNROwnedAppliance** will also have a set containing the names of its owners.

Figure 33.1 **BNRAppliance** and its subclass, **BNROwnedAppliance**

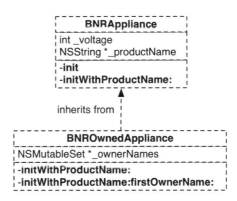

Create a new file: an **NSObject** subclass named **BNRAppliance**. In BNRAppliance.h, create property declarations for productName and voltage:

```
#import <Foundation/Foundation.h>

@interface BNRAppliance : NSObject

@property (nonatomic, copy) NSString *productName;
@property (nonatomic) int voltage;

@end
```

You would create an instance of **BNRAppliance** like this:

```
BNRAppliance *a = [[BNRAppliance alloc] init];
```

Note that because **BNRAppliance** does not implement an **init** method, it will execute the **init** method defined in **NSObject**. When this happens, all the instance variables specific to **BNRAppliance** are zeroed out. Thus, the productName of a new instance of **BNRAppliance** will be nil, and voltage will be zero.

A basic init method

In some cases, an initial value of zero for your instance variables may work fine. In others, however, you will need instances of your class to come into the world with their instance variables initialized to non-zero values.

Let's say that every instance of **BNRAppliance** should start its life with a voltage of 120. In BNRAppliance.m, override **NSObject**'s **init** method by adding a new implementation of **init**.

```
- (instancetype)init
{
    // Call the NSObject's init method
    self = [super init];

    // Did it return something non-nil?
    if (self) {

        // Give voltage a starting value
        _voltage = 120;
    }

    // Return a pointer to the new object
    return self;
}
```

Now when you create a new instance of **BNRAppliance**, it will have a voltage of 120 by default. (Note that this does not change anything about the accessor methods. After the instance is initialized, it can be changed just as before using **setVoltage:**.)

instancetype

This **init** method returns an instancetype. The instancetype keyword tells the compiler to expect an instance of the class to which a method belongs. Any initializers you write or override should always return instancetype.

Why not return BNRAppliance * from **BNRAppliance**'s initializer? Doing so could cause problems if **BNRAppliance** were subclassed. Imagine there was an **BNRAppliance** subclass named **BNROven**. **BNROven** would inherit an initializer declared as:

```
- (BNRAppliance *)init;
```

However, if an **init** message were sent to an instance of **BNROven**, an instance of **BNROven** would be returned. While an **BNROven** is technically a **BNRAppliance**, the discrepancy could cause problems later that would be hard to figure out. Using instancetype ensures that initializers can be safely inherited.

Sometimes you will see initializers returning id. Before Xcode 4.3 (when instancetype was introduced), developers returned id from initializers. Recall that id means "any object," so id also provides flexibility for subclassing when writing your own initializers. However, instancetype is the better option. It provides flexibility but still lets the compiler check the type of what is returned against the rest of your code.

Using and checking the superclass initializer

Your **init** method begins with two checks:

- In the first line of **init**, you set self to point to the object returned from the superclass's **init** method.

- You check that the superclass's initializer returns a valid object and not nil.

What do these checks do? A few classes have deviant **init** methods. There are two possible forms of deviance:

- The **init** method figures out a clever optimization that it can do, deallocates the original object, allocates a different object, and returns the new object.

  To address this possibility, Apple *requires* that you set self to point to the object returned from the superclass's initializer.

- The **init** method fails, deallocates the object, and returns nil.

  To deal with this possibility, Apple *recommends* that you check that the superclass's initializer returns a valid object and not nil. After all, there is no point in performing custom set-up on an object that does not exist.

Truthfully, these sorts of checks are only necessary in a couple of very specific cases. Thus, in practice, many Objective-C programmers often skip the second check. In this book, however, we will always do both because it is the Apple-approved way to implement **init** methods.

init methods that take arguments

Sometimes an object cannot be initialized properly without some information from the method that is calling it. For example, imagine that an appliance cannot function without a name. (nil does not count.) In this case, you need to be able to pass the initializer a name to use.

You cannot do this with **init** because, for now and always, **init** has no arguments. So you have to create a new initializer instead. Then, when another method creates an instance of **BNRAppliance**, it would look like this:

```
BNRAppliance *a = [[BNRAppliance alloc] initWithProductName:@"Toaster"];
```

The new initializer for **BNRAppliance** is **initWithProductName:**, and it accepts an **NSString** as an argument. Declare this new method in BNRAppliance.h:

```
#import <Foundation/Foundation.h>

@interface BNRAppliance : NSObject

@property (nonatomic, copy) NSString *productName;
@property (nonatomic) int voltage;
- (instancetype)initWithProductName:(NSString *)pn;

@end
```

In BNRAppliance.m, find the implementation of **init**. Change the name of the method to **initWithProductName:** and set productName using the passed-in value.

```
- (instancetype)initWithProductName:(NSString *)pn
{
    // Call NSObject's init method
    self = [super init];

    // Did it return something non-nil?
    if (self) {

        // Set the product name
        _productName = [pn copy];

        // Give voltage a starting value
        _voltage = 120;
    }
    return self;
}
```

Before you continue, build the project to make sure the syntax is right.

Now you can create an instance of **BNRAppliance** with a given name. However, if you give BNRAppliance.h and BNRAppliance.m to another programmer, this programmer may not know to call **initWithProductName:**. What if the programmer creates an instance of **BNRAppliance** in the most common way?

```
BNRAppliance *a = [[BNRAppliance alloc] init];
```

This is not an unreasonable action. As a subclass of **NSObject**, an instance of **BNRAppliance** is expected to do anything an instance of **NSObject** can do. And instances of **NSObject** respond to **init** messages. However, it causes a problem here because the above line of code creates an instance of **BNRAppliance** that has nil for a product name and zero for voltage. And we decided earlier that every instance of **BNRAppliance** needs a voltage of 120 and an actual name to function correctly. How can you prevent this from happening?

The solution is simple. In BNRAppliance.m, add an **init** method to call **initWithProductName:** with a default value for the name.

```
- (instancetype)init
{
    return [self initWithProductName:@"Unknown"];
}
```

Notice that this new overridden **init** does not do much work – it just calls the **initWithProductName:** method, which does the heavy lifting.

To test out your two initializers, you will need a **description** method. Implement **description** in BNRAppliance.m:

```
- (NSString *)description
{
    return [NSString stringWithFormat:@"<%@: %d volts>",
                                           self.productName, self.voltage];
}
```

Now, in main.m, exercise the class a bit:

```
#import <Foundation/Foundation.h>
#import "BNRAppliance.h"

int main (int argc, const char * argv[])
{

    @autoreleasepool {

        BNRAppliance *a = [[BNRAppliance alloc] init];
        NSLog(@"a is %@", a);
        [a setProductName:@"Washing Machine"];
        [a setVoltage:240];
        NSLog(@"a is %@", a);

    }
    return 0;
}
```

Build and run the program.

Using accessors

You have a perfectly good initializer for **BNRAppliance**, but let's take a moment to look at a variation that you will see in other people's code. We typically do a plain assignments in an initializer, but many programmers will use the accessor methods. Change **initWithProductName:** to do this:

```
- (instancetype)initWithProductName:(NSString *)pn
{
    // Call NSObject's init method
    self = [super init];

    // Did it return something non-nil?
    if (self) {

        // Set the product name
        [self setProductName:pn];

        // Give voltage a starting value
        [self setVoltage:120];
    }
    return self;
}
```

In most cases, there is little reason to do one over the other, but it makes for a great argument. The argument goes like this: The assign guy says, "You cannot use an accessor method in an **init** method! The accessor assumes that the object is ready for work, and it is not ready for work until *after* the **init** method is complete." Then the accessor method guy says, "Oh, come on. In the real world that is almost never an issue. My accessor method might be taking care of other stuff for me. I use my accessor anytime I set that variable."

Either approach will work in the vast majority of cases. Build and run the program.

At Big Nerd Ranch, we tend to set the instance variables directly and we typically do the assignment and check for the superclass's initializer in one line. Do this in your **initWithProductName:** method:

```
- (instancetype)initWithProductName:(NSString *)pn
{
    if (self = [super init]) {

        _productName = [pn copy];
        _voltage = 120;
    }
    return self;
}
```

Multiple initializers

Create a new file: a subclass of **BNRAppliance** named **BNROwnedAppliance**. In BNROwnedAppliance.h, add a mutable set of owner names and three methods.

```
#import "BNRAppliance.h"

@interface BNROwnedAppliance : BNRAppliance
@property (readonly) NSSet *ownerNames;
- (instancetype)initWithProductName:(NSString *)pn
                     firstOwnerName:(NSString *)n;
- (void)addOwnerNamesObject:(NSString *)n;
- (void)removeOwnerNamesObject:(NSString *)n;

@end
```

Notice that one of the methods that you have declared is an initializer that takes two arguments.

Implement the methods in BNROwnedAppliance.m:

```objc
#import "BNROwnedAppliance.h"

@interface BNROwnedAppliance ()
{
    NSMutableSet *_ownerNames;
}

@implementation BNROwnedAppliance

- (instancetype)initWithProductName:(NSString *)pn
                     firstOwnerName:(NSString *)n
{
    // Call the superclass's initializer
    if (self = [super initWithProductName:pn])

        // Create a set to hold owners names
        _ownerNames = [[NSMutableSet alloc] init];

        // Is the first owner name non-nil?
        if (n) {
            [_ownerNames addObject:n];
        }
    }
    // Return a pointer to the new object
    return self;
}

- (void)addOwnerName:(NSString *)n
{
    [_ownerNames addObject:n];
}

- (void)removeOwnerName:(NSString *)n
{
    [_ownerNames removeObject:n];
}

- (NSSet *)ownerNames
{
    return [_ownerNames copy];
}


@end
```

Note that this class does not initialize voltage or productName. The **initWithProductName:** in **BNRAppliance** takes care of those. When you create a subclass, you typically only need to initialize the instance variables that the subclass introduced; let the superclass take care of the instance variables that it introduced.

Now, however, you face the same situation as you did with **BNRAppliance** and its superclass's initializer, **init**. At the moment, one of your co-workers might create a terrible bug with this line of code:

```objc
OwnedAppliance *a = [[OwnedAppliance alloc] initWithProductName:@"Toaster"];
```

This code will cause the **initWithProductName:** method in **BNRAppliance** to run. This method knows nothing about the ownerNames set, which means ownerNames will not get properly initialized for this **BNROwnedAppliance** instance.

The fix here is the same as before. In BNROwnedAppliance.m, add an implementation of the superclass's initializer **initWithProductName:** that calls **initWithProductName:firstOwnerName:** and passes a default value for firstOwnerName.

```
- (instancetype)initWithProductName:(NSString *)pn
{
    return [self initWithProductName:pn firstOwnerName:nil];
}
```

Quiz time: Do you also need to implement **init** in **BNROwnedAppliance**? No. At this point, the following code will work fine:

```
OwnedAppliance *a = [[OwnedAppliance alloc] init];
```

Why? There is no implementation of **init** in **BNROwnedAppliance**, so this line will trigger the **init** method implemented in **BNRAppliance**, which calls [self initWithProductName:@"Unknown"]. self is an instance of **BNROwnedAppliance**, so it calls **initWithProductName:** in **BNROwnedAppliance**, which calls [self initWithProductName:pn firstOwnerName:nil].

What you wind up with is a chain of initializers that call other initializers.

Figure 33.2 Initializer chain

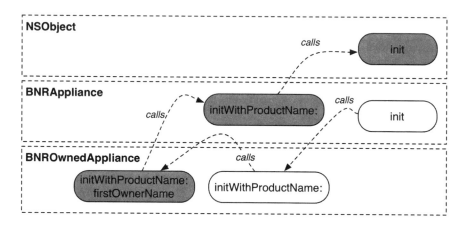

Notice that Figure 33.2 shows one shaded initializer for each class. This initializer is the *designated initializer* for that class. **init** is the designated initializer for **NSObject**, **initWithProductName:** is the designated initializer for **BNRAppliance**, and **initWithProductName:firstOwnerName:** is the designated initializer for **BNROwnedAppliance**.

The designated initializer acts as a funnel-point. A class has only one designated initializer method. If the class has other initializers, then the implementation of those initializers must call (directly or indirectly) the designated initializer.

When you create a class whose designated initializer has a different name than its superclass's designated initializer (as you did in **BNRAppliance** and **BNROwnedAppliance**), you have a responsibility to document that in the header file. Add the appropriate comment in BNRAppliance.h:

```
#import <Foundation/Foundation.h>

@interface BNRAppliance : NSObject

@property (nonatomic, copy) NSString *productName;
@property (nonatomic) int voltage;

// The designated initializer
- (instancetype)initWithProductName:(NSString *)pn;

@end
```

and in BNROwnedAppliance.h:

```
#import "BNRAppliance.h"

@interface BNROwnedAppliance : BNRAppliance

@property (readonly) NSSet *ownerNames;

// The designated initializer
- (instancetype)initWithProductName:(NSString *)pn
           firstOwnerName:(NSString *)n;
- (void)addOwnerName:(NSString *)n;
- (void)removeOwnerName:(NSString *)n;

@end
```

Thus, we arrive at the rules that all stylish Objective-C programmers follow when writing initializers:

- If a class has several initializers, only one should do the real work. That method is known as the designated initializer. All other initializers should call, either directly or indirectly, the designated initializer.

- The designated initializer will call the superclass's designated initializer before initializing its instance variables.

- If the designated initializer of your class has a different name than the designated initializer of its superclass, you must override the superclass's designated initializer so that it calls the new designated initializer.

- If you have several initializers, clearly document which is the designated initializer in the header.

Deadly init methods

Every once in a while, however, you cannot safely override the superclass's designated initializer. Let's say that you are creating a subclass of **NSObject** called **BNRWallSafe**, and its designated initializer is **initWithSecretCode:**. However, having a default value for secretCode is not secure enough for your application. This means that the pattern we have been using – overriding **init** to call the new class's designated initializer with default values – is not acceptable.

So what do you do? An instance of **BNRWallSafe** will still respond to an **init** message. Someone could easily do this:

```
BNRWallSafe *ws = [[BNRWallSafe alloc] init];
```

The best thing to do is to override the superclass's designated initializer in a way that lets developers know that they have made a mistake and tells them how to fix it:

```
- (instancetype)init
{
    [NSException raise:@"BNRWallSafeInitialization"
                format:@"Use initWithSecretCode:, not init"];
}
```

Throwing an exception like this will crash the program. In the console output, developers will see their mistake that led to the crash.

34

More about Properties

By now, you have used properties in many programs. In this chapter, you will learn a few more things about properties and what you can make them do.

More on property attributes

First let's take a closer look at the different attributes you can use to control how the accessors will be created.

Mutability

A property can be declared `readwrite` or `readonly`. The default is `readwrite`, which means that both a setter and a getter method are created. If you do not want a setter method to be created, you mark the property as `readonly`:

```
@property (readonly) int voltage;
```

Lifetime specifiers

A property can also be declared `unsafe_unretained`, `assign`, `strong`, `weak`, or `copy`. This option determines how the setter handles the property's memory management.

`assign` is the default for non-object types and the simplest: it just assigns the passed-in value to the property. Imagine this declaration and definition:

```
@property (assign) int averageScore;
// "@property int averageScore" would also work here
```

This would result in a setter method that is pretty much equivalent to:

```
- (void)setAverageScore:(int)d
{
    _averageScore = d;
}
```

In **BNRAppliance**, `voltage` is an assigned property. You will always use `assign` for properties that hold non-objects. Because it is the default for non-object types, you do not have to add it to your property declaration.

strong, as you learned in Chapter 23, will ensure that a strong reference is kept to the passed-in object. It will also let go of ownership of the old object (which will then deallocate itself if it has no other owners). For object properties, strong is the default for object pointers, and that is usually what you want.

weak does not imply ownership of the object pointed to. If this object is deallocated, then the property will be set to nil. This is a neat feature that keeps you safe from *dangling pointers*. A dangling pointer points to an object that no longer exists. Sending a message to a dangling pointer usually crashes your program.

unsafe_unretained properties, like weak properties, do not imply ownership. However, an unsafe_unretained property is not automatically set to nil when the object that it points to is deallocated.

copy forms a strong reference to a copy of the passed-in object. But there is a detail in this that most people misunderstand …

copy

The copy option makes a copy of an object and then changes the pointer to refer to this copy. Imagine you had a property declaration and definition like this:

```
@property (copy) NSString *lastName;
```

The generated setter method would look pretty much like this:

```
- (void)setLastName:(NSString *)d
{
    _lastName = [d copy];
}
```

Use of the copy attribute is most common with object types that have mutable subclasses. For example, **NSString** has a subclass called **NSMutableString**. You can imagine that your **setLastName:** method might be passed a mutable string:

```
// Create a mutable string
NSMutableString *x = [[NSMutableString alloc] initWithString:@"Ono"];

// Pass it to setLastName:
[myObj setLastName:x];

// 'copy' prevents this from changing the lastName
[x appendString:@" Lennon"];
```

What if the object passed in is *not* mutable? It seems wasteful to make a copy of an immutable object. The **copy** method just calls **copyWithZone:** and passes nil as the argument. For example, in **NSString**, the **copyWithZone:** method is overridden to look like this:

```
- (id)copyWithZone:(NSZone *)z
{
    return self;
}
```

That is, it does not make a copy at all. (Note that **NSZone** and memory zoning in general are all but deprecated, vestigial features of Cocoa programming, so we will not go further into them here. **copyWithZone:** still has some use, however, and has not been entirely phased out.)

For objects that come in mutable and immutable versions, the **copy** method returns an immutable copy. For example, **NSMutableString** has a **copy** method that returns an instance of **NSString**. If you want the copy to be a mutable object, use the **mutableCopy** method.

There is no property lifetime specifier called mutableCopy. If you wish for your setter to set the property to be a mutable copy of an object, you must implement the setter yourself so that it calls the **mutableCopy** method on the incoming object. For example, in **BNROwnedAppliance**, you might create a **setOwnerNamesInternal:** method:

```
- (void)setOwnerNamesInternal:(NSSet *)newNames
{
    _ownerNamesInternal = [newNames mutableCopy];
}
```

More about copying

Most Objective-C classes that did not come from Apple have no **copyWithZone:** method at all. Objective-C programmers make fewer copies than you might think.

Curiously, the **copy** and **mutableCopy** methods are defined in **NSObject** like this:

```
- (id)copy
{
    return [self copyWithZone:NULL];
}

- (id)mutableCopy
{
    return [self mutableCopyWithZone:NULL];
}
```

Thus, if you have some code like this:

```
BNRAppliance *b = [[BNRAppliance alloc] init];
BNRAppliance *c = [b copy];
```

You will get an error like this:

```
-[BNRAppliance copyWithZone:]: unrecognized
 selector sent to instance 0x100110130
```

The **copyWithZone:** and **mutableCopyWithZone:** methods are declared in the **NSCopying** and **NSMutableCopying** protocols, respectively. Many of the classes in the Foundation framework conform to one or both of these protocols. You can find out what protocols a class conforms to in its class reference in the developer documentation.

If you want your classes to be compatible with the copy property lifetime specifier, then you must ensure that they conform to the **NSCopying** protocol.

Advice on atomic vs. nonatomic

This is an introductory book on programming, and the `atomic/nonatomic` option relates to a relatively advanced topic known as multithreading. Here is what you need to know: the `nonatomic` option will make your setter method run a tiny bit faster. If you look at the headers for Apple's UIKit, every property is marked as `nonatomic`. You should always make your `readwrite` properties `nonatomic`, too.

(I give this advice to everyone. In every group, however, there is someone who knows just enough to be a pain. That person says, "But when I make my app multithreaded, I'll need the protection that atomic setter methods get me." And I *should* say, "I don't think you will write multithreaded code any time soon. And when you do, I don't think atomic setter methods are going to help." But what I really say is "OK, then you should leave your setters atomic." Because you can't tell someone something they aren't ready to hear.)

Unfortunately, the default for properties is `atomic`, so you will need to explicitly mark each of your properties `nonatomic`.

Implementing accessor methods

By default, the compiler synthesizes accessor methods for any property you declare. Usually, accessor method implementations are straightforward and thus well-suited to being handed off to the compiler.

However, there are times where you will need an accessor to do something out of the ordinary. When this is the case, you can implement the accessor yourself in the implementation file.

There are two reasonable cases to implement an accessor yourself:

- You need to update the app's user interface when the change occurs.

- You need to update some cached info when the change occurs.

For example, say you declared a property in a header file:

```
@property (nonatomic, copy) NSString* currentState;
```

When an object calls the **setCurrentState:** method, you want this method to do more than simply change the value of the property. In this case, you can explicitly implement the setter.

```
- (void)setCurrentState:(NSString *)currentState
{
    _currentState = [currentState copy];

    // Some code that updates UI
    ...
}
```

The compiler will see your implementation of **setCurrentState:** and will not create a setter for you. It will still create the getter method **currentState**.

If you declare a property and implement both accessors yourself, the compiler will *not* synthesize an instance variable.

If you still want an instance variable (and you usually do), you must create it yourself by adding an `@synthesize` statement to the class's implementation.

```
#import "Badger.h"

@interface Badger : NSObject ()
@property (nonatomic) mushroom;
@end

@implementation Badger;

@synthesize mushroom = _mushroom;

- (Mushroom *)mushroom
{
    return _mushroom;
}

- (void)setMushroom::(Mushroom *)mush
{
    _mushroom = mush;
}

...
```

The @synthesize statement tells the compiler that an instance variable named _mushroom is the backing variable for the **mushroom** and **setMushroom:** methods and that the instance variable should be created if it does not already exist.

If you left out the @synthesize statement in this case, the compiler would complain that _mushroom is undefined.

When you declare a readonly property, the compiler automatically synthesizes only a getter method and an instance variable. Thus, if you implement the getter method for a readonly property yourself, the effect is the same as implementing both accessors for a readwrite property. The compiler will not synthesize an instance variable, and you will need to synthesize it yourself.

You may be wondering, why declare a property at all in these cases? Declaring the property is still good shorthand for the accessor declarations and leads to visual consistency in your code.

35

Key-Value coding

Key-value coding is the ability to read and set a property using its name. The key-value coding methods are defined in **NSObject**, and thus every object has this capability.

Open main.m and find the line:

```
[a setProductName:@"Washing Machine"];
```

Rewrite the same line to use key-value coding:

```
[a setValue:@"Washing Machine" forKey:@"productName"];
```

In this case, the **setValue:forKey:** method, as defined in **NSObject**, will go looking for a setter method named **setProductName:**. If the object does not have a **setProductName:** method, it will access the instance variable directly.

You can also read the value of a variable using key-value coding. Add a line to main.m that prints out the product name:

```
int main (int argc, const char * argv[])
{
    @autoreleasepool {

        BNRAppliance *a = [[BNRAppliance alloc] init];
        NSLog(@"a is %@", a);
        [a setValue:@"Washing Machine" forKey:@"productName"];
        [a setVoltage:240];
        NSLog(@"a is %@", a);

        NSLog(@"the product name is %@", [a valueForKey:@"productName"]);

    }
    return 0;
}
```

In this case, the **valueForKey:** method, as defined in **NSObjcct**, goes looking for an accessor named **productName**. If there is no **productName** method, the instance variable is accessed directly.

This use of the word "key" seems to bother some readers. You can imagine the problem: the engineer who named these methods needed a word that could mean the name of an instance variable or the name of a property or the name of a method. "Key" was the most specific word that he could come up with.

If you type the name of the property wrong, you will not get a warning from the compiler, but there will be a runtime error. Make this mistake in main.m:

```
    NSLog(@"the product name is %@", [a valueForKey:@"productNammmme"]);
```

When you build and run it, you will see an error:

```
*** Terminating app due to uncaught exception 'NSUnknownKeyException',
reason: '[<BNRAppliance 0x100100dd0> valueForUndefinedKey:]:
this class is not key value coding-compliant for the key productNammmme.'
```

Fix the error before you go on.

Why is key-value coding interesting? Anytime a standard framework wants to push data into your objects, it will use **setValue:forKey:**. Anytime a standard framework wants to read data from your objects, it will use **valueForKey:**. For example, Core Data is a framework that makes it easy to save your objects to a SQLite database and then bring them back to life. It manipulates your custom data-bearing objects using key-value coding.

To prove that key-value coding will manipulate your variables even if you have no accessors, explicitly declare an instance variable for the productName and comment out the @property declaration for productName in BNRAppliance.h:

```
#import <Foundation/Foundation.h>

@interface BNRAppliance : NSObject
{
    NSString *_productName;
}
// @property (nonatomic, copy) NSString *productName;
@property (nonatomic) int voltage;

// The designated initializer
- (instancetype)initWithProductName:(NSString *)pn;

@end
```

Also, remove all use of the methods **setProductName:** and **productName** from BNRAppliance.m:

```
@implementation BNRAppliance

- (instancetype)initWithProductName:(NSString *)pn
{
    if (self = [super init]) {
        _productName = [pn copy];
        _voltage = 120;
    }
    return self;
}

- (instancetype)init
{
    return [self initWithProductName:@"Unknown"];
}

- (NSString *)description
{
    return [NSString stringWithFormat:@"<%@: %d volts>", _productName, self.voltage];
}

@end
```

Build and run the program. Note that even though you have no accessor methods for productName, the variable can still be set and read from other methods. This is an obvious violation of the idea of *object encapsulation* – methods of an object are public, but the instance variables are delicate and should be kept private. If key-value coding was not astonishingly useful, no one would tolerate it.

Non-object types

The key-value coding methods are designed to work with objects, but some properties hold a non-object type, like an int or a float. For example, voltage is an int. How do you set voltage using key-value coding? You use an **NSNumber**.

In main.m, change the line for setting the voltage from this:

```
[a setVoltage:240];
```

to this:

```
[a setValue:[NSNumber numberWithInt:240] forKey:@"voltage"];
```

Add an explicit accessor to BNRAppliance.m so that you can see it getting called:

```
- (void)setVoltage:(int)x
{
    NSLog(@"setting voltage to %d", x);
    _voltage = x;
}
```

Build and run the program.

Similarly, if you ask for the valueForKey:@"voltage", you will get back an **NSNumber** containing the value of voltage.

Key paths

Most applications end up with a relatively complex object graph. For example, you might have a **BNRDepartment** object that has a manager property that is a pointer to an **BNREmployee** object which has an emergencyContact property which is a pointer to a **BNRPerson** object which has a phoneNumber property.

Figure 35.1 Complex object graph

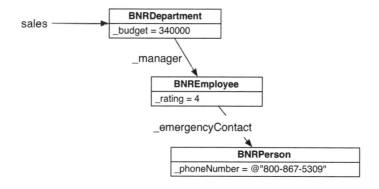

Imagine that you are asked, "What is the phone number of the emergency contact for the manager of the sales department?" You could use key-value coding to traverse these relationships one at a time:

```
BNRDepartment *sales = …;
BNREmployee *sickEmployee = [sales valueForKey:@"manager"];
BNRPerson *personToCall = [sickEmployee valueForKey:@"emergencyContact"];
NSString *numberToDial = [personToCall valueForKey:@"phoneNumber"];
```

However, there is an easier way. Using a key path, you can make the system traverse the relationships for you. Put the keys that you want followed in one long string separated by dots. The order is important; the first relationship you want traversed comes first:

```
BNRDepartment *sales = …;
NSString *numberToDial =
                  [sales valueForKeyPath:@"manager.emergencyContact.phoneNumber"];
```

You can also set the property at the end of a key path:

```
BNRDepartment *sales = …;
[sales setValue:@"555-606-0842" forKeyPath:@"manager.emergencyContact.phoneNumber"];
```

is equivalent to:

```
BNRDepartment *sales = …;
BNREmployee *sickEmployee = [sales valueForKey:@"manager"];
BNRPerson *personToCall = [sickEmployee valueForKey:@"emergencyContact"];
[personToCall setValue:@"555-606-0842" forKey:@"phoneNumber"];
```

36

Key-Value Observing

Key-value observing is a technique that lets you get a notification when a particular property of an object changes. Although you will not use it everyday, key-value observing (or KVO) is a crucial part of what makes Cocoa bindings and Core Data possible.

Essentially, you tell an object, "I want to watch your fido property. If it changes, let me know." When the **setFido:** method gets called, you will get sent a message from the object you are observing: "Hey, my fido property has a new value."

When you add yourself as an object's observer, you specify the name of the property you are observing. You can also specify some options. In particular, you can tell the object to send you the old and/or new value of the property when you are notified of the change.

(Unfortunately, the language used when discussing key-value observing and when discussing **NSNotificationCenter** is very similar. In this chapter, we are not talking about **NSNotification** or **NSNotificationCenter**, even if we use the word "notify" or "notification".)

Open your Callbacks project. You are going to create a new object that will observe the lastTime property of your **BNRLogger** class. Start by creating a new Objective-C class, a subclass of **NSObject** named **BNRObserver**.

In main.m, create an instance of **BNRObserver** and make it an observer of the logger's lastTime property:

```
__unused NSTimer *timer =
            [NSTimer scheduledTimerWithTimeInterval:2.0
                                             target:logger
                                           selector:@selector(updateLastTime:)
                                           userInfo:nil
                                            repeats:YES];

__unused BNRObserver *observer = [[BNRObserver alloc] init];

// I want to know the new value and the old value whenever lastTime is changed
[logger addObserver:observer
         forKeyPath:@"lastTime"
            options:NSKeyValueObservingOptionNew | NSKeyValueObservingOptionOld
            context:nil];

[[NSRunLoop currentRunLoop] run];
```

Do not forget to import BNRObserver.h at the top of main.m.

Next, implement the method that will get called when `lastTime` is changed. Open `BNRObserver.m` and add this method:

```
#import "BNRObserver.h"

@implementation BNRObserver

- (void)observeValueForKeyPath:(NSString *)keyPath
                      ofObject:(id)object
                        change:(NSDictionary *)change
                       context:(void *)context
{
    NSString *oldValue = [change objectForKey:NSKeyValueChangeOldKey];
    NSString *newValue = [change objectForKey:NSKeyValueChangeNewKey];
    NSLog(@"Observed: %@ of %@ was changed from %@ to %@",
          keyPath, object, oldValue, newValue);
}

@end
```

Build and run the program. Every two seconds `lastTime` should get a new value, and your observer should be informed.

Using the context in KVO

Notice that when you register as an observer, you can pass a pointer to anything as context. When you are notified of the change, you will receive that same pointer with the notification. The most common use of this is to answer "Is this really the notification that I asked for?" For example, your superclass may use KVO. If you override **observeValueForKeyPath:ofObject:change:context:**, how do you know which notifications should be forwarded on to the superclass's implementation? The trick is to come up with a unique pointer, use it as context when you start observing and check it against the context each time you are notified. The address of a static variable works well. Thus, if you are subclassing a class that might have already registered for KVO notifications, it will look something like this:

```
static int contextForKVO;
…

[petOwner addObserver:self
          forKeyPath:@"fido"
             options:0
             context:&contextForKVO];
…

- (void)observeValueForKeyPath:(NSString *)keyPath
                      ofObject:(id)object
                        change:(NSDictionary *)change
                       context:(void *)context
{
    // Is this not mine?
    if (context != &contextForKVO) {

        // Pass it on to the superclass
        [super observeValueForKeyPath:keyPath
                             ofObject:object
                               change:change
                              context:context];

    } else {
        // Handle the change
    }
}
…
```

Triggering the notification explicitly

The system can automatically inform the observer if you use the accessor method to set the property. What if you, for some reason, choose not to use the accessor? You can explicitly let the system know that you are changing a property. Change your BNRLogger.m so that it does not use the accessor to set lastName:

```
- (void)updateLastTime:(NSTimer *)t
{
    NSDate *now = [NSDate date];
    _lastTime = now;
    NSLog(@"Just set time to %@", self.lastTimeString);
}
```

Build and run the program. Notice that the **Observer** never gets told that _lastTime has changed.

To fix this, explicitly tell the system before and after you change the property:

```
  (void)updateLastTime:(NSTimer *)t
{
    NSDate *now = [NSDate date];
    [self willChangeValueForKey:@"lastTime"];
    _lastTime = now;
    [self didChangeValueForKey:@"lastTime"];
    NSLog(@"Just set time to %@", self.lastTimeString);
}
```

Build and run the program. The observer should be notified correctly now.

Dependent properties

What if you want to observe lastTimeString instead of lastTime? Try it. In main.m, start observing lastTimeString:

```
__unused BNRObserver *observer = [[BNRObserver alloc] init];
[logger addObserver:observer
        forKeyPath:@"lastTimeString"
           options:NSKeyValueObservingOptionNew | NSKeyValueObservingOptionOld
           context:nil];
```

If you build and run the program, you will see that the notifications are not being sent properly. The system does not know that lastTimeString changes whenever lastTime changes.

To fix this, you need to tell the system that lastTime affects lastTimeString. This is done by implementing a class method. Open BNRLogger.m and add this class method:

```
+ (NSSet *)keyPathsForValuesAffectingLastTimeString
{
    return [NSSet setWithObject:@"lastTime"];
}
```

Note the name of this method: it is **keyPathsForValuesAffecting** plus the name of the key, capitalized. This is the canonical nomenclature for methods like this one, just as property setters are named **set** plus the property's name, capitalized.

There is no need to declare this method in BNRLogger.h; it will be found at runtime.

37
Categories

Categories let a programmer add methods to any existing class. For example, Apple gave us the class **NSString**. Apple does not share the source code to that class, but you can use a category to add new methods to it.

Create a new Foundation Command Line Tool called VowelCounter. Then create a new file that is an Objective-C category. Name the category BNRVowelCounting and make it a category on NSString.

Now open NSString+BNRVowelCounting.h and declare a method that you want to add to the **NSString** class:

```
#import <Foundation/Foundation.h>

@interface NSString (BNRVowelCounting)
- (int)bnr_vowelCount;

@end
```

Now implement the method in NSString+BNRVowelCount.m:

```
#import "NSString+BNRVowelCounting.h"

@implementation NSString (BNRVowelCounting)

- (int)bnr_vowelCount
{
    NSCharacterSet *charSet =
            [NSCharacterSet characterSetWithCharactersInString:@"aeiouyAEIOUY"];

    NSUInteger count = [self length];
    int sum = 0;
    for (int i = 0; i < count; i++) {
        unichar c = [self characterAtIndex:i];
        if ([charSet characterIsMember:c]) {
            sum++;
        }
    }
    return sum;
}
@end
```

Now use the new method in main.m:

```
#import <Foundation/Foundation.h>
#import "NSString+BNRVowelCounting.h"

int main (int argc, const char * argv[])
{
    @autoreleasepool {

        NSString *string = @"Hello, World!";
        NSLog(@"%@ has %d vowels", string, [string bnr_vowelCount]);

    }
    return 0;
}
```

Build and run the program. Nifty, eh? Categories turn out to be very useful.

It is important to note that only this program has the category. If you want the method available in another program, you must add the files to your project and compile the category in when you build that program.

Notice also that the method that you wrote begins with **bnr_**. When you implement a method using a category, it replaces any method with the same name that already exists on the class. So if, in the future, Apple implements a method called **vowelCount** on **NSString**, you don't want your method to stomp on theirs. Thus, it is a good idea to add a prefix like this to the names of any methods you add to Apple's classes using a category.

You should use categories to add functionality to existing classes. Do not use them to replace functionality in existing classes; use subclassing instead.

Challenge

Create a new Foundation Command Line Tool called DateMonger. Add an **NSDate** category named BNRDateConvenience.

In the category, add a class method to **NSDate** that takes three integers (year, month, and day) and returns a new **NSDate** instance that is initialized to midnight on the passed-in day.

Test it in **main()**.

Hint: You will want to refer to the **NSDateComponents** class that you learned about in Chapter 14.

Part VI
Advanced C

To be a competent Objective-C programmer, you must also be a competent C programmer. In our rush to get you familiar with objects, we skipped a few things that you might want to know about C. These topics are not ideas that you will use everyday, but you will encounter them occasionally, so we want to introduce you to them here.

38
Bitwise Operations

In the first part of this book, we described the memory of a computer as a vast meadow of switches (billions of switches) that could be turned on or off. Each switch represents one bit, and we usually use 1 to mean "on" and 0 to mean "off."

However, you never address a single bit. Instead, you deal with byte-sized chunks of bits. If you think of a byte as an unsigned 8-bit integer, each bit represents another power of two:

Figure 38.1 One byte representing the decimal number 60

128	64	32	16	8	4	2	1
0	0	1	1	1	1	0	0

32 + 16 + 8 + 4 = 60

As a side-effect of evolving to have 10 fingers, people like to work with decimal numbers (base-10). Computers, as a side-effect of evolving to use switches that could only be on or off, like powers of 2. Programmers often use a base-16 number system ($16 = 2^4$) known as *hexadecimal* or just "hex." This is especially true when dealing with individual bits of an integer.

We use the letters a, b, c, d, e, and f for the extra digits. Thus, counting in hex goes like this: 0, 1, 2, 3, 4, 5, 6, 7, 8, 9, a, b, c, d, e, f, 10, 11, ...

To make it clear when we are writing in hex, we prefix the number with 0x. Here is the same number and byte expressed using hex:

Figure 38.2 One byte representing the hex number 0x3c

0x80	0x40	0x20	0x10	0x8	0x4	0x2	0x1
0	0	1	1	1	1	0	0

0x20+ 0x10+0x8 + 0x4 = 0x3c

Note that one byte can always be described as a two-digit hex number (like 3c). This makes hex a reasonable way to look at binary data. A tough-guy programmer thing to say is "I reverse-engineered the file format by studying the document files in a hex editor." Want to see a file as a list of hex-encoded bytes? In Terminal, run `hexdump` on the file:

```
$ hexdump myfile.txt
0000000 3c 3f 78 6d 6c 20 76 65 72 73 69 6f 6e 3d 22 31
```

```
0000010 2e 30 22 3f 3e 0a 3c 62 6f 6f 6b 20 78 6d 6c 6e
0000020 73 3d 22 68 74 74 70 3a 2f 2f 64 6f 63 62 6f 6f
0000030 6b 2e 6f 72 67 2f 6e 73 2f 64 6f 63 62 6f 6f 6b
0000040 22
0000041
```

The first column is the offset (in hex) from the beginning of the file of the byte listed in the second column. Each two digit number represents one byte.

Bitwise-OR

If you have two bytes, you can bitwise-OR them together to create a third byte. A bit on the third byte will be 1 if at least one of the corresponding bits in the first two bytes is 1.

Figure 38.3 Two bytes bitwise-ORed together

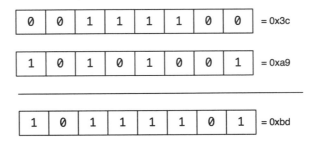

This is done with the | operator. To try your hand at manipulating bits, create a new project: a C Command Line Tool (not Foundation) named bitwize.

Edit main.c:

```c
#include <stdio.h>

int main (int argc, const char * argv[])
{
    unsigned char a = 0x3c;
    unsigned char b = 0xa9;
    unsigned char c = a | b;

    printf("Hex: %x | %x = %x\n", a, b, c);
    printf("Decimal: %d | %d = %d\n", a, b, c);

    return 0;
}
```

When you run this program, you will see the two bytes bitwise-ORed together:

```
Hex: 3c | a9 = bd
Decimal: 60 | 169 = 189
```

What is this good for? In Objective-C, we often use an integer to specify a certain setting. An integer is always a sequence of bits, and each bit is used to represent one aspect of the setting that can be turned on or off. We create this integer (also known as a *bit mask*) by picking and choosing from a set of constants. These constants are integers, too, and each constant specifies a single aspect of the setting by having only one of its bits turned on. You can bitwise-OR together the constants that represent the particular aspects you want. The result is the exact setting you are looking for.

Let's look at an example. iOS comes with a class called **NSDataDetector**. Instances of **NSDataDetector** go through text and look for common patterns like dates or URLs. The patterns an instance will look for are determined by the bitwise-OR result of a set of integer constants.

NSDataDetector.h defines these constants: NSTextCheckingTypeDate, NSTextCheckingTypeAddress, NSTextCheckingTypeLink, NSTextCheckingTypePhoneNumber, and NSTextCheckingTypeTransitInformation. When you create an instance of **NSDataDetector**, you tell it what to search for. For example, if you wanted it to search for phone numbers and dates, you would do this:

```
NSError *e;
NSDataDetector *d = [NSDataDetector dataDetectorWithTypes:
                        NSTextCheckingTypePhoneNumber|NSTextCheckingTypeDate
                                    error:&e];
```

Notice the bitwise-OR operator. Each of the numbers being ORed together has exactly one bit on, so the resulting bit mask would have two bits on. You will see this pattern a lot in Cocoa and iOS programming, and now you will know what is going on behind the scenes.

Bitwise-AND

You can also bitwise-AND two bytes together to create a third. In this case, a bit on the third byte is 1 only if the corresponding bits in the first two bytes are *both* 1.

Figure 38.4 Two bytes bitwise-ANDed together

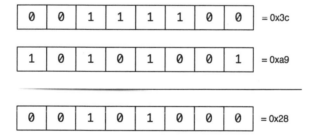

This is done with the & operator. Add the following lines to main.c:

```
#include <stdio.h>

int main (int argc, const char * argv[])
{
    unsigned char a = 0x3c;
    unsigned char b = 0xa9;
    unsigned char c = a | b;

    printf("Hex: %x | %x = %x\n", a, b, c);
    printf("Decimal: %d | %d = %d\n", a, b, c);

    unsigned char d = a & b;

    printf("Hex: %x & %x = %x\n", a, b, d);
    printf("Decimal: %d & %d = %d\n", a, b, d);

    return 0;
}
```

When you run it, you will see the two bytes bitwise-ANDed together:

```
Hex: 3c & a9 = 28
Decimal: 60 & 169 = 40
```

In Objective-C, we use bitwise-AND to see if a certain bit, or *flag*, is on. For example, if you were handed an instance of **NSDataDetector**, you could check if it was set to look for phone numbers like this:

```
if ([currentDetector checkingTypes] & NSTextCheckingTypePhoneNumber) {
    NSLog(@"This one is looking for phone numbers");
}
```

The **checkingTypes** method returns an integer that is the bitwise-OR result of all the flags this instance of **NSDataDetector** has on. You bitwise-AND this integer with a particular NSTextCheckingType constant and check the result. If the bit that is on in NSTextCheckingTypePhoneNumber is not on in the data detector's setting, then the result of bitwise-ANDing them will be all zeroes. Otherwise, you will get a non-zero result, and you will know that this data detector does look for phone numbers.

Note that when we use bits this way, we do not care what the integers in these cases equate to numerically.

Other bitwise operators

For completeness, here are the other bitwise operators. These are less commonly used in Objective-C but good to know.

Exclusive-OR

You can exclusive-or (XOR) two bytes together to create a third. A bit in the third byte is 1 if exactly one of the corresponding bits in the input bytes is 1.

Figure 38.5 Two bytes bitwise-XORed together

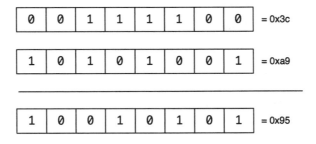

This is done with the ^ operator. Add to main.c:

```
    unsigned char e = a ^ b;

    printf("Hex: %x ^ %x = %x\n", a, b, e);
    printf("Decimal: %d ^ %d = %d\n", a, b, e);

    return 0;
}
```

When you run it you will see:

```
Hex: 3c ^ a9 = 95
Decimal: 60 ^ 169 = 149
```

This operator sometimes causes beginners some confusion. In most spreadsheet programs, the ^ operator is exponentiation: 2^3 means 2^3. In C, we use the **pow()** function for exponentiation:

```
double r = pow(2.0, 3.0); // Calculate 2 raised to the third power
```

Complement

If you have a byte, the complement is the byte that is the exact opposite: each 0 becomes a 1 and each 1 becomes a 0.

Figure 38.6 The complement

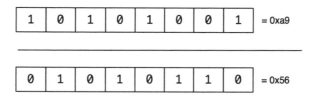

This is done with the ~ operator. Add a few lines to main.c:

```
    unsigned char f = ~b;
    printf("Hex: The complement of %x is %x\n", b, f);
    printf("Decimal: The complement of %d is %d\n", b, f);

    return 0;
}
```

You should see:

```
Hex: The complement of a9 is 56
Decimal: The complement of 169 is 86
```

Left-shift

If you left-shift the bits, you take each bit and move it toward the most significant bit. The ones that are on the left side of the number are forgotten, and the holes created on the right are filled with zeros.

Figure 38.7 Left-shifting by 2

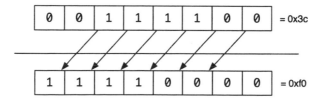

Left-shift is done with the << operator. Add a shift of two places to main.c:

```
unsigned char g = a << 2;
printf("Hex: %x shifted left two places is %x\n", a, g);
printf("Decimal: %d shifted left two places is %d\n", a, g);

return 0;
}
```

When this code runs, you will see:

```
Hex: 3c shifted left two places is f0
Decimal: 60 shifted left two places is 240
```

Every time you left-shift a number one place, you double its value.

Right-shift

The right-shift operator should not be much of a surprise.

Figure 38.8 Right-shifting by 1

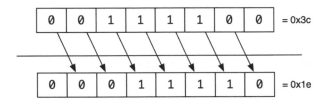

Add code to main.m:

```
unsigned char h = a >> 1;
printf("Hex: %x shifted right one place is %x\n", a, h);
printf("Decimal: %d shifted right one place is %d\n", a, h);

return 0;
}
```

When run:

```
Hex: 3c shifted right one place is 1e
Decimal: 60 shifted right one place is 30
```

Every time you right-shift a number one place, you halve its value. (If it is odd, round down.)

Using enum to define bit masks

Often you will want to define a list of constants, each representing an integer with one bit turned on. Then, these integers can be bitwise-ORed together and tested for using bitwise-AND, as described above.

The elegant way to do this is to define an enum that uses the left-shift operator to define the values. Here is how the constants for the **UIDataDetector** are defined:

```
enum {
    UIDataDetectorTypePhoneNumber   = 1 << 0,
    UIDataDetectorTypeLink          = 1 << 1,
    UIDataDetectorTypeAddress       = 1 << 2,
    UIDataDetectorTypeCalendarEvent = 1 << 3,
    UIDataDetectorTypeNone          = 0,
    UIDataDetectorTypeAll           = NSUIntegerMax
};
```

More bytes

In this chapter, you worked with unsigned char, which is one 8-bit byte. Any unsigned integer type will work the same way. For example, NSTextCheckingTypePhoneNumber is actually declared uint64_t, a 64-bit unsigned number.

Challenge

Write a program that creates an unsigned 64-bit integer such that every other bit is turned on. (There are actually two possible resulting numbers: one is even, the other is odd. Create the odd one.) Display the number. To check your work, the answer is 6,148,914,691,236,517,205.

39

C Strings

Given the choice, an Objective-C programmer will always choose to work with **NSString** objects rather than C strings. However, sometimes we do not have a choice. The most common reason we end up using C strings? When we access a C library from within our Objective-C code. For example, there is a library of C functions that lets your program talk to a PostgreSQL database server. The functions in that library use C strings, not instances of **NSString**.

char

In the last section, we talked about how a byte could be treated as a number. We can also treat a byte as a character. As mentioned earlier, there are many different string encodings. The oldest and most famous is ASCII. ASCII (American Standard Code for Information Interchange) defines a different character for each byte. For example, 0x4b is the character 'K'.

Create a new C Command Line Tool and name it yostring. In this program, you are going to list some of the characters in the ASCII standard. Edit main.c:

```
#include <stdio.h>

int main (int argc, const char * argv[])
{
    char x = 0x21; // The character '!'

    while (x <= 0x7e) { // The character '~'
        printf("%x is %c\n", x, x);
        x++;
    }

    return 0;
}
```

Build and run it. You may be wondering "Hey, a byte can hold any one of 256 numbers. You just printed out 94 characters. What happened to the rest?" Well, ASCII was written to drive old teletype-style terminals that printed to paper instead of to a screen, so characters 1 - 31 in ASCII are unprintable control codes. For example, the number 7 in ASCII makes the terminal bell ring. Number 32 is the space character. Number 127 is the delete – it causes the previous character to disappear. What about characters 128 – 255? ASCII only uses 7 bits. There is no ASCII character for the number 128. Nor is there an ASCII character for the number 0.

You can use ASCII characters as literals in code. Just put them inside single quotes. Change your code to use these:

```
int main (int argc, const char * argv[])
{
    char x = '!'; // The character '!'

    while (x <= '~') { // The character '~'
        printf("%x is %c\n", x, x);
        x++;
    }

    return 0;
}
```

Build it and run it.

The non-printable characters can be expressed using escape sequences that start with \. You have already used \n for the newline character. Here are some other common ones:

Table 39.1 Common escape sequences

\n	new line
\t	tab
\'	single-quote
\"	double-quote
\0	null byte (0x00)
\\	backslash

char *

A C string is just a bunch of characters right next to each other in memory. The string ends when the character 0x00 is encountered.

Figure 39.1 The word "Love" as a C string

0x4c	0x6f	0x76	0x65	0x00
'L'	'o'	'v'	'e'	'\0'

Functions that take C strings expect the address of the string's first character. **strlen()**, for example, will count the number of characters in a string. Try building a string and using **strlen()** to count the letters:

```c
#include <stdio.h>  // For printf
#include <stdlib.h> // For malloc/free
#include <string.h> // For strlen


int main (int argc, const char * argv[])
{
    char x = '!'; // The character '!'

    while (x <= '~') { // The character '~'
        printf("%x is %c\n", x, x);
        x++;
    }

    // Get a pointer to 5 bytes of memory on the heap
    char *start = malloc(5);

    // Put 'L' in the first byte
    *start = 'L';

    // Put 'o' in the second byte
    *(start + 1) = 'o';

    // Put 'v' in the third byte
    *(start + 2) = 'v';

    // Put 'e' in the fourth byte
    *(start + 3) = 'e';

    // Put zero in the fifth byte
    *(start + 4) = '\0';

    // Print out the string and its length
    printf("%s has %zu characters\n", start, strlen(start));

    // Print out the third letter
    printf("The third letter is %c\n", *(start + 2));

    // Free the memory so that it can be reused
    free(start);
    start = NULL;

    return 0;
}
```

Build and run it.

Notice the places where you added a pointer and a number together. start is declared to be a char *. A char is one byte. So start + 1 is a pointer one byte further in memory than start. start + 2 is two bytes further in memory than start.

Figure 39.2 The address of each character

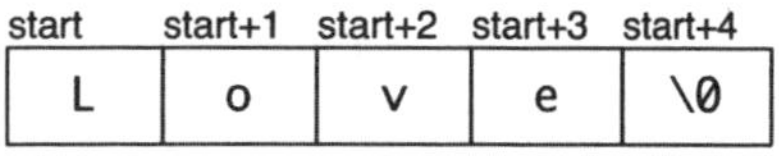

start	start+1	start+2	start+3	start+4
L	o	v	e	\0

This adding to a pointer and dereferencing the result is so common that there is a shorthand for it: start[2] is equivalent to *(start + 2). Change your code to use it:

```c
char *start = malloc(5);
start[0] = 'l';
start[1] = 'o';
start[2] = 'v';
start[3] = 'e';
start[4] = '\0';

printf("%s has %zu characters\n", start, strlen(start));
printf("The third letter is %c\n", start[2]);

free(start);
start = NULL;

return 0;
}
```

Build and run it.

It should be mentioned that this works with any data type. Here, for example, I can make a list of my favorite 3 floating point numbers and print them out:

```c
int main (int argc, const char * argv[])
{
    // Claim a chunk of memory big enough to hold three floats
    float *favorites = malloc(3 * sizeof(float));

    // Push values into the locations in that buffer
    favorites[0] = 3.14158;
    favorites[1] = 2.71828;
    favorites[2] = 1.41421;

    // Print out each number on the list
    for (int i = 0; i < 3; i++) {
        printf("%.4f is favorite %d\n", favorites[i], i);
    }

    // Free the memory so that it can be reused
    free(favorites);
    favorites = NULL;

    return 0;
}
```

The only interesting difference here is that favorites is typed as a float *. A float is 4 bytes. Thus favorites + 1 is 4 bytes further in memory than favorites.

Figure 39.3 An array of three floats

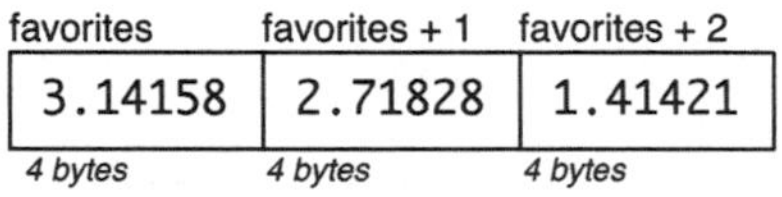

favorites	favorites + 1	favorites + 2
3.14158	2.71828	1.41421
4 bytes	*4 bytes*	*4 bytes*

String literals

If you were dealing with C strings a lot, malloc-ing the memory and stuffing the characters in one by one would be a real pain. Instead, you can create a pointer to a string of characters (terminated with the zero character) by putting the string in quotes. Change your code to use a string literal:

```
int main (int argc, const char * argv[])
{
    char x = '!'; // The character '!'

    while (x <= '~') { // The character '~'
        printf("%x is %c\n", x, x);
        x++;
    }

    char *start = "Love";
    printf("%s has %zu characters\n", start, strlen(start));
    printf("The third letter is %c\n", start[2]);

    return 0;
}
```

Build it and run it.

Notice that you do not need to malloc and free memory for a string literal. It is a constant and appears in memory only once, so the compiler takes care of its memory use. As a side-effect of it being a constant, bad things happen if you try to change the characters in the string. Add a line that should crash your program:

```
char *start = "Love";
start[2] = 'z';
printf("%s has %zu characters\n", start, strlen(start));
```

When you build and run it, you should get a EXC_BAD_ACCESS signal. You tried to write into memory that you are not allowed to write in.

To enable the compiler to warn you about writing to constant parts of memory, you can use the const modifier to specify that a pointer is referring to data that must not be changed. Try it:

```
const char *start = "Love";
start[2] = 'z';
printf("%s has %zu characters\n", start, strlen(start));
```

Now when you build, you should get an error from the compiler.

Delete the problematic line (start[2] = 'z';) before continuing.

You can use the escape sequences mentioned above in your string literals. Use a few:

```
const char *start = "A backslash after two newlines and a tab:\n\n\t\\";
printf("%s has %zu characters\n", start, strlen(start));
printf("The third letter is \'%c\'\n", start[2]);

return 0;
}
```

Build and run it.

Converting to and from NSString

If you are using C strings in an Objective-C program, you will need to know how to make an **NSString** from a C string. The **NSString** class has a method for this:

```
char *greeting = "Hello!";
NSString *x = [NSString stringWithCString:greeting encoding:NSUTF8StringEncoding];
```

You can also get a C string from an **NSString**. This is a little trickier because **NSString** can handle some characters that certain encodings cannot. It is a good idea to check that the conversion can occur:

```
NSString *greeting = "Hello!";
const char *x = NULL;
if ([greeting canBeConvertedToEncoding:NSUTF8StringEncoding]) {
    x = [greeting cStringUsingEncoding:NSUTF8StringEncoding];
}
```

You do not own the resulting C string; the system will eventually free it for you. You are guaranteed that it will live at least as long as the current autorelease pool, but if you are going to need the C string to live for a long time, you should copy it into a buffer you have created with **malloc()**.

Challenge

Write a function called **spaceCount()** that counts the space characters (ASCII 0x20) in a C string. Test it like this:

```
#include <stdio.h>

int main (int argc, const char * argv[])
{
    const char *sentence = "He was not in the cab at the time.";
    printf("\"%s\" has %d spaces\n", sentence, spaceCount(sentence));

    return 0;
}
```

Remember: when you run into '\0', you have reached the end of the string!

40

C Arrays

In the last chapter, you worked with C strings. A C string turned out to be a list of characters packed one next to the other in memory. C arrays are lists of other data types packed one next to the other in memory. Just as with strings, you deal with the list by holding onto the address of the first one.

Imagine that you wanted to write a program that would calculate the average of 3 grades. Create a new C Command Line Tool project and name it gradeInTheShade.

Edit `main.c`:

```
#include <stdio.h>
#include <stdlib.h> // malloc(), free()

float averageFloats(float *data, int dataCount)
{
    float sum = 0.0;
    for (int i = 0; i < dataCount; i++) {
        sum = sum + data[i];
    }
    return sum / dataCount;
}

int main (int argc, const char * argv[])
{

    // Create an array of floats
    float *gradeBook = malloc(3 * sizeof(float));
    gradeBook[0] = 60.2;
    gradeBook[1] = 94.5;
    gradeBook[2] = 81.1;

    // Calculate the average
    float average = averageFloats(gradeBook, 3);

    // Free the array
    free(gradeBook);
    gradeBook = NULL;

    printf("Average = %.2f\n", average);

    return 0;
}
```

Build and run it.

Figure 40.1 Pointers on the stack to a buffer of floats

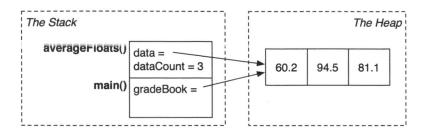

`malloc()` allocates a buffer on the heap, so you need to make sure that you free it when you are done. Wouldn't it be great if you could declare that buffer as part of the frame (on the stack) so that it would be deallocated automatically when the function is done executing? You can. Change `main.c`:

```
import <stdio.h>

float averageFloats(float *data, int dataCount)
{
    float sum = 0.0;
    for (int i = 0; i < dataCount; i++) {
        sum = sum + data[i];
    }
    return sum / dataCount;
}

int main (int argc, const char * argv[])
{

    // Declares the array as part of the frame
    float gradeBook[3];

    gradeBook[0] = 60.2;
    gradeBook[1] = 94.5;
    gradeBook[2] = 81.1;

    // Calculate the average
    float average = averageFloats(gradeBook, 3);

    // No need to free the array!
    // Cleanup happens automatically when the function returns

    printf("Average = %.2f\n", average);

    return 0;
}
```

Build and run it.

The string literal made it easy to pack an array with characters. There are also array literals. Use one to initialize gradeBook:

```
int main (int argc, const char *argv[])
{
    float gradeBook[] = {60.2, 94.5, 81.1};

    float average = averageFloats(gradeBook, 3);

    printf("Average = %.2f", average);

    return 0;
}
```

Build and run the program.

Notice that you did not need to specify the length of gradeBook as 3; the compiler figures that out from the array literal. You can use this type in many places where you might use *. For example, change the declaration of **averageFloats()** to do this:

```
float averageFloats(float data[], int dataCount)
{
    float sum = 0.0;
    for (int i = 0; i < dataCount; i++) {
        sum = sum + data[i];
    }
    return sum / dataCount;
}
```

Build and run the program.

Challenge

Before reading this book, you had probably used hexadecimal notation: Nearly every software license key or coupon code given out is written in hexadecimal. You have probably seen this "Type this into the coupon code field: 4af812e660ba8c123ee." It is a common way to get a user to type in a seemingly random set of bytes.

However, hexadecimal notation is fraught with peril when these values must work with speech recognition. "B", "C", "D" and "E" sound a lot alike to humans and machines. Big Nerd Ranch had a client with this problem, who asked me to come up with a license key system that would allow them to easily recite license keys over the phone.

Our solution was a system based on a set of internationally recognized words. What words are these? Mostly, international brands, like "Honda," "Google," and "Nike." The idea for using brand names came from a passage in Don DeLillo's *White Noise*. The narrator is listening to a child recite car brands in her sleep. He says "She was only repeating some TV voice. Toyota Corolla, Toyota Celica, Toyota Cressida. Supranational names, computer-generated, more or less universally pronounceable. Part of every child's brain noise, the substatic regions too deep to probe. Whatever its source, the utterance struck me with the impact of a moment of splendid transcendence."

This solution allowed our client to create and understand strings made of numbers and brand names. These strings could be transferred into a byte of data. Your challenge is to create a similar system. Warning: This is the final challenge of this book, and it is quite challenging.

The leftmost 3 bits of each byte will be encoded as a digit between 2 and 9 inclusive. You are avoiding 0 and 1 because in writing these are easily confused with the letters O and l. The remaining five bits will be represented by a brand name. 2^5 is 32. So you will need 32 international brand names. Here is a list you can use:

0. Camry
1. Nikon
2. Apple
3. Ford
4. Audi
5. Google
6. Nike
7. Amazon
8. Honda
9. Mazda
10. Buick
11. Fiat
12. Jeep
13. Lexus
14. Volvo
15. Fuji
16. Sony
17. Delta
18. Focus
19. Puma
20. Samsung
21. Tivo
22. Halo
23. Sting
24. Shrek
25. Avatar
26. Shell
27. Visa
28. Vogue
29. Twitter
30. Lego
31. Pepsi

So, for example, four bytes of random data might be rendered in hexadecimal as 53ec306f. In our system, the same data would become the string "4 Puma 9 Jeep 3 Sony 5 Fuji". When parsing the string, we would ignore whitespace and capitalization.

The challenge, then, is to create a new command-line tool that includes two methods:

- Take a buffer of bytes and return a string that represents those bytes

- Take a string and return the buffer of bytes it represents

You will add these methods to **NSData** as a category. Here is the declaration of the category:

```
@interface NSData (Speakable)
- (NSString *)encodeAsSpeakableString;
+ (NSData *)dataWithSpeakableString:(NSString *)s
                              error:(NSError **)e;
@end
```

The first method is considerably easier to write than the second.

Here is a main.m that will test those methods:

```
#import <Foundation/Foundation.h>
#import "NSData+Speakable.h"

int main(int argc, const char * argv[])
{

    @autoreleasepool {

        // Generate 8 bytes of random data
        srandom((unsigned int)time(NULL));
        int64_t randomBytes = (random() << 32) | random();

        // Pack it in an NSData
        NSData *inData = [NSData dataWithBytes:&randomBytes
                                       length:sizeof(int64_t)];
        NSLog(@"In Data = %@", inData);

        // Convert to a speakable string
        NSString *speakable = [inData encodeAsSpeakableString];
        NSLog(@"Got string \"%@\"", speakable);

        // Converting it back to an NSData
        NSError *err;
        NSData *outData = [NSData dataWithSpeakableString:speakable
                                                   error:&err];
        if (!outData) {
            NSLog(@"Unexpected error: %@", [err localizedDescription]);
            return -1;
        }
        NSLog(@"Out data: %@",  outData);

        // outData better be the same as inData
        if (![outData isEqual:inData]) {
            NSLog(@"Data coming out not the same as what went in.");
            return -1;
        }

        // Test a misspelling ("Teevo" not "Tivo")
        speakable = @"2 Jeep 3 Halo 7 Teevo 2 Pepsi 2 Volvo";
        outData = [NSData dataWithSpeakableString:speakable
                                           error:&err];
        if (!outData) {
            NSLog(@"Expected error: %@", [err localizedDescription]);
        } else {
            NSLog(@"Missed bad string");
            return -1;
        }
    }
    return 0;
}
```

This program should produce output like this:

```
In Data = <53ec306f 955c6668>
Got string "4 Puma 9 Jeep 3 Sony 5 Fuji 6 Tivo 4 Vogue 5 Nike 5 Honda"
Out data: <53ec306f 955c6668>
Expected error: Unable to parse
Program ended with exit code: 0
```

At some point, you will find yourself asking, "Where is the next digit?" You can use **NSCharacterSet** to find it.

```
NSString *string =

// Get the digit character set
NSCharacterSet *digits = [NSCharacterSet decimalDigitCharacterSet];
NSRange searchRange;
searchRange.location = 0;
searchRange.length = [string length];

// Find the location of the first digit in the string
NSRange digitRange = [str rangeOfCharacterFromSet:digits
                                          options:NSLiteralSearch
                                            range:searchRange];

// Are there no digits?
if (digitRange.length == 0) {
    NSLog(@"Searched whole string and found no digits");
} else {
    NSLog(@"Character %d is a digit", digitRange.location);
}
```

You will need to look at the documentation for **NSString** and **NSMutableString** to find some of the ways that you can manipulate substrings using NSRange.

In **dataWithSpeakableString:error:**, you will need to deal with badly formatted strings by creating an **NSError** and returning nil. This will look something like this:

```
// Did the parse fail?
if (!success) {

    // Did the caller give me a place to put the error?
    if (e) {
        NSDictionary *userInfo = @{NSLocalizedDescriptionKey : @"Unable to parse"};
        *e = [NSError errorWithDomain:@"SpeakableBytes"
                                  code:1
                              userInfo:userInfo];
        return nil;
    }
}
```

You will use several bitwise operations.

Good luck!

41

Running from the Command Line

In this book, you have built and run many command-line tools in Xcode. Running in Xcode works great for testing programs and for learning programming. However, if you create a command-line tool to use in real life, then you will want to run it from the command line.

In a Mac, you typically use Terminal to run programs from the command line. The Terminal app is just a pretty interface to what is called a *shell*. There are a few different shells with catchy names like csh, sh, zsh, and ksh, but nearly all Mac users use bash.

To run a program from the command line, you enter the path of the program's executable file in Terminal and press Return.

In Xcode, return to your gradeInTheShade project from Chapter 40. In the project navigator, reveal the contents of the Products folder and find a file named gradeInTheShade. This is your executable file. Right-click this file and choose Show In Finder.

Figure 41.1 Showing executable in Finder

Copy the gradeInTheShade file from Finder to your desktop.

Next, open Terminal and type the following command:

```
$ ~/Desktop/gradeInTheShade
```

Press Return, the program will run, and the output will appear in the Terminal window. Your command-line tool has now lived up to its name.

Command-line arguments

A command-line tool can have one or more *command-line arguments*. A command-line argument provides information to the tool about what you want it to do.

None of the tools that you have created so far have had command-line arguments, but useful command-line tools typically do. In this chapter, you are going to create another command-line tool called Affirmation. It will not be particularly useful, but it will have command-line arguments.

Here is what running Affirmation will look like when you are finished:

```
$ Affirmation awesome 4
You are awesome!
You are awesome!
You are awesome!
You are awesome!
```

This tool has two command-line arguments: an inspiring adjective and the number of times to display the affirmation. Command-line arguments are typed in just after the file path, separated by whitespace. These arguments will be read into the Affirmation program as strings, and then the program will use that information to get its work done.

In Xcode, create a new C Command Line Tool project called Affirmation. Open main.c and check out this familiar code:

```
int main (int argc, const char * argv[])
{
...
```

The **main** function has two arguments. The second argument, argv, is an array of C strings. This is where command-line arguments are stored. Each command-line argument becomes a C string and is packed into argv before **main()** is called. The first argument, argc, is the number of strings in argv.

In main.c, edit **main()** to print out the contents of argv:

```
#include <stdio.h>

int main (int argc, const char * argv[])
{
    for (int i = 0; i < argc; i++) {
        printf("arg %d = %s\n", i, argv[i]);
    }

    return 0;
}
```

Use Command-B to build (but not run) this program. From the project navigator, select the executable file and show it in Finder. Copy the file to your desktop. Then, in Terminal, enter the following command:

```
$ ~/Desktop/Affirmation terrific 3
```

Here is your output:

```
arg 0 = /Users/mward/Desktop/Affirmation
arg 1 = terrific
arg 2 = 3
```

Surprise! The first item in argv is not the first command-line argument; it is the path to the executable file. This item is always in argv even in programs that do not accept command line arguments.

Figure 41.2 argv and argc in Affirmation

In Xcode, modify **main()** to print out affirmations instead. Use **atoi()** to convert the argv item string to an int that you can use.

```
#include <stdio.h>
#include <stdlib.h>

int main (int argc, const char * argv[])
{

    int count = atoi(argv[2]);

    for (int j = 0; j < count; j++) {
        printf("You are %s!\n", argv[1]);
    }

    return 0;
}
```

To run the modified code, you could follow the same process you did before: build, show in Finder, copy to Desktop, run from Terminal. Fortunately, however, there is a way to feed command-line arguments to Xcode so that you can build and run without leaving the comfort of home.

From Xcode's menu bar, select Product → Scheme → Edit Scheme.... On the sheet that appears, select Run Affirmation on the lefthand side. Then select Arguments from the choices at the top of the sheet. Find the list entitled Arguments Passed On Launch and use the + button to add two specific arguments:

Figure 41.3 Adding arguments

Click OK to dismiss the sheet. The build and run the program. The console will show the output based on the two command-line arguments that you included in the scheme.

Note that there is nothing currently in the code that checks the number of the command-line arguments entered. Usually, it is important to check to ensure that the program will have the information it needs to run.

In Xcode, edit main.c to check for the correct number of command-line arguments. Do not forget about argv[0] (the executable file path) when testing the value of argc.

```
#include <stdio.h>

int main (int argc, const char * argv[])
{
    if (argc != 3) {
        fprintf(stderr, "Usage: Affirmation <adjective> <number>\n");
        return 1;
    }

    int count = atoi(argv[2]);

    for (int j = 0; j < count; j++) {
        printf("You are %s!\n", argv[1]);
    }

    return 0;
}
```

Edit the scheme again to test your error case (Product → Scheme → Edit Scheme...). Remove one of the arguments and build and run again.

Command-line arguments do not have to be single words. You can use quotation marks to pass a multiple-word argument. For instance, you could edit the scheme again and make the first argument `"the best"`:

Figure 41.4 Adding a multi-word argument

More convenient running from the command-line

What if you wanted to run Affirmation from the command line on a regular basis? Your best option is to move the executable to one of the standard directories for executables. This will allow you to run from the command line using only the name of the executable:

```
$ Affirmation "the best" 4
```

The standard directories for executables are determined by the PATH environment variable.

In Terminal, find your PATH environment variable:

```
$ echo $PATH
/usr/bin:/bin:/usr/sbin:/sbin:/usr/local/bin:/usr/X11/bin
```

The /usr/local/bin directory a good home for Affirmation; by convention, it is the directory for user-installed tools on Unix and Unix-based systems, like OS X.

Even though the /usr/local/bin directory is in your PATH environment variable, it may not exist on your Mac. If this is the case, then you will need to create the /usr/local/bin directory. Type the following command to make the directory if it does not already exist:

```
$ mkdir -p /usr/local/bin
```

Next, type the following command to open the /usr/local/bin directory in Finder:

```
$ open /usr/local/bin
```

In Finder, copy Affirmation into `/usr/local/bin`.

Now that Affirmation is in `/usr/local/bin`, you no longer have to provide the complete path to the executable in Terminal; you can use just its name:

```
$ Affirmation "good enough" 3
```

The system will scan the directories in the PATH environment variable, and find and run Affirmation.

42

Switch Statements

It is not uncommon to check a variable for a set of values. Using `if-else` statements, it would look like this:

```
int yeastType = ...;

if (yeastType == 1) {
   makeBread();
} else if (yeastType == 2) {
   makeBeer();
} else if (yeastType == 3) {
   makeWine();
} else {
   makeFuel();
}
```

To make this sort of thing easier, C has the `switch` statement. The code above could be changed to this:

```
int yeastType = ...;

switch (yeastType) {
    case 1:
        makeBread();
        break;
    case 2:
        makeBeer();
        break;
    case 3:
        makeWine();
        break;
    default:
        makeFuel();
        break;
}
```

Notice the `break` statements. Without the `break`, after executing the appropriate `case` clause the system would execute all the subsequent `case` clauses. For example, if you had this:

```
int yeastType = 2;

switch (yeastType) {
    case 1:
        makeBread();
    case 2:
        makeBeer();
    case 3:
        makeWine();
    default:
        makeFuel();
}
```

then the program would run **makeBeer()**, **makeWine()**, and **makeFuel()**. A switch statement works this way so that you can have more than one value trigger the same code:

```
int yeastType = ...;

switch (yeastType) {
    case 1:
    case 4:
        makeBread();
        break;
    case 2:
    case 5:
        makeBeer();
        break;
    case 3:
        makeWine();
        break;
    default:
        makeFuel();
        break;
}
```

As you can imagine, forgetting to put the break at the end of the case clause is a common programmer error, and it is only discovered when your program starts acting strangely.

In C, switch statements are for a very specific situation: the value of each case must be a constant integer. As such, you do not see a lot of switch statements in most Objective-C programs. Which is why we snuck it in here just before the book ends.

Appendix
The Objective-C Runtime

"Any sufficiently advanced technology is indistinguishable from magic." —Arthur C. Clarke

"Magic is dumb." —Every engineer, ever

People who become programmers are often the sort of people who are dissatisfied with magic and with the statement, "It just works." We want to know *how* and *why* it works.

This chapter will reveal some of the underlying mechanisms that make Objective-C programs "just work." These mechanisms are part of the Objective-C Runtime.

The term "runtime" has multiple meanings. So far, we have used it to describe the time period during which your application is running on a user's computer. Runtime is contrasted with "compile-time," which is the period before running when you build your program using Xcode.

Objective-C developers also refer to "the Runtime" (often with a capital 'R'). This is the part of OS X and iOS that executes Objective-C code. The Objective-C Runtime is responsible for dynamically keeping track of which classes exist, what methods they have defined, and seeing that messages are passed properly between objects.

Introspection

One feature of the Runtime is *introspection*: the ability for an object to answer questions about itself while the program is running. For example, there is an **NSObject** method named **respondsToSelector:**.

```
- (BOOL)respondsToSelector:(SEL)aSelector;
```

Its one argument is a selector (the name of a method). The return value will be YES if the object implements the named method and NO if it does not. Using **respondsToSelector:** is an example of introspection.

Dynamic method lookup and execution

A running Objective-C application consists largely of objects sending messages to each other. When an object sends a message, it kicks off a search for the method to execute. The search normally starts with the class referenced by the receiver's isa pointer and then proceeds up the inheritance hierarchy until it finds a method of that name.

The dynamic search and the execution of the found method make up the basis of every Objective-C message send and are another feature of the Runtime.

Performing this lookup and executing the method is the job of the C function `objc_msgSend()`. This function's arguments are the receiver of the message, the selector of the method to be executed, and any arguments for the method.

For example, consider this short program that logs the uppercase version of a string:

```
#import <Foundation/Foundation.h>

int main (int argc, const char * argv[])
{
    @autoreleasepool {
        NSString *nameString = @"Mikey Ward";
        NSString *capsName = [nameString uppercaseString];
        NSLog(@"%@ -> %@",nameString,capsName);
    }
    return 0;
}
```

When the compiler sees your **uppercaseString** message, it replaces the message with a call to `objc_msgSend()`:

```
#import <Foundation/Foundation.h>
#import <objc/message.h>

int main (int argc, const char * argv[])
{
    @autoreleasepool {
        NSString *nameString = @"Mikey Ward";
        NSString *capsName = objc_msgSend(nameString, @selector(uppercaseString));
        NSLog(@"%@ -> %@",nameString,capsName);
    }
    return 0;
}
```

The `objc_msgSend()` function is one of a family of functions that lie at the heart of every message sent in an Objective-C program. These functions are declared in `objc/message.h`. For more information on these and other runtime functions, head to the developer documentation and browse the Objective-C Runtime Reference.

Management of classes and inheritance hierarchies

The Runtime is responsible for keeping track of which classes you're using, as well as those being used by the libraries and frameworks included in your application. There are a number of functions that exist in order to manipulate the classes loaded by the Runtime.

Create a new Foundation Command Line Tool named ClassAct.

In main.m, update the **main** function with the following code. Make sure you import `objc/runtime.h` at the top.

```objc
#import <Foundation/Foundation.h>
#import <objc/runtime.h>

int main(int argc, const char * argv[])
{

    @autoreleasepool {
        // Declare a variable to hold the number of registered classes
        unsigned int classCount = 0;

        // Get a pointer to a list of all registered classes
        // currently loaded by your application.
        // The number of registered classes is returned by reference
        Class *classList = objc_copyClassList(&classCount);

        // For each class in the list...
        for (int i = 0; i < classCount; i++) {

            // Treat the classList as a C array to get a Class from it
            Class currentClass = classList[i];

            // Get the class's name as a string
            NSString *className = NSStringFromClass(currentClass);

            // Log the class's name
            NSLog(@"%@",className);
        }

        // We're done with the class list buffer, so free it
        free(classList);
    }
    return 0;
}
```

The **objc_copyClassList** function returns a C array of pointers to **Class** objects. Recall from Chapter 12 that memory obtained by calling **malloc()** must be freed when you are done with it. By convention, memory obtained by calling a function with "copy" or "create" in its name, such as **objc_copyClassList** should be treated the same way. This is called the *create rule*. Similarly, memory obtained by calling any other function, such as one with "get" in its name, is not owned by you and you do not need to free it. This one is the *get rule*. Notice that these rules are similar to those used for manual memory management (discussed at the end of Chapter 23).

Build and run your program.

Browse through the list of classes that have been logged by your program. It is very impressive how many different classes have been written that provide the basis for the programs that we write. You should also see lots of class names that begin with underscores. These are internal-only classes that exist deep in the bowels of Apple's frameworks, making our programs work.

Next, you are going to add functions to your program to show the class hierarchies of each of the listed classes as well as list all of the methods implemented by each class.

In main.m, add a helper function to create an **NSArray** of **Class**es that represents the inheritance hierarchy of a passed-in **Class**:

```
#import <Foundation/Foundation.h>
#import <objc/runtime.h>

NSArray *BNRHierarchyForClass(Class cls) {

    // Declare an array to hold the list of
    // this class and all its superclasses, building a hierarchy
    NSMutableArray *classHierarchy = [NSMutableArray array];

    // Keep climbing the class hierarchy until we get to a class with no superclass
    for (Class c = cls; c != Nil; c = class_getSuperclass(c)) {
        NSString *className = NSStringFromClass(c);
        [classHierarchy insertObject:className atIndex:0];
    }

    return classHierarchy;
}

int main(int argc, const char * argv[])
{
    ...
```

This function will take a **Class** object and get its superclass. Then it will get *that* class's superclass, and proceed up the hierarchy until it reaches a class with no superclass, which is usually **NSObject**.

Now write a function to get a list of all of the methods that are implemented on a given class.

```
    ...
    return classHierarchy;
}

NSArray *BNRMethodsForClass(Class cls) {

    unsigned int methodCount = 0;

    Method *methodList = class_copyMethodList(cls, &methodCount);

    NSMutableArray *methodArray = [NSMutableArray array];

    for (int m = 0; m < methodCount; m++) {
        // Get the current Method
        Method currentMethod = methodList[m];
        // Get the selector for the current method
        SEL methodSelector = method_getName(currentMethod);
        // Add its string representation to the array
        [methodArray addObject:NSStringFromSelector(methodSelector)];
    }

    return methodArray;
}

int main(int argc, const char * argv[])
{
    ...
```

This code looks similar to the code that you wrote to get the class list. There is a new type here that you have not seen before: Method. In this context, Method is the name of a type of struct whose members include a method's selector (variable of type SEL) as well as a *function pointer* – a pointer to the actual hunk of code to execute in the program's data segment of memory. This function pointer is a variable of type IMP.

Now edit **main()** to make use of you helper functions:

```
int main(int argc, const char * argv[])
{

    @autoreleasepool {

        // Create an an array of dictionaries, where each dictionary
        // will end up holding the class name, hierarchy, and method list
        // for a given class
        NSMutableArray *runtimeClassesInfo = [NSMutableArray array];

        // Declare a variable to hold the number of registered classes
        unsigned int classCount = 0;

        // Get a pointer to a list of all registered classes
        // currently loaded by your application
        // The number of registered classes is returned by reference
        Class *classList = objc_copyClassList(&classCount);

        // For each class in the list...
        for (int i = 0; i < classCount; i++) {

            // Treat the classList as a C array to get a Class from it
            Class currentClass = classList[i];

            // Get the class's name as a string
            NSString *className = NSStringFromClass(currentClass);

            // Log the class's name
            NSLog(@"%@",className);

            NSArray *hierarchy = BNRHierarchyForClass(currentClass);

            NSArray *methods = BNRMethodsForClass(currentClass);

            NSDictionary *classInfoDict = @{    @"classname" : className,
                                                @"hierarchy" : hierarchy,
                                                @"methods"   : methods };

            [runtimeClassesInfo addObject:classInfoDict];
        }

        // You are done with the class list buffer, so free it
        free(classList);

        // Sort the classes info array alphabetically by name, and log it.
        NSSortDescriptor *alphaAsc = [NSSortDescriptor sortDescriptorWithKey:@"name"
                                                                   ascending:YES];
        NSArray *sortedArray = [runtimeClassesInfo
                                    sortedArrayUsingDescriptors:@[alphaAsc]];
        NSLog(@"There are %ld classes registered with this program's Runtime.",
                                                            sortedArray.count);

        NSLog(@"%@",sortedArray);

    }
```

```
    return 0;
}
```

Build and run your program.

Now you should have a whole lot of output where you can see the class name, inheritance hierarchy, and method list for every class registered with the Runtime by your program.

How KVO works

One example of an Apple API that relies on runtime functions like those above is Key-Value Observing. When you learned about KVO in Chapter Chapter 36, you learned that an observer is automatically notified of a change in a property if the affected object's accessors are used.

At runtime, when an object is sent the **addObserver:forKeyPath:options:context:** message, this method:

- determines the class of the observed object and defines a new subclass of that class using the **objc_allocateClassPair** function

- changes the object's isa pointer to point to the new subclass (effectively changing the type of the object)

- overrides the observed object's accessors to send KVO messages

Figure A.1 KVO dynamic subclass

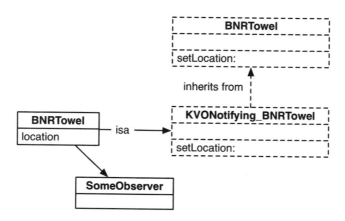

For example, consider a class's setter for a location property:

```
- (void)setLocation:(NSPoint)location
{
    _location = location;
}
```

In the new subclass, this accessor would be overridden like this:

```
- (void)setLocation:(NSPoint)location
{
    [self willChangeValueForKey:@"location"];
    [super setLocation:location];
    [self didChangeValueForKey:@"location"];
}
```

The subclass's implementation of the accessor calls the original class's implementation and wraps it in explicit KVO notification messages. These new classes and methods are all defined at runtime by using the Objective-C Runtime functions. No magic here.

To see the subclassing in action, add a new class to your ClassAct program called **BNRTowel**. Give it a single property:

```
@interface BNRTowel : NSObject
// Always know where your towel is!
@property (nonatomic, assign) NSPoint location;
@end
```

Build and run your program. Search the debugger output for "Towel," and you will find that just by having defined the class in your program you have a new entry in your output – even though you haven't instantiated one or implemented any methods yourself:

```
{
    classname = BNRTowel;
    hierarchy =          (
        NSObject,
        BNRTowel
    );
    methods =          (
        location,
        "setLocation:"
    );
}
```

Now, add a nil KVO observer to an instance of **BNRTowel**:

```
int main(int argc, const char * argv[])
{

    @autoreleasepool {

        // You don't have an object to do the observing, but send
        // the addObserver: message anyway, to kick off the runtime updates
        BNRTowel *myTowel = [BNRTowel new];
        [myTowel addObserver:nil
                forKeyPath:@"location"
                    options:NSKeyValueObservingOptionNew
                    context:NULL];

        ...
```

Build and run your program. Search the output again for "Towel." This time, in addition to the **BNRTowel** class, you should see its shiny new subclass in the list:

```
{
    classname = "NSKVONotifying_BNRTowel";
    hierarchy =          (
        NSObject,
        BNRTowel,
        "NSKVONotifying_BNRTowel"
    );
    methods =           (
        "setLocation:",
        class,
        dealloc,
        "_isKVOA"
    );
}
```

Final notes

If you would like to learn even more about the Objective-C Runtime, head to the documentation and look up the *Objective-C Runtime Programming Guide* and the *Objective-C Runtime Reference*.

Now that you have learned some of the magic, you probably want to try out some of these functions in your code.

Don't do this.

Knowing that these functions exist helps draw back the curtain to understand what is going on under the hood of your programs. However, the runtime functions are primarily for use by Apple's developers to support Apple's APIs, and can be very unwieldy when used by us mortals.

Challenge: instance variables

Modify your program to also log all of the instance variables that each class has.

Next Steps

Well, that is everything you will ever need to know to write brilliant applications for iOS and OS X.

That is what we wish we could tell you. We know you have worked hard to get to this point.

The truth is that you have completed the first leg of a fun and rewarding journey. It is, however, a very long journey. It is now time for you to spend some time studying the standard frameworks that Apple makes available to Objective-C developers like you.

Let us repeat that last phrase so you can relish it: "Objective-C developers like you." Congratulations.

If you are learning to develop applications for iOS, I recommend that you work through *iOS Programming: The Big Nerd Ranch Guide,* but there are several other books on iOS, and you are ready for any of them.

If you are learning to develop applications for OS X, we recommend that you work through *Cocoa Programming for Mac OS X*, but, here again, there are several other books on Cocoa, and you are ready for any of them.

There are groups of developers who meet every month to discuss the craft. In most major cities, there are iOS Developers Meetups and CocoaHeads chapters. The talks are often surprisingly good. There are also discussion groups online. Take some time to find and use these resources.

Shameless plugs

You can find both of us on Twitter. Aaron is @AaronHillegass, and Mikey is @wookiee. You can also follow Big Nerd Ranch: @bignerdranch.

Keep an eye out for future guides from Big Nerd Ranch. We also offer week-long courses for developers. And if you just need some code written, we do contract programming. For more information, visit our website at www.bignerdranch.com.

It is you, dear reader, who makes our lives of writing, coding, and teaching possible. So thank you for buying our book.

Index

Symbols

! (logical NOT) operator, 26
!= (not equal) operator, 26
\" escape sequence, 318
#define, 189-192, 195
#import, 191
#include, 191
% (tokens), 43, 44
% operator, 50
%= operator, 51
%@, 147
%d, 44
%e, 52
%f, 52
%ld, 49
%lo, 49
%lu, 49
%o, 48
%p, 66
%s, 44
%u, 49
%x, 48
%zu, 68
& operator, retrieving addresses, 65
&& (logical AND) operator, 26
( )
   cast operators, 50
   in function names, 15
   for function parameters, 30
   order of operations and, 24
* (asterisk)
   arithmetic operator, 49
   pointer operator, 67
*= operator, 51
+ (plus sign), 49
++ (increment operator), 51
+= operator, 51
- (minus sign), 49
-- (decrement operator), 51
-= operator, 51
-> (dereference) operator, 81
.h files (see header files)
.m (implementation files), 129
.pch (pre-compiled header), 191

.xib (XML Interface Builder) files, 262
/ (division operator), 49
/* ... */ (comments), 13
// (comments), 13
/= operator, 51
; (semicolon), 13
   do-while loop and, 60
< (less than) operator, 26
< > (angle brackets)
   conforming to protocols, 230
   importing files, 191
<< operator, 314
<= operator, 26
= operator, 26
== operator, 26
> (greater than) operator, 26
>= operator, 26
>> operator, 314
? (ternary operator), 28
@
   format string token, 147
@interface
   class extensions, 161
   header files, 130
   visibility of, 162
@property, 137
@selector(), 216
@synthesize, 294
\ (backslash), 318
   escape character, 44
\n, 44
\\ escape sequence, 318
^ (caret)
   exclusive-or operator, 312
   identifying blocks, 217
{ }
   in conditional expressions, 27
   in functions, 13
   scope of, 34
|| (logical OR) operator, 26
~ (tilde), 313

A

abs(), 51
absolute value, 51
accessor methods
   about, 133